A Traveller's History of Italy

THE AUTHOR Valerio Lintner was born in London of Italian and Polish parents. He studied at the Universities of Reading and Bologna, and at the European University Institute in Florence. He has strong personal and cultural ties with Italy, where he lived for several years and which he now visits frequently. He is a Principal Lecturer at London Guildhall University.

SERIES EDITOR Professor Denis Judd is a graduate of Oxford, a Fellow of the Royal Historical Society and Professor of History at the University of North London. He has published over 20 books including the biographies of Joseph Chamberlain, Prince Philip, George VI and Alison Uttley, historical and military subjects, stories for children and two novels. His most recent book is the highly praised *Empire: The British Imperial Experience from 1765 to the Present.* He has reviewed and written extensively in the national press and in journals, has written several radio programs and is a regular contributor to British and overseas radio and television.

Other Titles in the Series

A Traveller's History of the Caribbean
A Traveller's History of France/Fifth Edition
A Traveller's History of Paris/Second Edition
A Traveller's History of England/Fourth Edition
A Traveller's History of Scotland/Third Edition
A Traveller's History of Ireland/Third Edition
A Traveller's History of London/Second Edition
A Traveller's History of Spain/Third Edition
A Traveller's History of Greece/Third Edition
A Traveller's History of Turkey/Third Edition
A Traveller's History of India/Second Edition
A Traveller's History of China/Second Edition
A Traveller's History of Russia/Third Edition
A Traveller's History of Japan/Second Edition
A Traveller's History of North Africa

Cover illustration: detail of 'Guido Riccio da Fogliano' *by Simone Martini. By kind permission of The Bridgeman Art Library, London.*

A Traveller's History of Italy

FIFTH EDITION

VALERIO LINTNER

Series Editor DENIS JUDD
Line drawings JOHN HOSTE

INTERLINK BOOKS
An Imprint of Interlink Publishing Group, Inc.
NEW YORK

To Sue, Anna and Dominic

First American edition published 1998 by
INTERLINK BOOKS
An imprint of Interlink Publishing Group, Inc.
99 Seventh Avenue • Brooklyn, New York 11215 and
46 Crosby Street • Northampton, Massachusetts 01060

Library of Congress Cataloging-in-Publication Data

Lintner, Valerio
A traveller's history of Italy/Valerio Lintner; line drawings, John Hoste. — 1st American ed.
p. cm.
Bibliography; p.
Includes index.
ISBN 1-56656-296-1
1. Italy—History. 2. Historic sites—Italy. I. Title.
DG467.L586 1998
945-dc20 89-15345
CIP

Printed and bound in Canada

Table of Contents

Preface

The history of Italy is central to the European experience, but also curiously detached from it. It was, of course, through the supremacy of Rome that Italy enjoyed its greatest influence. Roman power stretched from the Atlantic to the borders of Mesopotamia, and from the Scottish Lowlands to the Sahara Desert. It is understandable that the Mediterranean was believed to lie at the centre of the civilized world, or that early twentieth-century Russian and German emperors assumed a local variation of the title Caesar. Nor did Italian influence vanish with the collapse of Rome: a new, spiritual Caesar exercised a global sway from the Vatican; Italian banking techniques and artistic genius shaped European and world attitudes; a Genovese discovered the Americas in 1492, and Machiavelli was to statecraft what Marconi became to radio communications.

Yet modern Italy has often been on the sidelines of world events. Despite its nineteenth and twentieth century pretensions Italy was of little account in the European balance of power, and its empire consisted largely of the scraps left over by the major imperial predators. To travel down the length of Italy is a reminder that though the country's northern regions are thoroughly European, its southern extremities are almost North African in character and climate. Today, even within the European Economic Community, comparatively few schoolchildren study Italian as their main foreign language. The British in particular find it difficult to take the Italians seriously, except perhaps as footballers or, on an equally seasonal basis, as lovers.

It is one of the major strengths of this lucid, knowledgeable and, always readable, book that both the foibles and the virtues of the Italians are given their proper historical weight. This is just as well, for Italy remains a traveller's dream – from its Alpine ski resorts to the Greek temples of Sicily, from the incomparable wealth of its art galleries and museums to the serenity and beauty of its cypress topped hills. In Italy, Communism and Catholicism, urban chic and peasant simplicity, an almost shocking self-regard and great personal generosity, are part of a uniquely satisfying whole. This intelligent and accessible book will help you to understand why.

Denis Judd

CHAPTER ONE

Early Italy: From Cave-Dwellers to Etruscan Civilisation

The Stone Age

The first Italians shared the land with elephants, hippopotami and rhinoceros. This was the warm second interglacial period, around 200,000 BC, and tropical creatures such as these roamed wild in the plains and forests of the Italian peninsula. No direct remains have been found of these Lower Palaeolithic humans, but it is generally thought that they were of the Homo Erectus type. Some of their tools, notably hand axes, have been found near Verona and near Imola, and an actual settlement, complete with traces of huts and left-overs of meals, has been discovered at Torrimpietra, near Rome. In the Middle Palaeolithic period, around 60,000 BC, Italy was populated by the Neanderthal race of humans. Like their predecessors, the people of this period were primitive creatures, similar to apes, probably with low intelligence. Life was undoubtedly short, basic and not particularly sweet, almost entirely taken up with the struggle for survival and the quest for food. Unlike their predecessors, the Italians of the Neanderthal period buried their dead in graves and cemeteries, traces of which have been found in caves south of Rome. Further evidence of their presence comes from archaeological finds of skeletal remains in the relevant geologic strata, and of flint weapons and tools in caves, notably near Chieti in the Abruzzi and at Venosa. Perhaps more striking are two of their footprints which have been found in the clay floor of the Basura cave in Liguria. Human life on the island of Sicily seems to date back to the beginning of the Upper Palaeolithic period, around 30,000 BC, when people probably first crossed the Straits of Messina from the mainland.

By about 10,000 BC other types of somewhat more advanced humans had found their way into Italy, probably from Asia and Africa. These Upper Palaeolithic peoples were essentially nomadic cave-dwellers and food gatherers. They used fire, but kept no animals and grew no crops. They were scattered and not very numerous, and were probably of the Cro-Magnon type, to judge by the skull found in the Fucino area. We know of them mainly through the discovery of their caves and rock dwellings, many of which contain the primitive animal art which links them culturally with similar peoples in the Spanish Peninsula and Southern France. The oldest of these dwellings date from about 10,000 BC and can be found on the island of Livanzo off western Sicily, at Addaura on Mount Pellegrino on the northern coast of the island, at del Ramito in Calabria, and at the grotto Polesini near Tivoli. Slightly later examples exist in the form of the Romanelli cave near Otranto in Puglia, and the Grimaldi caves at Balzi Rossi on the north-west coast. A Palaeolithic 'Venus' has also been found near Lake Trasimeno, but in general their art is unspectacular when compared to that of their French and Spanish contemporaries. The Addaura caves, discovered by chance when a Second World War bomb store blew up accidentally, contain what are probably the most impressive of the mysterious late Palaeolithic paintings so far discovered in Italy. The best of these depicts what has been interpreted as either a human sacrifice or some kind of sexual initiation ceremony.

Around 5000 BC, these peoples of the glacial age were gradually displaced by Mesolithic or Middle Stone Age cultures who had by then entered Italy. The latter enjoyed the superiority in war and hunting which came from the possession of fine flint and bone implements and, above all, the bow and arrow. It was also then that the climate, flora and fauna of Italy settled into the pattern which we know today.

The economic history of Italy took its first major step forward between 3500 and 2500 BC with the coming of the Neolithic or New Stone Age. For it was at this time that, with the introduction of agriculture, the early Italians moved from being food gatherers to being food producers.

This had the important consequences of both permitting a substantial increase in the population and encouraging communal settlement.

Farmers and animal keepers probably landed at the Gargano from the Near East, where they seem to have existed as far back as 7000 BC. They settled, notably at Coppa Nevigata, and lived in huts grouped into compounds which were in turn often grouped into villages. These villages can be seen from the air in the Tavoliere plain near Foggia in Puglia, where they were discovered by RAF reconnaissance in 1943. The Neolithic Italians were also weavers and potters, and some curious square-mouthed pottery has been discovered at Molino Casarotto in the Veneto. Skeletal remains show them to be of the long and narrow-headed, short-statured Mediterranean stock. An important characteristic of their culture is their burial customs, which consisted of placing corpses in a contracted position, either in caves or in pits or trenches covered with stones. The flesh was often stripped from the bones, which were painted red and buried with vases full of food and drink and with ornaments, clothes and weapons. They were still to some extent nomadic, moving on when the land close to them was exhausted, and they thus spread in south-east Italy, and eventually throughout the peninsula, diffusing their economic methods as they went.

The Copper and Bronze Ages

Between 2000 and 1800 BC copper began to be used in the Italian peninsula, probably coming into the south from Cyprus and into the Po valley and the area around the Alps from Bohemia. Indigenous stocks were not exploited until much later. With it from central Europe came 'Alpine' peoples with round heads. Italy had moved into the Chalcolithic or Copper Age, or more accurately the Copper-Stone Age, since copper was scarce and supplemented rather than replaced flint. The new culture gradually spread throughout Italy, co-existing with Neolithic groups; evidence of it exists at Guado near Salerno, Remedello near Brescia, and Rinaldone in Tuscany. It is from around this period that the large stone tombs built above ground in central–southern Italy, Sicily and Sardinia date. These often consist of dolmens, or chambers made from huge stone slabs, together with menhirs, single large monumental stones fixed in the ground. A good example are the 'giant graves' in Sardinia, which were probably collective burial places spanning several generations.

TERRAMARICOLI AND ALPINE CULTURES

The knowledge that by adding tin to copper it was possible to produce a superior alloy was discovered in the Near East before 3000 BC, and it reached Italy around 1800 BC, propelling the land into the Bronze Age. The principal cultural groups which existed around this time were the Palafitte peoples, who probably developed into the Terramaricoli in the north, and the Apennine Cultures or Extraterramaricoli in the centre and south. The former date back to late Neolithic times, and probably came to Italy from the Danube by way of the central Alpine passes. The name Palafitte comes from their principal characteristic, which was that they lived in villages built on piles or stakes on the edge of the north Italian lakes such as Maggiore and Garda (where a major settlement was discovered at Polada), and on the rivers in the Po valley. The Terramaricoli take their name from terramara, which is the local dialect for the rich black earth in which the remains of their settlements have been discovered. They flourished in the Copper and Bronze Ages, being accomplished metal workers, and were principally farmers and herdsmen who also hunted, fished and traded to the north and south. They used wheeled carts, weaved, were potters, and were further characterised by the fact that they cremated their dead and buried the remains close together in rows of pottery urns in cemeteries near to their villages. They probably spoke some form of Indo-European language.

The Extraterramaricoli, on the other hand, were less advanced. They lived along the Apennine belt from Bologna to Puglia, and were essentially nomadic shepherds, moving from high ground in the summer to lowlands in the winter – not unlike their modern counterparts. Unlike the northern Bronze Age people, they buried their dead, although they too probably spoke an Indo-European language. Primitive trade and migration gradually led to the development of peaceful links between the Apennine peoples and Terramara, and by about 1200 BC there had been considerable cultural cross-fertilisation, as can be seen at Pianello near Ancona, and at Scoglio del Tonno near Taranto.

It is very interesting to note that a fusion of Terramara and Apennine cultures also existed in the Bronze Age in Sicily at Milazzo and on the island of Lipari. This is sometimes referred to as the Ausonian culture, after the legend that Liparus, a prince of the Ausonians from central–southern Italy, landed on Lipari and settled there. Like Sicily, the island of Sardinia was in general culturally isolated, and here the most noteworthy Bronze Age culture developed towards the end of the period, around 1400 BC, and lasted until the arrival of the Romans in the third century BC. This was the Nuraghic culture, named after the huge stone forts and towers which they built. A staggering 6000 of these have been found, and doubtless many more have disappeared. They became more elaborate as time went on, by the sixth century BC probably being used as defences against Carthaginian invaders who came to Sardinia for the island's mineral deposits. A good example of *nuraghe* can be found at Barumini, where the construction is very intricate and is surrounded by a system of huge walls.

The Iron Age

THE VILLANOVANS

The transition from the Bronze Age to the Iron Age in Italy took place between 1000 and 800 BC. The main feature of the Iron Age in Italy was the emergence of several regional cultures. By far the most important was the Villanovan, named after the settlement discovered at Villanova, just east of Bologna, in 1853. The Villanovans can be seen as consisting of two closely linked, but in some ways culturally diverse, peoples: a northern group which was centred around Bologna and stretched eastwards through Verucchio and San Marino in eastern Romagna towards Rimini and down to Fermo in the Marche; and a southern group which was based in Tuscany, in the environs of Rome, and which extended as far south as Salerno. They had an advanced sense of social development and lived in villages of round huts, used iron weapons, and produced relatively high-quality bronze helmets, armour and domestic articles. A room in the Museo Civico in Bologna contains 15,000 bronze objects which were found by chance together in a massive pot near the church of San Francesco in the centre of the city in 1877. They are, however, mainly remarkable for the curious biconical urns in which they buried the ashes of their cremated dead. In the north these were generally covered with pottery; in the south, they were later replaced by urns shaped like the huts they lived in, and were more commonly covered with helmets. The urns were usually surrounded by ornaments and buried in round holes covered with stones (*tombe a pozzo*).

The Villanovans were early traders and gathered in clusters of villages, forming larger settlements than had hitherto been seen. The settlement at Bologna was possibly the first Italian town, and has been described as 'the Birmingham of early Italy' since it was effectively the economic centre of the time. Remains of Villanovan huts were recently, and again by chance, found in the centre of Bologna, between Piazza Nettunno and Via Rizzoli, during the excavation of the pedestrian underpass where they are now displayed. Their huts have also been found in several other places, notably in Rome on the Palatine, and at Veii, just north of the capital. One can only speculate about Villanovan social structure; the evidence from their ossuaries, however, would suggest a roughly equal distribution of wealth at first, with the gradual emergence of dominant individuals and groups in later periods. The northern Villanovan culture remained substantially intact and unchanged by events around it until it eventually died out some time after the Etruscans founded Felsina on the site of Bologna in 500 BC. In

A Villanovan hut-shaped cinerary urn

the south, the Villanovans were gradually absorbed and dominated by Etruscan culture, for example burying their dead rather than cremating them, and placing them in rectangular trenches (*tombe a fossa*).

OTHER IRON AGE PEOPLES

Apart from the Villanovans, the most significant cultures in Italy around the Iron Age were the following:

The Ligurians. Wild and primitive mountain peoples on the north-west coast, who also seem to have spread into parts of Corsica. They are a mysterious people about which very little is known except that they fought bitterly against the Romans for 200 years, and that their beer and honey were held in some esteem. An eighth-century Ligurian cemetery, discovered in 1959 at Chiavari, revealed some decorated cinerary urns.

The Golasecca-Comacines. A warrior people in Piedmont and Lombardy and around Lake Maggiore and Lake Como, who were gradually invaded by Celtic peoples.

The Veneti (or Atestines). Around Este in Venetia, a comparatively advanced, apparently egalitarian people who probably originated in Illyria, and who were also eventually overrun by the Celts. They are sometimes referred to as the Situla people, after the situlae, or decorated bronze wine buckets, for which they are best known. An interesting collection of their artefacts is kept at the Museo Civico in Este.

The Picenes. A conservative and culturally independent race of warlike sea-traders who lived in the Marche near Ancona, and who probably originated from Illyria. Good examples of their unsophisticated but powerful art are the human-shaped clay vase handle recently found in excavations at Campovallano, the stone head of a warrior from Numana, and a huge statue of a warrior from Capestrano. An interesting selection of remains from their culture is to be found in the Museo Nazionale delle Marche in Ancona.

The Umbrians. Settled between Gubbio and Todi, and after whom the region of Umbria ('the green heart of Italy') is named. They were culturally isolated, to a large extent avoiding Etruscan influence, until the Roman unification of the peninsula. They lived in small settlements and had their own separate language, Umbrian, which they continued to use until the third century BC and which was to some extent influenced by Etruscan and Latin. The most famous remains of their culture are the seven inscribed bronze Eugubian tablets found at Gubbio, and the 'Mars of Todi' sculpture in the Vatican Museum in Rome.

The Fossa Grave. A trading culture in Calabria and Campania who have left important evidence of their lives at Cumae and on the island of Ischia. In a generally rather confused situation around and south-west of Rome, the Samnites, the Oscans, the Volscians, the Sabines, the Latins, the Sabellians, and the Sikels in Sicily, are also peoples worthy of mention. Most of these were Italic peoples and were possibly descended from the Apennine cultures; they were often culturally linked, but displayed little signs of unity and made no attempt at federation – indeed, they were often hostile to one another.

The Messapians, Peucetians and Daunians in Puglia. These were also Illyrian in origin, produced interesting pottery and, like the Fossa Grave, were eventually dominated by Greek migrants.

Thus in the Iron Age Italy consisted of a series of fairly discrete peoples formed by a series of migrations and infiltrations, most of whom spoke Indo-European dialects. The general level of culture was rudimentary, with comparatively low levels of social organisation, limited material resources, and pleasant but very basic art. There was little evidence of what was to come within a few hundred years when the Romans would dominate Italy, and indeed most of the known world.

Greek Influences

A major theme which runs through the the whole of Italian history is Italy's openness to migration and invasion because of its geographical characteristics. Its elongated peninsula has, of course, a great deal of coastline, which has rendered it vulnerable to infiltration from the sea. The Alps and the Dolomites contain sufficient accessible crossing points to ensure that migration from France and northern Europe has also been relatively easy. Migrants have therefore consistently had a key impact on

Italy's culture and destiny. There were probably population movements into Italy in very early times, but the first migrants to arrive in considerable numbers were the Mycenaeans, whose presence in Sicily and Lipari can be traced back to around 1400 BC, and who established a colony at Tarantum from which they traded with the Adriatic and as far afield as Luni in Etruria. Apart from the Mycenaeans, the Phoenicians also settled in Sicily, and later traded with Italic peoples, mainly through their colony at Carthage.

However, the first invaders to exert a really important and lasting influence on the Italic peoples were the Greeks. Their presence in Italy can be traced back to just after 800 BC, and during the next 200 years they established roots in Sicily and on the west coast of the mainland between Tarantum (Taranto) and Neapolis (Naples). On the island they dominated the Sikels and the Sikanians, the main indigenous populations, and made a number of settlements, including ones at Naxos near Taormina, Acragas (Agrigento), Selinus (Selinunte), Catana (Catania), Syracuse (Siracusa), and Messina. Of the many remains of Greek civilisation in Sicily, perhaps the most striking are the magnificent and well-preserved temples at Agrigento and Selinunte. On the mainland, they also founded several settlements, the most important of which were at Cumae, Naples and Posidonia (Paestum). There were also a number of cities along the 'toe' of Italy, such as Sybaris (Sibari), Croton (Crotone) and Rhegium (Reggio Calabria), which are sometimes collectively known as Magna Graecia. From these bases they traded extensively with the rest of Italy, exporting their bronze products and pottery, notably to Tuscany. They also founded a number of outlying cities such as Ancona, which was established in the fourth century BC as an outpost of Syracuse.

The Greeks, like everybody else in Italy, eventually fell under the domination of Rome, but they contributed much to the development of the country. For a start, it was they who introduced the systematic cultivation of vines and olive trees into the peninsula (and it is fairly obvious what the impact of this has been on life in Italy over the years!). They contributed to the development of the written language, introducing an improved form of alphabet which most Italic peoples to some extent copied.

They were responsible for the very name of Italy, which is derived from Fitalia, or 'land of cattle', the name by which the Greeks referred to the south-west coast of the peninsula in the fifth century BC; by the first century BC Italia had become the name of the whole country.

Most obviously Greek influence led to important developments in Italian artistic and cultural life. Apart from the effects of their trade, there is evidence that some Greek craftsmen migrated to various parts of Italy, deeply influencing local practice. Demaratus of Corinth, for example, emigrated to Tarquinia in Etruria in the middle of the seventh century BC with an entourage of potters and painters; he married the daughter of a local nobleman and legend has it that their son moved to Rome and became King Tarquin the Elder. Philosophy also developed under the Greeks, with Pythagoras and Elia living at Croton. Furthermore, the Greeks handed down important lessons in military tactics to the Italians, using a phalanx, or battle-line, of infantry or hoplites, instead of the individualistic 'heroic' methods. They were also responsible for important advances in the way in which towns were fortified, as the Etruscans found to their cost when attempting to extend their influence into Greek territory. Ultimately this, acting as a bulwark against an Etruscan unification of Italy, may well be the single most important impact which the Greeks had on early Italian history. Why, then, was it that a culture so superior to the indigenous Italic ones did not have a far greater political impact? The answer, perhaps predictably, lies in lack of unity: the Greek cities were continually fighting amongst themselves, and there was considerable internecine strife within the cities. This clearly dissipated any energy the Greeks might have had for further penetration of the Italian peninsula.

The Etruscans

> 'The long-nosed, sensitive-footed, subtly-smiling Etruscans,
> Who made so little noise outside the cypress groves ...'
>
> D. H. LAWRENCE, '*Cypresses*'

The pre-Roman Italian culture which had the greatest influence and left the most important mark on Italian history, however, is without doubt the Etruscan one. The traveller to Italy should note that there is a wealth of often fascinating evidence of Etruscan culture to be seen in Italy's 'Etruscan belt', between Florence and Rome, which is full of truly remarkable tombs, temples and other remains of the civilisation. These even today are sometimes neglected, out of the way and underexploited, which in many ways adds to their attractiveness and offers interesting possibilities for the slightly more adventurous tourist.

Around the sixth century BC much of Italy, and in particular central Italy, was dominated by the Etruscans. The Romans knew them as Etrusci or Tusci, the Greeks as Tyrsenoi or Tyrrhenoi. They called themselves, so Greek tradition has it, Rasenna. The Greek version of their name survives in the form of the Tyrrhenian Sea (Tirreno) which separates the west coast of Italy from the islands of Sicily and Sardinia. The Roman version has given rise to Tuscany (Toscana), the modern name for Etruria, their homeland.

ORIGINS

There has always been an air of fascination and mystery surrounding the Etruscans. This is as much the result of what we don't know about them as it is of our knowledge of their characteristics and customs. To start with, there is a good deal of uncertainty and controversy surrounding where they actually came from. The Greek historian Herodotus wrote in the fifth century BC that they were Lydians who had migrated to Italy from western Asia Minor to escape famine, and this became the recognised wisdom, even accepted by the Etruscans themselves. A dissenting view was put forward in the first century BC by Dionysius of Halicarnassus who claimed that they must in fact be native Italians, as their language and institutions were in many ways radically different from those of the Lydians. The debate continues to the present day, substantially unresolved despite the use of modern scientific methods to study the human remains that have been discovered by archaeologists. Those who favour the indigeneity thesis point to the fact that Etruscan towns usually replaced former Villanovan settlements, a good example of this being Veii near Rome. Furthermore, their burial practices often seem to be a logical progression of Villanovan ones. The oriental flavour of Etruscan culture can, according to this view, be explained by the

Greek influence which was, as we have seen, significant at this time. The proponents of the immigration view, on the other hand, consider that to make the transition from the villages of the Villanovans to the cities which the Etruscans founded required new skills which did not exist in Italy at the time, and which must therefore have been brought in from outside. They additionally point to the many parallels between eastern and Etruscan culture, and to linguistic evidence.

The Etruscan language, such as we know of it, was not Indo–European and is remarkably similar to that which archaeological evidence has shown to have been used on the Aegean island of Lemnos in pre-Greek

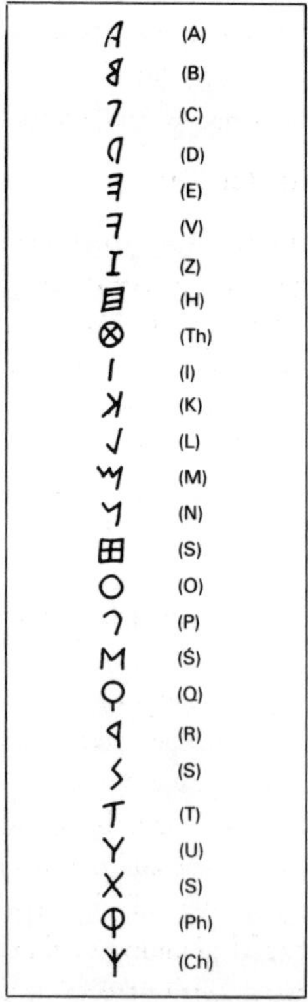

The Etruscan Alphabet with its phonetic equivalents

times. This also has links with the languages of Asia Minor and tempts one to see Lemnos as a staging-post for the Etruscans between Asia Minor and Italy. The 'Cippo Perugino', bearing one of the longest known Etruscan inscriptions, is perhaps the best-known source of evidence on the language. (It is in the National Archaeological Museum in Perugia which, incidentally, also contains some interesting specimens from the Palaeolithic and metal ages.) Almost equally controversial is the date of the Etruscan invasion, if invasion it was. The traditional view is that they came to Italy around 1200 BC, but archaeological evidence points to the early eighth century BC as the most likely date of their settlement in Italy. It is also likely that such a migration took place gradually over an extended period of time. No matter where the Etruscans originated, or when and how they arrived, the salient fact is that Etruscan culture as we know it developed in Italy, in Etruria proper.

CITIES, TOMBS AND RELIGION

The early Etruscans founded the cities of Populonia, Tarquinia, Vetulonia, Vulci and Caere at key points along the west coast. They later moved inland and imposed themselves as the rulers of Villanovan settlements, establishing the cities of Volsinii (Orvieto), Volaterrae (Volterra), Cortona, Arretium (Arezzo), Clusium (Chiusi), Perusia (Perugia), Veii, and others. They were very much pioneers, organising the Villanovans to clear and reclaim the thick forests and macchia which characterised central Italy at the time, to gain land for cultivation and enable cities to be built. They also used their superior engineering abilities to drain land and build roads, which of course further facilitated the city building process.

In line with the Etruscan propensity for mysticism and ritual, the cities were founded according to religious rules, which were contained in Ritual Books. So, for example, it was necessary to protect citizens from external dangers, real or imaginary, by building sacred boundaries (*pomeria*) around cities, and temples and public buildings were carefully planned and sited. The geographical characteristics of many of the earlier cities precluded careful planning of their layout, but later cities were arranged meticulously, with streets built on a grid system, a practice which probably influenced Roman town planning later on. (An excellent example can be found at Marzabotto, near Bologna.) Most private houses were made from wood and rudimentary bricks and were rectangular in shape, larger ones having two floors and sometimes gabled roofs. The aristocracy lived in large and stylish houses (*domus*) which were built around a courtyard in the Greek style – probably the forerunner of the Roman atrium style of luxury house.

Etruscan temples were generally square buildings on top of a high stone plinth, with a large colonnaded portico to the front and a cella, or interior chamber, inside. The cella was often divided into three parts in accordance with the Etruscan belief in a triad of deities, although occasionally there would be one central cella flanked by two wing chambers (*alae*). A feature of these temples is that the mainly wooden interior often contained gaily coloured terracotta ornamentation and figures.

The Etruscans' burial rites consisted of both cremation and interment, and their tombs, which are one of the main sources of our knowledge of their civilisation, are sometimes splendid affairs. The poor were interred in holes or trenches, but the nobility were usually buried in style in chambers covered by mounds of earth (*tumuli*), round stone vaults set in hillsides (*tholoi*), or in corridor tombs cut out of solid rock. These last were often family tombs, laid out in rows of streets so that they have been termed 'cities of the dead' (*necropoleis*), striking examples being the cemeteries at Caere and at Volsinii (modern Orvieto). The necropoleis had vaulted roofs and were decorated with often spectacular frescoes depicting scenes of everyday Etruscan life, while individual tombs were sometimes shaped like houses, luxuriously furnished, and contained high-quality pottery, jewellery and metalware. There is an outstanding example at Tarquinii which contains some magnificent brightly-coloured murals depicting dancing, banqueting, music, hunting, fishing and horse racing, as well as some mysterious underworld scenes. Besides the major burial sites, central Italy contains many minor, relatively unheralded, often neglected but nonetheless extremely interesting, remains of the Etruscans. An example is the site just outside the small town of Sovana where, apart from rock tombs, there is a well-preserved temple and other remains of a settlement.

Religion is a major contributor to the aura of mystery which surrounds Etruscan culture. The Etruscans believed in many gods, some of them adopted from the Greeks, and also in malicious spirits: in particular, they worshipped the triad of Tinia, Uni and Menerva, corresponding to Jupiter, Juno and Minerva in the Roman pantheon. They believed that the 'Etrusca disciplina' had been revealed to them by seers, and religious practice was laid out in books of ritual. The 'libri fulgurales' dealt with the way in which thunder and lightning could be interpreted, while the 'libri haruspicini' contained instructions on how 'haruspices', or professional diviners, could interpret the omens to be found in the livers of sacrificed animals – another example of the way in which the Etruscans influenced the Romans, who were to follow similar practices. These books also contained instructions on how to perform most important private and public functions, including how to build temples, found cities and wage war. Ritual and religion dominated most things the Etruscans did. Their religion, unlike that of the Greeks and other Italians, was cruel and sombre. A particularly macabre practice was that of human sacrifice to placate the gods and protect themselves from the kind of torment meted out by demons in the underworld which is depicted in their tomb paintings. Victims were forced to kill each other off in gladiatorial duels which took place at funerals, and prisoners of war were frequently massacred to enhance the peace of mind of their captors.

ART AND COMMERCE

The Etruscans also left many examples of their art. The frescoes on the walls of their tombs have already been mentioned, but fine painting can also be found on their vases. Their pottery was mostly imported in large quantities from Greece, but there are some good examples of work based on the traditional black clay (bucchero). They were high-quality metal-workers, producing impressive incised decorations on their funerary paraphernalia and on mirrors, and makers of gold and silver jewellery which they widely exported. The Capitoline wolf in Rome and the Chimera of Arezzo are fine examples of the artistic metal-work which they were capable of producing. Also of note is a beautifully intricate and ornate candelabra which, together with other Etruscan bronze artefacts, can be found in the Etruscan Museum in Cortona. Other

Etruscan Bronze Stud from a tomb at Tarquinia

interesting Etruscan pieces are kept at the Archaeological Museum in Florence, and at the Vatican Museums in Rome. The Etruscans were not particularly impressive stone sculptors, but produced magnificent terracotta sculpture, the best known of which is from the Apollo in Veii, which yielded life-size terracotta figures often referred to as the 'Contest for the Sacred Hind'. Etruscan art was clearly strongly influenced by the Greeks, and some Greek artists are thought to have settled and founded schools in Etruria. However, this imported influence was fused with native Italic practice to produce a style which is truly original and which is characterised by its life and naturalness.

Apart from being a spiritual and artistic people the Etruscans were also great traders and seafarers. At home the basis of their economic efforts was agriculture, fishing and hunting; this was supplemented by the exploitation of mineral deposits such as copper and iron, and of building stone. These enabled a large population to be supported and an advanced civilisation to be developed, as well as providing the basis for trade. From early days they traded with the Phoenicians and the Carthaginians, and by the seventh century BC they had established strong links with Greece, trading directly with Athens using their own ships. There was also substantial trade within Italy, notably with the Greek cities of the south. This development of trade led to the introduction of coins as a medium of exchange around the end of the sixth century BC. These replaced lumps of copper which had been used earlier; at first coins of Greek cities were used, but later Etruscan cities started issuing their own gold, silver and copper coins based on the Greek standard which was in use in Campania.

Closely related to the Etruscan prowess in trade was their naval power, which also of course played a central part in their expansion in Italy. In alliance with Carthage they controlled the Tyrrhenian and the western Mediterranean, and in 536 BC even managed to expel Greek colonists from the coast of Corsica and to set up a colony there, following a naval battle at Aleria. The collapse of their sea power was later to be an important factor in their downfall.

POLITICS AND SOCIETY

The Etruscans did not spread their influence through force of numbers. There would typically be small groups of warriors who possessed organisation, techniques and culture superior to that of the indigenous peoples. This enabled them to establish themselves as ruling aristocracies in the places they took over, imposing their language and ways on the native population. This is the way they remained, not merging with the native Italic peoples as other conquerors might have done, but keeping them subjugated, remaining aloof, and organising and exploiting their resources for their own purposes. Not surprisingly, therefore, the political and social structure of Etruscan society was highly élitist and rigid. At first the city states were ruled by kings, or *lucumones*, who lived in remarkable luxury and magnificence. They wore crowns of gold and purple robes and sat on ivory thrones; their henchmen carried a collection of rods, or fasces, as a symbol of the power which the king wielded over his subjects. Again much of this acted as a model for the Romans in years to come. Later the cities were ruled by the nobility, who collectively formed a powerful and wealthy aristocracy which was surrounded by large numbers of clients and slaves. This ruling class seems to have treated its subjects with great cruelty and oppression, and was often hated by them. The middle class consisted of a series of closely-knit families in which, interestingly enough, women enjoyed a high status and played a key role; descent, for example, was often on the mother's side. Not surprisingly, little is known about the serfs, who were of course the majority of the population. Each city was an independent and autonomous state, but they were linked by the Etruscan League, which was an organisation through which the leaders of twelve cities met from time to time at the Fanum Voltumnae (named after the main Etruscan god), near Volsinii. This resulted in some joint action and co-operation, but fundamentally individual cities were not prepared to surrender the amount of local sovereignty required to achieve any real degree of national unity, and no real federation seems to have emerged.

ETRUSCAN ROME

During the late seventh century and the early part of the sixth century BC the Etruscans conquered much of Latium, including towns such as Tusculum (Frascati) in the Alban hills, and they occupied Rome. Some of them pushed as far south as Campania, settling in various places, including Capua, Nola and Pompeii.

Rome provides a good case study of the functioning and influence of Etruscan civilisation. In Rome, the Etruscans ruled through a succession of three kings: Lucius Tarquinius Priscus (616–579 BC), Servius Tullius (578–535), and Tarquinius Superbus (534–510). Lucius is credited with the introduction of drainage and games to the city. The latter probably consisted largely of horse-racing, for which the Etruscans had a weakness, and were held at the Circus Maximus, between the Palatine and the Aventine. Servius is chiefly known for his reorganisation of the Roman state and army, significantly increasing the power of the middle classes; he also founded a sanctuary dedicated to the goddess Diana on the Aventine hill, and possibly built a defensive wall around the city. Superbus' main achievement was probably a temple to Jupiter on the Capitoline hill which was adorned with statues by Vulca from Veii. Under the Etruscan kings Rome was developed to a considerable extent, becoming a real city with an advanced cultural life. Industry and commerce began to develop in what was still a predominantly agricultural city, and traditional Roman religion was to a large extent 'Etruscanised' during this period. Following the reforms implemented by Servius, an embryonic form of political assembly emerged. Many remains of Etruscan Rome survive to this day, notably in the Forum and on the Capitoline hill. The Etruscan domination of Rome finally came to an end around 510 BC when Tarquinius Superbus, who is often portrayed as a cruel tyrant, was expelled, in all probability after his son Sextus had raped Lucretia, the wife of Collatinus, thereby provoking a rebellion led by Iunius Brutus. Superbus tried to recapture the city with the help of Lars Porsenna from Clusium. According to Livy he failed and was defeated by Horatius. According to Tacitus and other later Roman writers, however, Lars Porsenna actually retook Rome, tried to replace Superbus, and was eventually defeated by the Latins under Aristodemus at Aricia in 506 BC.

END OF ETRUSCAN RULE

This defeat was an important stage in the decline of Etruscan power in Italy, for it cut off the land links between Etruria and its settlements in Campania. The same Aristodemus had been responsible for blocking the Etruscan expansion in southern Italy by preventing them from taking the Greek city of Cumae in 524 BC. When Etruscan naval control was smashed in 474 at a battle off Cumae, the proverbial writing was very much on the wall for the Etruscans in the south since they were now isolated by sea as well as by land. By 420 the cities in Campania had been overrun by Sabellian tribesmen descending from the mountains; ironically, they also captured Cumae.

In the north meanwhile, late in the sixth century the Etruscans crossed the Apennines into the Po valley and conquered a good deal of central–northern Italy from the Adriatic up to near the Alps. Their main city in this part of Italy was at Felsina, near Bologna, but important settlements were also to be found at Spina, north of Ravenna, and at Marzabotto, which has not been built over since and provides important evidence of the structure of an Etruscan city. Another noteworthy settlement was at Adria, near the mouth of the Po, and after which the

Adriatic sea is named. However, Etruscan domination of the north of Italy was also relatively short-lived, and they were gradually swept aside by Celtic tribes descending from further north from about 400 BC. In 350 BC Felsina fell, and Etruscan power was at an end in what the Romans were to call Gallia Cisalpina. By this time Etruria itself was in the process of being conquered by the Romans. In 396 Veii was taken after a siege lasting ten years, in 308 Tarquinia was lost, and the final blow came in 265 BC when the Romans captured Volsinii, the last Etruscan city.

As has already been suggested, the Etruscans came very close to bringing about the first unification of Italy, and they were certainly responsible for a massive leap in Italian civilisation. They began the process of urbanisation in Italy, they precipitated economic progress, they disseminated their alphabet, and greatly influenced the development of town planning, art, architecture, road building, religion, warfare, and political structures. Why did they, then, ultimately fail to unify Italy? Several reasons can be put forward, the first of which is that their cities lacked unity and political organisation between one another. Despite the Etruscan League they remained, partly because of geographic factors, quite discrete entities who rarely acted in a cohesive fashion. Thus, among other things, they were unable to defend their gains when these came under threat. Secondly, because they subjugated rather than absorbed or mixed with the people they conquered, and because they often treated their serfs cruelly, they never managed to win the true loyalty of their subjects. There were armed risings among the underprivileged classes in Etruscan cities, and Etruscan hold on their conquests became more tenuous as the area they controlled grew larger. Add to this the corrupting effect on an élite of too much wealth and the picture is complete. Very colourful Greek and Latin accounts of Etruscan debauchery are probably overstated; nevertheless, this was probably an important factor in their downfall. The scene was now set for the rise of Rome.

CHAPTER TWO

The Romans

The years of Roman hegemony constitute without doubt the first truly great period in Italian history, in which the country was united for the first time, and came to rule over most of the known world, spreading its culture far and wide and making a fundamental and lasting contribution to the development of civilisation as we know it. Contemporary Italian life is deeply influenced by the events of Roman times, and the remains of their culture are still widely to be found throughout the country. In particular, Rome itself is of course something of an open-air living museum, brimming over with famous and easily accessible features such as the colosseum, the forum, and the temples at Largo Argentina. Outside the capital one can visit the unique cities of Pompeii and Herculaneum, where an eruption of Vesuvius in AD 79 tragically engulfed whole Roman towns and left them perfectly preserved for posterity. Also worthy of particular note are the breathtaking mosaics from Roman times which are to be found on the east coast at Ravenna, and in Sicily in the Roman villa at Piazza Armerina.

The period of Roman ascendancy can conveniently be divided into three phases: the early monarchic era (foundation–510 BC), the republic (509–31 BC), and the principate, or empire (31 BC–AD 476). First we must consider the very beginnings of the city.

The Foundation of Rome and the Period of Monarchy

ROMULUS AND REMUS

A famous legend has it that the city of Rome was founded by two brothers, Romulus and Remus, who were the children of Rhea Silvia by the god Mars. The two children were cast afloat on a raft on the River Tiber by some well-wishers, to escape the clutches of their wicked uncle Amulius, who had condemned them to death. They ended up on the Palatine hill, where they were suckled and cared for by a female wolf. Hence the famous image which has become the symbol of Rome (much in evidence on the interminable souvenir stalls which today inevitably surround the tourist venues in the city). Romulus and Remus were brought up by a shepherd, and eventually they set out from Alba Longa, where they had been raised, to found a city. However, they could not agree on the exact site of the proposed settlement, Romulus wanting it to be on the Palatine hill, and Remus preferring the Aventine hill. They consulted the gods, and were each told to stay on their chosen site to await an omen. Romulus apparently saw twelve white vultures, whereas Remus saw six of them. A quarrel ensued, during which Romulus killed his brother and then proceeded to found the city of Rome on the Palatine. This colourful story dates back to Rome's earliest days and has always been a part of Roman folklore.

According to ancient Greek historians, however, it was Aeneas, escaping from the sack of Troy, who landed in Latium and founded the city. The best-known account of Aeneas' travels is to be found in Virgil's *Aeneid*, in which the mythical adventurer married a princess called Lavinia on his arrival in Italy, and founded the city of Lavinium, named after her. This equally colourful tale is almost certainly fictitious, as the sack of Troy took place some 400 years before the likely foundation of Rome. Nevertheless it became popularly accepted, not least in Rome itself.

Later Roman historians such as Fabius Pictor and Livy (in his influential history of Rome written at the time of Augustus) fused the local traditional story with the account in Greek mythology, to produce, in the third century BC, the 'official' synthesis which became the widely accepted version of events. According to this, Romulus and Remus were the grandchildren of Aeneas, who himself was the offspring of the goddess Venus. Lavinium was founded by Aeneas, and Alba Longa by his son Ascanius. Romulus, after his unconventional upbringing and experiences with fratricide, founded Rome on 21 April 753 BC, and was the first of a line of seven kings who ruled Rome for 243 years up to the beginning of the republic. The implication of this version of the origin of the city is that the Romans were descended from the gods, which no doubt added to its popular appeal.

An early problem which Romulus had to face was the lack of nubile women in the embryonic city, which he solved by inviting local tribes, including the Sabines, to a celebration and then proceeding to abduct their young females. Hence the well-known works of art on the theme of the 'Rape of the Sabine Women'. According to Livy, Romulus eventually reconciled the Sabines after raping their daughters, and ruled jointly for a period with their king Titus Tatius, expanding the city to include the Aventine and Capitoline hills and founding the Senate, the calendar, and the Roman army. He is variously depicted as a good man or a tyrannical despot who was killed by the senate, but the traditional story is that during a storm he rose into the heavens shrouded in a thick mist and became a god. He then reappeared briefly to announce that 'by the will of the gods my Rome shall be the capital of the world', before returning to the heavens.

THE ROMAN KINGS

The historical validity of these wonderful accounts is clearly dubious, but it certainly adds to the mystery surrounding ancient Rome. However, it seems that there was in fact a period of monarchical rule in Rome from about 753 to around 510 BC, and someone known as Romulus was probably the first king, reigning until 715. He was succeeded by Numa Pompilius (715–713), Tullus Hostilius (673–641), Ancus Marcius (641–616), and then by the three Etruscan kings Tarquinius Priscus (616–579), Servius Tullius (579–534) and Tarquinius Superbus (534–510). Numa was a peace-loving Sabine from Cures, and under him Rome enjoyed a period of stability with little quest for territorial expansion. He is supposed to have divided Rome's land among its citizens, and to have established many religious ceremonies and the twelve-month calendar. Tullus, on the other hand, was a quite different proposition, waging war against the Sabines, conquering Alba Longa, and gaining control of the holy Alban hill, thereby establishing Rome as the leader of the Latin League of cities. Under him the population of Rome was doubled by the forced resettlement of people from Alba Longa. His successor Ancus continued to fight with the Latins, conquering a number of their towns and continuing the resettlement process, which clearly has several parallels in modern times, further to increase the population of Rome. The three Etruscan kings and the impact of the Etruscans on the city have already been discussed in chapter 1 (pp. 18–19).

An interesting characteristic of Rome under the monarchy was the sophisticated political structure which was put into place. The king (*rex*) was endowed with overall power, or *imperium*, which was essentially underpinned by a form of divine right. Unlike other positions of privilege, the monarchy was not passed on by a system of inheritance. The kings were chosen according to largely religious criteria with the help of omens from the gods, although no doubt in practice political wheeling and dealing must also have played an important part. In the period between kings, the city was ruled by a series of *interreges*, chosen from the ranks of the senate. The senate, which was basically the body which represented the aristocracy, consisted of *patricians*, who were supposedly descended from the original one hundred wise men whom Romulus, so the story goes, had chosen to act as counsellors. These elders in turn represented the *gens*, important groups of people sharing common ancestry, who controlled large numbers of dependants (*clientes*). The senate's role remained largely one of providing advice to the king, but it also enjoyed *auctoritas*, or influence, which derived from religion and played a crucial part in the process of king-making. A significant political role was also played by the *curiae*, which can be thought of as representing the populace. These originally consisted of thirty groups based on the three tribes (Ramnes, Tities, and Luceres) into which Romulus was supposed to have organised the Roman population, and they met in rudimentary form of political assembly called *comitia curiata*. The tribes also provided the basic organisation of the army, each contributing one third of the total infantry, cavalry and tribunes (or commanders). Under the later Etruscan kings, the power of the *curiae* was to a large extent diluted, and their assembly was largely superseded by the *comitia centuriata*, an alternative body in which the franchise was mainly determined by the wealth and military potential of individual members.

The social structure was basically dominated by extended families (*familia*), which were strongly patriarchal in their organisation. The head of the family (*paterfamilias*) had virtually unlimited power over the rest of the family, including the sons, who eventually inherited the position. Summarising, one could say that heredity and patriarchy were two of the essential bastions of the Roman monarchic period.

The Roman Republic

After the tyrant Tarquinius Superbus had been expelled, Etruscan rule of the city came to an end and the Roman republic was established in or around 510 BC. At first the republic was effectively run by the aristocracy, the patrician *gentes*. The position of head of state was, curiously, shared equally by two men known as *praetors* or *consuls*. They were elected by the people, in the form of the *comitia centuriata*, for a fixed and not renewable term of one year, and they had to a large extent the same *imperium* and duties which the kings had previously enjoyed. Consuls were chosen from the senate and returned to it at the end of their period of office. They were subject to what we might today refer to as strong checks and balances to their power. The most obvious of these was their limited term of appointment; however, there is also some evidence that citizens could appeal to the people against their decisions (*provocatio*), and they operated on a principle of unanimity or collegiality, which effectively meant that one consul could veto the decisions of the other. All this meant that the real power rested very much with the senate, which of course was in the control of the aristocracy. The only exception to these arrangements was that, from around 500 BC, in times of emergency the senate took powers to appoint a *dictator*, who for six months had unlimited and unrestrained authority to deal with the crisis.

Another important position in the republic was that of the *quaestors*, early bureaucrats who assisted the consuls. At first these were appointed, but from 447 BC they were elected; their number gradually increased, from two to about forty by the end of the republic. There were also *censors*, who held office for eighteen months and who were, from 443 BC onwards, elected to carry out population counts, but also to determine the social position of citizens and remove unworthy ones from office.

Most intriguing, however, was the *rex sacrorum*, who took over the king's previous religious functions, presumably in order to help keep power in the hands of the aristocracy by removing the temptation for consuls to claim divine right and assume absolute control over the state.

RISE OF THE PLEBS

It is perhaps not surprising that this intricate system of government, carefully designed to keep the aristocracy in power, from time to time precipitated sometimes unseemly attempted coups by individuals, many of whom in fact kept private armies. For example, Appius Herdonius attempted such a coup in 460 BC, with moderate success. Most crucially, however, the monopoly of power held by the aristocracy was challenged, during the first two centuries of the republic, by what may be seen as an early form of class struggle. The hereditary ruling class, usually known as *patricians*, were taken on by the *plebs*. One may regard these as the underprivileged majority, but they included many of what we would now term the middle classes, that is artisans, traders and the like. They were driven to challenge the political power of the hereditary aristocracy by the crippling burden of debt which they faced and by the resentment which they felt at the unequal distribution of wealth. Debt was particularly onerous, since under the *nexus* system loans were secured directly by a person's labour. Default meant that the principal and interest had to be repaid with the borrower's work, which resulted in many people living much of their lives in a form of economic bondage. The problem of wealth distribution concerned mainly land ownership. The patricians, predictably owned most of the land and exploited the poor by charging in kind for its use.

The plebs managed to organise themselves, with the objective of removing these two forms of iniquity, and further of demanding a codified and public system of law designed to give equal rights to all. In 494 BC they moved en masse out of the city to the Aventine hill, where they created an alternative state. They set up a separate assembly, the *concilium plebis*, and elected *tribunes*, officials who were protected by the oath of their peers under the *lex sacrata* (hallowed law). This quasi-revolutionary form of mass protest or withdrawal of support (*cessatio*) was an extremely powerful weapon which was used five times before

287 BC. Thus the plebs established a strong solidarity among themselves which was the source of their strength, and the tribunes, whose number gradually grew from two to as many as ten, became very influential people. They wielded power (*potestas*) comparable to that of the consuls, and could use sanctions (*coercitio*) such as fines and imprisonment to enforce it. They interceded in favour of plebeians in disputes with the consuls, and eventually exercised what amounted to a power of veto (*intercessio*) over the functioning of the official state.

Given these circumstances, the rise of the plebeians was more or less inevitable, and they inexorably managed to acquire a share of power in the Roman republic. The *lex publilia* of 471 BC and the Valerio–Horatian laws of 449 set in motion the process whereby plebeian institutions and methods were gradually recognised and incorporated into the official state, and by 287 the plebeian assembly had won the right to make universally accepted law. In the meantime, the plebs had achieved representation in the senate and had been given access to the consulship by the Licino–Sextian laws of 367 BC, which are remarkable for introducing what would now be called a formal system of power-sharing between the patricians and the plebs. Additionally, the objective of legal codification was achieved around 450, and the much despised *nexum* was abolished in 326. What basically emerged from this process was a new, more meritocratic élite of patrician and plebeian nobles.

Over nearly 500 years of the republic there were inevitably variations and developments, but the foregoing can be regarded as the essence of how the republic was organised. This structure served the republic well over a remarkably long period, providing what was, for its time, a subtle compromise between effectiveness and personal liberty.

CONQUEST OF ITALY

The political and social structure of the republic was undoubtedly innovative, and it is clear that subsequent civilisations both within and without Italy were deeply influenced by it. However, the republic's most fundamental and enduring achievement was the conquest of the Italian peninsula and the first unification of Italy, together with the territorial acquisition outside Italy which laid the basis of one of the greatest empires the world has known.

The conquest of Italy was achieved in various stages over a period of four or five centuries. In general the tactic employed was one of wherever possible attempting to incorporate rather than subjugate. Many peoples were given partial citizen rights and privileges, known as 'Latin rights'; some, the *municipia*, were later allowed full Roman citizenship in return for essential contributions to the war effort. Other communities were given the status of allies (*socii*), which bestowed social and economic privileges and established mutual defence obligations. The objective was fundamentally to allow the ruling class in conquered territory to identify themselves directly with Rome and give them a vested interest in the preservation and expansion of Roman hegemony, thus enabling the Romans to use the resources of conquered peoples to fight wars and build the empire. Furthermore, the Romans would bolster the local ruling class by helping them to maintain their position in the face of revolts and popular uprisings, thereby increasing dependence on Rome. For example, local revolts at Arretium and Volsinii were put down by Roman soldiers in 302 and 264 BC respectively. Where there were no suitable communities to incorporate, the Romans would use resettlement as a means of control. Landless Roman citizens were given land in conquered areas to induce them to found settlements (*coloniae*) in these places – again a tactic often employed subsequently in history. These settlements usually consisted of 4500–6000 people and were laid out with meticulous precision in strategic points. The carefully planned and quasi-liberal approach which the Romans adopted towards conquered peoples was an important reason why Roman hegemony endured over an extended period of time, whereas the conquests of others such as the Etruscans were much more transient.

The first phase of the unification of Italy was naturally the establishment of control over the Latins and the immediate area around Rome. This process was interrupted briefly by the sack of the city by the Celts in 390 BC. However, these Gallic tribesmen were bought off with gold, order was relatively quickly re-established, and the subjugation of the Latins was completed by 348 when the Latin League was dissolved. Next the Romans expanded southwards into Campania, the Puglie and Lucania, defeating the Oscan-speaking Samnite tribes who controlled this area in a series of wars between 343 and 290.

After the successful war against Pyrrhus, King of Epirus, who had invaded Italy from the Near East in 282–275, and the capture of Tarentum in 272, Roman control of the south was almost complete, and an extensive process of colonisation was undertaken. The Greek states were given privileged treatment as allies, mainly because their ports were critical for the establishment of Roman naval power. Whilst all this was happening in the south, the Romans were also busy crushing the Etruscans in their own homeland, a task which was completed around 395. The Umbrians also capitulated without much resistance around this time.

THE PUNIC WARS

The next phase in the expansion of Rome is mainly centred around a bitter struggle with the city of Carthage in north Africa, Rome's fiercest and most tenacious rival at this time. This attrition took the form of three wars, usually known as the Punic wars, between 264 and 146 BC. With the first of these the Romans completed their domination of the south, expelling the Carthaginians from Sicily and forcing their leader, Hamilcar Barca, to sue for peace from his stronghold at Mount Eryx (Monte Erice) near Drepanum (Trapani), after a momentous siege. The captured island was made an overseas province of Rome, as were Sardinia, which was annexed in 239, and Corsica. This war was a real conflict of the titans, in which huge armies and fleets of 50–70,000 men were pitted against one another. Once created, the provinces were ruled by governors who were sent out annually, although the major Greek cities were allowed a large degree of independence.

The second Punic war (218–202 BC) is probably best known for Hannibal and his elephants crossing the Alps in the legendary expedition to challenge Rome in its own backyard. Hannibal was Hamilcar's son, and he began his amazing march in Spain in 218. Within two years he had employed his innovative and brilliant military tactics to defeat the Romans in four great battles: at Ticinus and Trebia in 218, at Lake Trasimeno (where he outflanked and annihilated the Roman forces led by C. Flaminius, pushing them into the lake) in 217, and at Cannae in 216 BC. Rome seemed to be at his mercy. However, he lacked the ability or inclination to push home his advantage at the crucial time, and Rome was saved. His brother Hasdrubal was sent to reinforce him but was defeated and killed at the battle of Metaurus (Metauro) in 207. The Romans now went onto the offensive: they stalled Hannibal in the south and Sicily and sent Scipio Africanus to north Africa, where he defeated the Carthaginians at Utica in 204 and Zama in 202.

Apart from the story of Hannibal's elephants, the second Punic war is remembered in folklore for the fabulous war machines of Archimedes – for example, huge cranes which could drop enormous weights on warships, which the Carthaginians used to frustrate the Roman siege of Syracuse over an extended period in 212 BC.

The war naturally consolidated Roman hold over central–southern Italy and Sicily, but it also marked the beginning of expansion into the rest of the Mediterranean. Spain fell under Roman domination, and the provinces of Hither and Further Spain (Hispania Citerior and Ulterior) were created in 197 BC. Much of the Balkans was added after wars with Macedonia in 200–196 and 172–167. Carthage, however, remained a source of insecurity, and the Romans finally resolved their problem by precipitating the third Punic war (149–146). Scipio Aemilianus, the adopted grandson of Scipio Africanus, was sent to Carthage where he kept up the family tradition by utterly devastating the city. It was captured and all of its inhabitants were killed. After burning for ten days, what remained of Carthage was razed to the ground and the scorched earth was scattered with salt and cursed to make sure that it would never threaten Rome again.

EXPANSION NORTHWARDS

While the Punic wars were being waged, the Republic was also busy conquering northern Italy. The Celtic-speaking Gauls who had settled there were defeated at the battles of Telamon (Talamone) in 225 BC and of Mediolanium (Milan) in 222, and by 160 their territory south of the Po had been captured, together with that of the Ligurian Apennine tribes. The Ligurian hill peoples around Genua (Genoa) were overcome between 220 and 118, when the Provincia Narbonensis (Provence) was created. By this time Rome's hold on Italy as we know it today was well established, although the official frontier was still along the Apennines and the famous Rubicon stream, which we shall encounter again later.

It was not until 90–89 BC that the whole of Italy south of the Po was incorporated in a unitary Roman state, and not until 27 BC that Augustus included the remainder of Gallia Cisalpina north of the River Po into the Roman state.

The unification of Italy under the Romans was clearly a major watershed in Italian history. The most obvious effect which it had on the Italian people was that they began the very gradual process of taking on a national identity. Much of this naturally consisted of assimilating the Roman way of life, including the Latin language, a process often referred to as the 'Romanisation' of Italy. The disappearance of many of the ethnic differences in the peninsula was largely complete by the first century AD, a process which was facilitated by the increased contact other Italians had with the Romans through long periods of shared military service, but also by improved communications, for the Romans were great builders of roads.

Roman roads were originally built for military purposes, were usually named after the people who had organised their construction, and one of their most striking features is the way they were built in straight lines, with little regard for the contours of the land. Many modern Italian arteries more or less follow the routes taken by these pioneering roads. There were, for example,

Via Latina (334 BC), from Rome to Campania (where it joined the Via Appia) via the Alban Hills;

Via Appia (312 BC), to Campania, by way of the coast, and extended (244 BC) to Brundisium (Brindisi);

Via Salaria (361 BC), to the central Apennines;

Via Flaminia (200 BC), to the Adriatic coast;

Via Aurelia (108 BC), to Pisa and Genoa;

Via Cassia (170 BC), which crossed Etruria.

THE REPUBLICAN CITY

The establishment of Rome as such a dominant and mighty force also had far-reaching implications for the city itself. It grew steadily in size, with about 150,000 inhabitants by the third century BC, and it also grew very rich on the land it seized from subjected peoples and from the spoils of war. This enabled public works to be undertaken on a grand scale.

Temples were built, including the one to Bellona started in 296 by Appius Claudius Caecus and the two which can still be seen at Largo Argentina in the centre of the city. So were the first of the famous Roman aqueducts, the Aqua Appia in 312 and the Anio Vetus in 272, which have become one of the best-known symbols of Roman prowess in engineering. Economic prosperity led to the emergence of a services sector and luxury goods industries to meet the demands of the wealthy. A convenient medium of exchange was naturally required, and so coins were introduced from around 280 BC, the idea being copied from the Greeks, and a mint was established, administered by a *triumvir monetalis*. The wealthy classes began to keep slaves, who were mainly prisoners of war, to work in their households and on their expanding estates. However, the children of freed slaves were absorbed into Roman society and were allowed full Roman citizenship.

Art flourished in this period, much of it heavily influenced by Greek culture, which was highly fashionable among the élite of the time. So did Latin literature, with great writers and poets such as Cato, Livius Andronicus, Ennius, Lucilius and Terentius Afer (Terence) emerging. This period also saw the emergence of the great Roman triumphs, or victory celebrations, accorded to commanders on their return from particularly successful missions. The *triumphator* would parade his army and his booty around the city from the Campus Martius to the Capitol, where he would offer thanks and sacrifices to Jupiter Optimus Maximus, amid wild scenes of public rejoicing and festivity.

On a political level, the military victories which the senate had organised, particularly over Hannibal, naturally boosted its prestige and control over Roman society. For about a century after the tribunate of C. Flaminius in 232 BC there was political stability and very little opposition to the established order in the city, a kind of halcyon period for the republic. Some of the credit for this must go to Cato (234–149 BC) who, as censor, set out to purge, by his influence and personal example, the excesses of the frivolous rich who often affected pro-hellenic snobbery and who tended to live grossly hedonistic lifestyles. There is, for example, the story of those who would vomit with the help of a feather into *vomitoriae* so as to prolong eating binges. Cato also acted to prevent powerful individuals, such as Scipio Africanus whom he forced out of office in 184 BC, from developing ideas above their station and threatening the oligarchy.

The Roman Revolution and the Transition from Republic to Empire

INTERNAL CRISIS

However, the storm clouds were gathering. War, although successful, was also costly, not only in terms of direct resources, but also because of the indirect effect which it had on agriculture and the countryside. Hannibal's invasion and the long war which followed, for example, had a devastating effect on the land, with many peasant families displaced or destroyed. Additionally, it was necessary for the Romans to keep a very large army, probably as numerous as 130,000, on an almost permanent basis. This was a huge slice of the adult male population of Italy, and most peasant families were therefore deprived of their menfolk for long periods, or even permanently if they perished in battle. Many farms were neglected or abandoned, and numerous peasant families were stripped of their livelihood. At the same time the Roman rich accumulated a kind of *latifundium* by investing their wealth in land, which was worked by slaves (supervised by managers called *vilici*) to produce food to meet the needs of the growing cities. This capitalism in the countryside produced profits for the landowners but resulted in the eviction of large numbers of peasants from the land. As one historian has written, 'Roman peasant soldiers were fighting for their own displacement.' This process naturally resulted in a flight from the countryside into the cities, including Rome, where there was work available servicing the demands of the nouveaux riches, and helping the new class of private contractors (*publicani*) to supply the army and build the temples, the aqueducts and the other conspicuous works which were being commissioned.

The result was that a basically disaffected under class was created in the cities of Roman Italy, which was supplemented by the growing number of slaves that had to be imported to meet the labour supply requirements of the system. This created a huge law and order problem and a potentially revolutionary situation; furthermore, the army, which had been traditionally drawn from the peasant class, now found itself short of recruits. Then, of course, there was the abject poverty which now existed among much of the lower classes, particularly in the countryside. The next century of the republic was consequently one of increasing strife, violence and disunity, and is frequently referred to as the Roman revolution. Essentially republican society was split between the *optimates*, the senatorial class of inherited wealth and position who clearly opposed any change to the status quo, and the *populares*, who, as their name implies, were the less fortunate mass, keen to change the system to their own advantage.

THE GRACCHI

This troubled century began with the tribunate of Tiberius Gracchus, a liberal and perceptive man, who realised the seriousness of the situation faced by the republic, and in 133 BC set about attempting to remedy it by an agrarian reform. He proposed to enforce the legal limit on the size of estates, which had up to now been conveniently ignored, to repossess the surplus and redistribute it to the poor. Of course this proposal met a wall of opposition from the landowners whose interests were seriously threatened, but it obviously enjoyed mass popular support and was approved, with people descending on Rome in their thousands to vote for it. A triumvirate of Tiberius Gracchus himself, his brother Gaius Gracchus, and his father-in-law Appius Claudius was set up to administer the scheme. When Tiberius then presented himself for re-election as tribune, this was stretching constitutional propriety and was all too much for some among the ruling élite. A mob led by Scipio Nasica disrupted the senate and started a riot in which Tiberius Gracchus and 300 of his followers were clubbed to death. This was the first infringement of the traditional rule, emanating from the *lex sacrata*, which protected tribunes from all threats to their personal safety.

Tiberius was followed by his younger brother Gaius Gracchus who continued the re-establishment of the tribunate as the protector of the populace. He set about improving the welfare of the *populares* by a number of measures, the most interesting of which were an extension of colonisation to spread land ownership, attempts to curb corruption in the senate, a widening of the franchise by giving Roman citizenship to the Latins and Latin rights to more Italian allies, improving conditions in the army, and fixing the price of grain for the poor. These were financed by fiscal reform aimed at maximising and stabilising revenues from the vastly rich province of Asia. Contracts to collect taxes were to be auctioned off by the censors to *publicani* who would guarantee to provide the state with a fixed income for five years. Needless to say, Gaius ended up in the same way as his brother: in 121 BC 3000 of his followers were slaughtered on the Aventine hill by troops under the consul Opimius; Gaius himself was stabbed by a faithful servant to prevent his capture; senatorial power was restored. Thus ended the sincere, but on reflection rather naive, attempt by the Gracchi brothers to reform the republic.

CIVIL WAR

The next development in what was by now fast becoming civil war was precipitated by a military crisis, which brought to prominence Gaius Marius, a self-made man from the Volscian area who made his name fighting Jugurtha in Africa and who first became a tribune in 119 BC and a consul in 108. Rome was at this time engaged in an almost continuous series of wars to protect its foreign conquests. There were, of course, defeats as well as victories, but what really impinged on Roman consciousness was the prospect of direct threat to the city itself, as at the time of Hannibal and the second Punic war. This time the threat was provided by the Cimbri and the Teutones, northern tribes who were in the process of migrating southwards and who meted out a succession of defeats to the Roman forces, the most disastrous of which was in 105 BC at Arausio (Orange), where as many as 80,000 men were massacred. Italy was at their mercy and the Romans were clearly terrified, as is shown by their increased offerings, perhaps including human sacrifice, to the gods. However, the German tribesmen failed to seize the moment, and did not attempt to invade Italy until 102 BC. By this time Marius had reorganised the army, as he had previously done in Africa, recruiting heavily among the *proletarii*, the lowest social class, and turning it into the efficient, self-reliant and professional force which was to characterise the later period of empire. Marius' new army smashed the northern invaders at Aquae Sextiae (Aix-en-Provence) in 102 and at Vercellae (Vercelli) in 101.

Marius himself was very much a hero of the people and contrary to law and tradition, was re-elected to the consulship in successive years between 104 and 102 BC, as well as on his return in 100. His importance in the revolutionary period lay in acting as a role model by emphasising that people from outside the ruling élite in fact possessed outstanding abilities and were capable of achieving great things. Most crucially, his military reforms resulted in the army developing a political dimension. Under his command the new proletarian soldiers began to demand economic security as a reward for their efforts. They failed to achieve this in the short run, when an attempt by Saturninus to reserve allotments of land for them in Africa was crushed, but thereafter the army was there to be used as a political weapon by ambitious commanders. The direct threat from the north exposed and exacerbated the internal divisions in the republic, both within the city itself and between Rome and its Italian allies who were growing increasingly unhappy at the unfair way in which they were treated. Thus the process of the collapse of the oligarchy was hastened.

An effort was made by Marcus Livius Drusus to avert the inevitable. He attempted to introduce reforms in the by now familiar fields of the franchise, agrarian structure, and the legal system. These moves were generally inept and never looked like having success. They were finally buried in 91 BC when Drusus was murdered and his principal ally Lucius Crassus also perished. By now armed revolt had broken out in Italy, as Rome's Italian allies (*socii*) fought for their liberties and rights in the bloody Social War. The Romans succeeded in putting this down by force within a couple of years, but at the cost of important political concessions, such as the granting in 90 BC of citizenship to all Italians who remained loyal or surrendered.

SULLA AND POMPEY

The republic's problems continued to pile up, however, next emanating from the province of Asia which Mithridates invaded in 88 BC from Pontus, massacring thousands of Roman citizens. The task of dealing with Mithridates was given to Cornelius Sulla, an unscrupulous and ambitious consul from an old patrician family, who had a distinguished military record. This greatly annoyed Marius, who relished what he saw as the chance of a quick and prestigious victory, and he therefore plotted, with the help of Sulpicius, to replace Sulla on the eastern campaign. Sulla countered this by appealing to his army, which then marched on Rome and captured the city, killing Sulpicius and forcing Marius to flee to Africa amid what was by now almost routine violence and chicanery. Sulla then left for Asia, but in his absence there was more intrigue and violence, with Marius returning and Cinna this time seizing power, which he proceeded to hold from 87 to 84 BC when he too came to a sticky end (Marius had died in 86). Before his demise Cinna sent his own alternative army to Asia under Valerius Flaccus, who was later murdered and replaced by his legate Flavius Fimbra. Sulla, however, defeated Mithridates, won over Fimbra's army (rewarding the soldiers with almost unlimited licence to plunder), and then returned to Rome in 83 BC.

With the help of Marcus Crassus, Metellus Pius and, most notably, Pompey (Gnaeus Pompeius), Sulla crushed his opponents in Italy and took control of Rome, carrying out the statutory purge in which forty senators and 1600 *equites* (knights) were murdered without trial. Pompey was awarded a triumph and given the title Magnus, the great. Sulla then assumed the position of dictator, now used for the first time since the days of Hannibal's invasion, and proceeded in 81 to attempt to fill the senate with his own supporters from the equestrian class, to emasculate the tribunate, and set up a series of tribunals to try public crime and restore law and order. Sulla's dictatorship, which he relinquished in 80 (he died in 78), had little chance of reversing the trend, and his measures were later reversed by Pompey. By now the oligarchy had lost control and was quite incapable of governing. Rome had become a merry-go-round of intrigue, in which almost farcical shifts in power regularly took place against a backcloth of bloodshed and hatred.

The oligarchy was now threatened by the revolt of Sertorius in Spain, which Pompey was dispatched to deal with in 77 BC. It took him five years and he returned just in time to finish putting down another revolt, this time led by Spartacus. The legendary Spartacus was a gladiator from Thrace who managed to free himself and in 73 amassed a rough and ready army of thousands of slaves on Mount Vesuvius. His was not an organised revolution, but rather the protest of a motley collection of oppressed people against their miserable lot. They roamed the countryside and pillaged at will for nearly two years, defeating in the process the Roman forces sent against them. Eventually they were well and truly routed in Bruttium (Calabria) in 71 by a huge army led by Crassus, who killed Spartacus and proceeded to crucify thousands of his wretched followers in a line which stretched from Rome to Capua.

On his return Pompey became extremely powerful. In three months in 67 he managed the extraordinary feat of clearing the seas around Rome of the pirates which had become a major menace to the city, and then he embarked on a major four-year campaign in Asia where he finally defeated Mithridates and added Anatolia, Syria and the surrounding territory to the empire before returning to Rome in 62. He acted without consulting the senate, virtually as a monarch, and secured the loyalty of the army by sharing with them a portion of the enormous quantity of booty which he brought back. Needless to say, there was further intrigue in Rome during his absence, notably the Catiline conspiracy which was mercilessly put down by Cicero. Back in Italy Pompey formed an alliance with Crassus and Julius Caesar. Known as the First Triumvirate, it effectively ruled Rome for about a year around 60 BC.

JULIUS CAESAR AND THE END OF THE REPUBLIC

Julius Caesar is clearly one of the best-known personalities in Italian history. A great orator and writer, who came from an old patrician family which claimed descent directly from Aeneas, he was related by marriage to both Marius and Cinna, and proved himself an able politician and soldier. Almost totally unscrupulous and immensely ambitious, he involved himself in various conspiracies before manipulating the triumvirate to land himself a prestigious command in Gaul. His remarkable victories there are chronicled in his famous *De Bello Gallico* (Gallic Wars), and they allowed him to build the prestige and popularity required to overthrow the republican system, which he had rejected as a viable form of government, and gain power for himself.

The triumvirate was renewed in 56, but by the time of its break-up and the death of Crassus in 53 Rome was sinking into further disarray and disorder, and was on the verge of anarchy. Pompey, by now the

Julius Caesar 100–44 BC

figurehead of the republican system, was appointed sole consul in 52, and in 49, when the senate voted that he should give up his command, Caesar took the much-chronicled step of crossing the Rubicon and invading Italy. Pompey retreated to the Balkans, leaving Caesar to enter Rome unopposed and establish himself as dictator. He then proceeded to secure his position by virtually eliminating the Pompeian dynasty, defeating Pompey's forces in Spain and Pompey himself at Pharsalus in Thessaly in 49. He pursued him to Egypt, where he arrived to find that Pompey had in fact been assassinated as he stepped ashore. After a famous affair with Cleopatra, whom he established as queen of Egypt, Caesar returned to Rome. (On the way he defeated Mithridates' son Pharnacus at Zela in Pontus, announcing his victory with the words 'Veni, vidi, vici'.) He finally defeated Pompey's sons at Munda in Spain in 45, executing Gnaeus Pompey and effectively removing the last vestiges of republican influence. He returned to Rome in triumph in October 45, and the republican era was now well and truly finished.

The republic had served Rome and Italy well, overseeing the first unification of the country, the creation of a vast and mighty empire, massive social, economic and political development, and establishing Rome as the 'centre of the world'. By Caesar's time the empire stretched over vast areas of the known world – North Africa, Spain, Gaul, central Europe, Greece and the East. Rome had grown into an impressive cosmopolitan city, with a rich and sophisticated cultural, economic, social and political life, as well as magnificent and advanced architectural features. The Roman way of life and system of government had spread and advanced civilisation throughout the whole of Italy and far beyond. Its language was exemplified not only by the writing of Julius Caesar, but by Sallust in his histories, by Cicero in his speeches and letters, and by poets such as Catullus and Lucretius. Ultimately the republic fell because it had outlived its usefulness, and was incapable of reconciling the conflicting interests which its very success had generated.

Caesar's ascendancy marks the transition from republic to principate. He ruled to all intents and purposes as a king, adopting much of the pomp of the monarchic period although he actually refused the title of *rex* when it was offered to him by Antony in 44. He enacted important economic, political and administrative reforms at home, including the use of the now widely accepted 365-day (Julian) calendar, which he introduced on 1 January 45 BC. His domestic achievements also included the building of a new forum. He built up enormous personal power, going as far as instituting cult honours for himself and having himself nominated ruler for life in 44. Life, however, turned out, not altogether surprisingly, to be not a very long time: he was murdered in a conspiracy of nobles led by Marcus Brutus and Cassius on the infamous Ides of March 44 BC.

'The Centre of the World': Rome and its Empire at their Zenith

AUGUSTUS

The stage now passed to Octavian (Gaius Octavius), Caesar's great-nephew, who was named in Caesar's will as his chief heir. At the age of nineteen, he returned from studies in Greece to claim his inheritance. After defeating Caesar's lieutenant Marcus Antonius (Mark Antony) at Mutina (Modena), he reached agreement with him, and in 43, with Marcus Lepidus, they were appointed triumvirs for five years. The following year, in two separate battles at Philippi, they defeated Cassius and Brutus (who both committed suicide), and in 36 Octavian defeated Sextus Pompey. The Second Triumvirate had been renewed in 37 but Lepidus was deposed in 36 and it was inevitable that sooner or later the two most powerful men in the world would clash. In 31 Antony and Cleopatra (who was having another illustrious affair) were defeated at Actium and fled to Alexandria. When Octavian followed them to Egypt they committed suicide, leaving Octavian to become the first Roman emperor (though never in name – in 27 he was awarded the title Augustus), a position he was to occupy for forty-five years from 31 BC to AD 14. The history of Rome and of Italy had moved into a new phase.

Augustus' first task was to re-establish order and stability in the strife-torn city and country which he now led. This he achieved with great political skill, completely reorganising the system of administration, revolutionising Roman morality, and in the process establishing in law his own personal control and position for life. Under the new system, power was in theory shared by the *princeps*, or chief, and the senate, but in practice the *princeps* was very firmly in control. The senate retained some power to govern the provinces, limited legislative powers, and partial control over taxation and public expenditure. Crucially, however, the *princeps* had complete control of the army, which he himself financed and deployed, and was personally protected from 27 BC by the highly trained and prestigious Praetorian Guard. He also had the backing of the new civil service which Augustus created; this was recruited from the *equites* and took over many of the functions previously exercised by the senate. The most important members of the new civil service were the *procuratori fisci*, who replaced the old corrupt private tax collectors and administered the *princeps'* personal wealth (*patrimonium*) and the treasury (*fiscus*). The *princeps* issued his own money in gold and silver, whereas the senate was only allowed to issue copper coins. Augustus did create a body of senior senators, known as the Council (*consilium*), to act as a sort of cabinet, advising the *princeps* and acting as an intermediary between him and the senate. The popular assemblies which had featured so prominently in the republic were dispensed with, although magistrates were still elected by the people. Fundamentally, Augustus underpinned his position by promoting the cult of the individual (himself!), just as Julius Caesar had done before him.

This system restored order and provided an effective means of governing the city, the country, and the vast empire which had been created. It effectively enabled the Roman hegemony to be extended for around 300 years, and this is perhaps the greatest testament to the importance of Augustus in Italian history. On the debit side, the new system made life extremely bureaucratic: for example, the Lex Julia, which was aimed at increasing the birth-rate, deprived unmarried or childless men of the right to inherit, and other measures provided tax incentives for large families. The arts, not surprisingly, suffered during the reign of Augustus from the restrictions imposed by this system, with

Augustus (Octavian) 63 BC–14 AD

dissidents often being banished and exiled. Despite this it was a golden age of poetry, with Virgil, Horace, Propertius and Ovid all writing during this period; Livy too produced his history of Rome.

DYNASTIC EMPERORS

By his death in AD 14, Augustus had secured what is now referred to as the Julio-Claudian dynasty of emperors (27 BC–AD 68) by arranging for his stepson Tiberius, whom he had adopted, to succeed him. Tiberius ruled until 37, living a life of paranoia and debauchery, and much under the influence of his ambitious mother Livia and of Agrippina, the wife of his popular nephew Germanicus, whom he probably had murdered, and then of Sejanus, the commander of the Praetorian Guard. He was followed by Gaius, better known as Caligula (37–41), who is chiefly noted for his massive vanity. Believing himself to be a god, he ordered the heads of Greek statues to be replaced by his own, and was eventually murdered by the Praetorian Guard. A more interesting character from this period was his uncle and successor Claudius (41–54), a shy and insecure personage who gradually grew into his position, although his achievements in it were rather limited (despite his addition of Britain to the empire). He is thought to have been poisoned by his fourth wife, his niece Agrippina – the system may have been more stable under the emperors, but the Roman instinct for intrigue and ruthlessness persisted! (A very readable account of the life and times of Claudius can be found in the books *I, Claudius* and *Claudius the God* by Robert Graves.) The Julio-Claudian period ended with Agrippina's son Nero, an unpopular character who was even blamed for the great fire of Rome in 64, and who died without leaving a son, thus bringing the dynasty to an end.

The achievements of the first dynastic period of the principate consisted, of course, mainly of Augustus' re-establishment of stable government. However, this was also a period of a large building programme in the city, which included famous developments such as the Arch of Augustus, the Forum of Augustus, the Baths of Agrippa, the rebuilt Pantheon, and the Theatre of Marcellus. The empire was expanded with the acquisition of north-west Spain (29–19 BC), Pannonia (12–9 BC), Cappadocia (AD 17–18), Mauretania (42), Britannia and Lycia (43) and Thrace (46).

The Julio–Claudians were followed, after a brief period of civil strife, by the Flavio–Trajan dynasty (69–117). This was only partly dynastic in nature since after the murder of Domitian in 96 emperors were chosen on merit by their predecessors. This period featured the industrious and efficient rule of Vespasian (69–79), who restored Rome after the great fire and built the Colosseum in 79, and the prosperous and expansionist reign of Trajan himself (98–117). This is principally remembered for growth in economic activity in general, and trade in particular, with the expansion of the ports of Ancona and Ostia. During his reign the frontiers of the empire were further expanded, the province of Dacia being created in 107, extensive settlement taking place in north Africa, and Armenia being annexed in 113 when Mesopotamia and Assyria were absorbed into the empire.

The next line of emperors was the so-called Antonine dynasty (117–193), the first of whom was Hadrian (117–138). Best known in Britain for the great wall which carries his name, built to keep the Picts

The Colosseum

and the Scots at bay, he was a very stable and wise character who during his reign travelled widely both in Italy and throughout the empire, which he consolidated with the introduction of a single legal framework applicable to all of Rome's sphere of influence. At home he is best remembered for his reform of the civil service, and for the magnificent villa he had built at Tivoli in 134, but it is generally accepted that his principate marked the very zenith of the empire. Another noteworthy emperor of this time was Marcus Aurelius (161–180), a devotee of Stoic philosophy, who personally repelled a menacing barbarian invasion of Roman territory. He was followed by his son Commodus (180–192); it is from his name that the modern Italian word for easy or comfortable (*comodo*) is derived, so it will come as no surprise that his period of office was characterised by corruption, financial extravagance and general misrule before he was murdered.

In art, sculpture reached its peak in Rome during the first two centuries AD, particularly in commemorative reliefs – good examples are to be found on the Arch of Titus and Trajan's Column. Among writers, those whose works have survived include the poet Martial, the historian Tacitus and the satirist Juvenal.

The Antonines were followed by the Severan emperors (193–235), who ruled until the murder of Severus Alexander. This period saw the extension of Roman citizenship in 212 to all free people living in the provinces by Caracalla (who also built the well-known *terme*, or baths, in Rome in 216), as well as the further rapid development of Roman town-building and architecture throughout Italy and the whole of the empire. Rome itself continued to increase in magnificence, rendering it a grand and impressive city fit to be the centre of a great empire. This period also marked the first signs of the serious problems which would eventually destroy the empire and the city, and can therefore in many ways be regarded as the beginning of the end.

BARBARIAN THREAT

As we have seen, the empire reached the height of its geographical extent and power between 70 and 235. But after 235, when Severus Alexander and his mother were murdered by disaffected troops, the Roman system again became prone to instability, and the city

BRITANNIA INFERIOR
BRITANNIA SUPERIOR
GERMANIA INFERIOR
BELGICA
LUGDUNENSIS
GERMANIA SUPERIOR
RAETIA
NORICUM
AQUITAINIA
NARBONENSIS
LUSITANIA
TARRCONENSIS
CORSICA
SARDINIA
BAETICA
DALM
SICILIA
MAURETANIA TINGITANA
MAURETANIA CAESARIENSIS
NUMIDIA
AFRICA
PROCONSUL

Legions ■
Major client kingdoms

1 ALPES POENINAE
2 ALPES COTTIAE
3 ALPES MARITIMAE
4 PANNONIA SUPERIOR
5 PANNONIA INFERIOR
6 LYCIA ET PAMPHYLIA
7 CILICIA

The Roman Empire at its height

BOSPORUS
MOESIA INFERIOR
THRACIA
PONTUS ET BITHYNIA
CAPPADOCIA
ARMENIA
ASIA
GALATIA
MESOPOTAMIA
6
7
CYPRUS
SYRIA COELE
SYRIA PHOENICE
CRETA ET CYRENE
SYRIA PALAESTINA
AEGYPTUS
ARABIA

experienced a period of near anarchy. The next fifty or so years saw an almost continuous power struggle, in which twenty-one emperors came and then went, the latter usually not by choice. This to an extent reflected, but also contributed to, an increasingly precarious external position, for the empire was coming under increasing threat from the various barbarian tribes who were massing on its borders. To the north, the Scots, the Picts, the Angles, the Saxones, the Franks, the Alamanni, the Burgundians and the Langobards were pressing. To the east, the threat came from the Vandals, the Visigoths, the Ostrogoths, the Huns, the Alani and the Sarmatae. And in Africa, the Mauri, or Moors, were proving increasingly difficult to handle.

This barbarian threat first came to the fore around 166, when the Langobards invaded Pannonia, only to be summarily dealt with by a Roman state and army which was at this time strong and organised enough to respond promptly and effectively. After 235, the internal divisions among the Romans meant that they were no longer in a position to make such a response, and the potential threat gradually became reality. Around 250 the Franks penetrated deep into Gaul, as far as the Pyrenees, and the Alamanni swept into Italy as far as Milan, where they were defeated by the emperor Gallienus, but only after a bitter struggle. Then the Ostrogoths invaded Thrace and Macedonia, slaughtering 100,000 people at Philippopolis (Plovdiv) in what is now Bulgaria.

The empire was in retreat, and Rome itself once again faced a potential threat. Memories must have turned to the days of Hannibal, when a senator returned from north Africa with a fresh fig to show how quickly Rome could be reached from the outreaches of the empire, and therefore how inherently insecure the position of the city was. A vain attempt to halt the slide was made by Valerian (253–260), who was the first to come up with the idea that the empire had become too large for one person to manage, and therefore should split in two. Valerian himself went east to deal with the increasing threat in Persia where he was eventually captured and killed, while his son Gallienus was appointed joint ruler and remained in Rome to deal with domestic matters. Although he clearly did not realise it at the time, Valerian's action of splitting the empire into two established a precedent and marks an important stage in the decline of the empire.

DIOCLETIAN

The collapse of the Valerian system brought the city closer still to the precipice. However, like a cat with several lives, Rome once again responded to the crisis and managed to come up with the right person at the right time to stop the rot. This time the saviour was Diocletian, who was appointed emperor in 284 by the Praetorian Guard. Diocletian came from a humble background in Illyria and rose to supreme power through sheer ability. A rather pompous character, who frequently wore the purple mantle of office and insisted that people always stand in his presence, he ruled for twenty years, orientalising the empire and having the unusual distinction in the Roman world of actually living to enjoy a peaceful retirement on the Adriatic coast. On assuming power he took strong and direct action on three fronts to tackle the problems of the empire, reforming the economic system, the army and the administrative and political structure.

The main problems which faced the economy were rampant inflation and underproduction, both exacerbated by the loss of the gold and silver mines in Dacia, and by the enormous military expenditure required by a great imperial power. In an attempt to deal with inflation, Diocletian introduced the first prices and incomes policy by his Edict on Prices in 301–302. It was somewhat more extreme than modern equivalents – the penalty for non-compliance was death! Like modern versions it was not altogether successful, since it restricted overt supply, but it did to some extent restore confidence in the currency. Rural depopulation and underproduction were also tackled by direct means, harsh edicts forcing people to remain in their trades and to work in their localities.

The army needed to be reorganised to render it more able to meet the growing barbarian challenge, and Diocletian tackled this problem by a complete overhaul of its structure. He divided it into *limitanei*, who were troops usually recruited from local conquered peoples and stationed in forts along the borders of the empire, and into *comitatenses*, highly mobile rapid-deployment forces which could be used quickly to reinforce threatened areas – again, these were largely recruited from conquered peoples, which meant that the empire was virtually defended by foreigners, clearly a high-risk strategy. To meet the administrative imperatives of the empire, Diocletian split Roman territory into two: he himself took over the east as Augustus, and appointed Galerius to rule the Balkans as his Caesar (and heir); Maximian became Augustus in the west, ruling Italy, Spain and Africa, while Constantius commanded Gaul and Britain as his Caesar. Thus a tetrarchy was effectively created. The four new regions of the empire were administered by *praefecti*, and were divided up into various *dioceses* run by *vicari*, which were themselves divided into *provinciae* ruled by governors. Military responsibility for each province was taken by a commander or *dux*.

Diocletian's reforms were tough but generally effective. They restored stability, and they substantially prolonged the life of the empire. However, they also required a massive civil service, which damaged the empire in the long run by increasing the tax burden and acting as a drain on the productive-goods sector of the economy.

CONSTANTINE AND CHRISTIANITY

Diocletian surrendered power, along with Maximian, in 305, and after some years of confusion Constantine, the son of Constantius, who had been Augustus in the west since his father's death in 306, took over as sole emperor in 324, a position which he held until his death in 337. He maintained the east–west division of the empire, appointing two of his sons to rule each part as Caesars, but he is best remembered for founding the city of Constantinople, and for his conversion to Christianity. After the death of Christ the number of his followers in the empire had steadily increased, and Christian communities in Rome itself date back to around 59. Their increasing number and influence were generally tolerated in the empire, but like many religious sects they were subject to periodic episodes of victimisation and persecution, since their rejection of traditional Roman gods was clearly uncomfortable for many people. Nero, for example, blamed them for the great fire and murdered many in bizarre fashion, using them as human torches to brighten the night, having them torn apart by dogs, and feeding them to the lions. In the third century, Christians were hounded by Decius and Valerian, and between 303–305 they were subjected to the 'great persecution', in which Diocletian savagely attempted to destroy them in order to appease the gods and persuade the latter to intercede in favour of the declining empire. Many, including Diocletian's own wife and daughter, were murdered or forced to sacrifice themselves. However, the sect survived, and after Constantine saw the light Christianity was officially recognised as a religion in 313. Thereafter it flourished and gradually, with a few hiccups such as the unsuccessful pagan revival under Julian in 361–363, became accepted as the dominant religion in the empire and in Rome itself.

DECLINE AND FALL

Despite Diocletian and Constantine, the long-term decline of the empire was now firmly established. Its economic and political system continued to flounder, and it was thus increasingly incapable of countering the barbarian threat. The only force which could now potentially stem the tide was the personal ability and charisma of the emperor but, after the death of Theodosius I at Milan in 395, no person with the necessary qualities emerged. The empire was finally divided in two and from then on the western empire inexorably disintegrated. The east, with its seat of power at Constantinople, remained strong for much longer, but lost its Roman character and became a Greek kingdom.

In the west, the imperial court had moved to Milan in 305, and then in 402 to Ravenna. In Rome itself the life of the ruling class continued essentially unchanged regardless of impending disaster. The city had become a centre of Christianity, with many churches of the new religion being built in this period. The absence of the restraining influence of an emperor led to strife, corruption, debauchery, and general excess the like of which had not been seen since the days of the republic, but this 'fiddling while Rome burned' was soon interrupted. The Vandals had swept across Africa, the Visigoths had taken the Danubian provinces and southern Gaul, the Saxones had captured Britain, the Suebi had occupied part of Spain, and the Franks, Alamanni and Burgundians had all settled in Roman territory. In 401–402 Alaric the Visigoth invaded Italy, and finally brought the party to an abrupt end by sacking Rome in 410. The shock must have been terrible for the senatorial class, but more was to come when in 455 the Vandals under Gaiseric (Genseric) took their turn to devastate the city. 476 is usually regarded as the very end of the western Roman empire. In this year the last emperor, Romulus Augustulus, was deposed by the German Odoacer (Odovacar), and

Germanic barbarian kings ruled Italy from their court at Ravenna. Odoacer was in turn overthrown in 493 by Theodoric the Ostrogoth, who ruled Italy through Roman officials and the senate until his death in 526. Ostrogothic rule continued until 540, when the bloody Byzantine reconquest of the country under Justinian, the emperor in the east, incorporated Italy into the Byzantine state (p. 55–56). As for the Roman senatorial class, they survived the sackings of the city and actually prospered under the Germans, only finally to disappear from history after Justinian's reconquest. Thus ended the great Roman episode of Italian history.

It only remains for us to consider why the empire declined and ultimately fell. The historian Gibbon has described the fall as '... the natural and inevitable effect of immoderate greatness ...'. There is probably some truth in this. One can look for immediate causes of decline: overindulgence, corruption, economic inefficiency, political bankruptcy, tactical failures, depopulation, diseases, internal divisions, the breakdown of an army excessively dependent on conquered peoples – all probably played their part. Fundamentally, however, the decline and fall of the Roman empire was probably an historical inevitability, especially in view of the increasing strength and aspirations of the so-called 'barbarian' peoples; one may perhaps more fruitfully ask why it was that it survived in all its greatness for so long. The legacy of Rome to Italy, and indeed to the whole world, cannot be overestimated. Its language, art, architecture, politics, administration, customs and religion have all profoundly and fundamentally influenced the development of the world we know today.

CHAPTER THREE

The Middle Ages: from Barbarians to City-States

With the demise of the Roman hegemony, the political unity of Italy effectively ended, not to return until the time of the Risorgimento. The ensuing medieval period, from the late fifth to about the fourteenth century, has traditionally been passed over by historians, partly because of the paucity of sources, especially for the period before 800 which has come to be referred to as the 'Dark Ages'. However, there has also been a tendency to acquiesce tacitly to the view which Renaissance scholars propounded in order to glorify their own period: that these 900 or so years were somehow an unfortunate and uncivilised break between the two culturally superior epochs of classical antiquity and the Renaissance. This view grossly belittles the Middle Ages in Italy which were, in fact, in a number of ways a period of great significance to the development of Italian society, and some knowledge of it is essential to an understanding of the evolution of Italy and of its people.

First of all, it saw the emergence of the Catholic Church and the Papacy as an independent and significant, if often corrupt, force, spawning some of the most interesting characters of the time. Secondly, and perhaps in the long run most crucially, it saw the development of the cities, initially as extensions of the settlements which had been established by the Romans, the Etruscans and the Greeks, and then as the great city-states of the early Renaissance. Associated with this was the consolidation and development, which took place during this period, of the regional and local cultures and identities which play such a crucial part in Italian history, and which still so centrally characterise the Italy of today. Thirdly, the medieval period was one in which Italy was exposed to a variety of foreign influences, mainly in the form of conquests and migratory movements, which have greatly influenced the shape and nature of present-day culture. Economically, the period is notable for the development, as was the case elsewhere in Europe, of a feudal pattern of land ownership, and, critically, for the emergence of the merchant capitalism which we now tend to associate with great city states such as Venice. Artistically, the second part of the period of course saw the beginnings of the Renaissance, and has bequeathed to us painting, architecture and literature of great importance and sensitivity, much of which is readily accessible to the traveller.

Early Medieval Times: Barbarians, Byzantines and Popes, 476–1024

Politically, the immediate post-Roman centuries were essentially characterised by the gradual division of Italy into two parts: much of the centre–south largely remained under the control of the Greek eastern kingdom, from its seat of power at Ravenna, and of the Church; while the north was gradually invaded and settled by 'barbarian' tribes of Franks, Goths and Lombards.

GERMANIC KINGS

The 'first blow' for the barbarians in the north was struck by Odoacer who, as we have seen (page 51), overthrew Romulus Augustulus and installed himself as king in 476. Although this event is seen as the end of the Roman empire in the west, the rise of Odoacer in fact made very little real difference to the status quo in Italy, apart from the fact, of course, that an Arian was now king. Odoacer respected Roman ways and traditions and to a large extent perpetuated the political life of Italy along Roman lines, courting the support of the old ruling élite such as the senatorial class in Rome. He even sought, unsuccessfully, to have himself recognised as a viceroy by the eastern emperor Zeno in Constantinople.

As we have also seen, Odoacer was overthrown by the Ostrogoth invader Theodoric in 493 after four years of bitter warfare, and there followed sixty years (493–552) of Gothic control of the kingdom of Italy During this time a considerable number of Goths settled in Italy, notably around Verona, Pavia, the central Apennines, Picenum and Samnium (today the Marche and Abruzzi), as well as in Rome and Ravenna and the area north of the River Po. Theodoric himself was to prove perhaps the greatest of the Germanic kings. He basically continued the policy of ruling through Roman institutions, including the senate, and he seems to have been an efficient and strong ruler who managed to preserve internal peace, and to facilitate the relatively harmonious co-existence of Goths and Romans during his reign, not least by administering justice in a racially unbiased fashion. He was also a distinguished builder, developing Rome and Ravenna, and constructing for himself palaces in Verona and Pavia, as well as in Ravenna itself. Perhaps his most significant legacy to the traveller in Italy is the superb unfinished monumental tomb in Ravenna, where the most magnificent mosaics in Europe, which also date from this period, can be found. On the debit side, he executed the philosopher Boethius (480–524), 'the last of the Romans', who wrote his famous work, *De consolatione philosophiae*, while in prison.

BYZANTINE RECONQUEST

Theodoric died in 526, and under his successors the Ostrogothic kingdom gradually declined. Tension between Goths and Romans increased in the kingdom during the reign of Athalaric (526–34), a minor who ruled through his mother Amalasuntha. The later was killed by Athalaric's successor Theodahad (534–36) in 535, and this prompted the eastern emperor Justinian to declare war on the Ostrogoths. There followed twenty years of bloody fighting which had a devastating effect on most of the Italian peninsula. The outcome of this Gothic war was that the Byzantine armies under Belisarius, who landed in Sicily in 535, and later Narses gradually defeated the Goths under a succession of leaders, the most notable of whom were Witigis (536–40) and Totila (541–52). Belisarius fought his way up through the peninsula, taking Ravenna in 540. Totila led a remarkably effective counterattack, recapturing most of Italy and Sicily, including even Rome, where he evicted all the inhabitants, leaving it deserted. Only Ravenna and some key coastal towns which enjoyed the protection of the Byzantine navy remained in Byzantine hands. However, Narses eventually recaptured the peninsula for the Byzantines, killing Totila and then Teias, the last Ostrogothic king, in 552. By 561 Narses had also defeated the Franks, who had since 540 been settling north of the River Po. The Byzantine reconquest of Italy was complete.

The native Italians seem largely to have been unwilling bystanders and victims in this bitter struggle between Goths and Byzantines which was being fought around them, not greatly caring who the victors were, since neither side would really make very much difference to their day-to-day reality. The war ravaged large areas of the country, the damage being particularly serious in Emilia, Picenum, Umbria and Campania. Here the countryside was severely disrupted, and there are accounts of serious famine and hardship. In the end the Goths were virtually wiped from the face of Italian history, disappearing a trifle mysteriously, hardly leaving a trace of their period in control. Justinian proceeded to turn the clock back, issuing in 554 what is now referred to as the Pragmatic Sanction, which re-established Italy as a province of the eastern empire, restored all property (including slaves!) to its pre-Gothic owners, and revived many Roman institutions. There is evidence that Justinian's reconquest was on the whole welcomed by many sections of the old Roman ruling class, but what is more certain is that he left his mark on Italian culture. Dante includes him in his *Paradise*, he appears in Raphael's frescoes in the Vatican, and, above, all, there are the great portraits of himself and his wife Theodora in the Church of San Vitale in Ravenna – fine examples, these, of the Byzantine art which was greatly to influence later Italian works. Additionally, Justinian is remembered for his codification of Roman law before his death in 565. His disappearance from the scene heralded the next important development of this early medieval period: the resurgence of the barbarians in the form of the Lombards.

THE LOMBARDS

The Lombards were originally a Germanic people, and they invaded northern Italy from Pannonia (modern Hungary) in 568 under their leader Alboin. They occupied the plain of the Po during 568–9 without encountering a great deal of opposition, establishing their dukes in the main cities, and then took Pavia in 572 following a three-year siege. They thus came to control what is now Venetia, Liguria and Tuscany.

Around 571, groups of them also occupied large areas of territory further down the peninsula, surprisingly without bothering to capture any of the land in between, and formed the duchies of Spoleto, under Faroald, and of Benevento, under Zotto (see Map below).

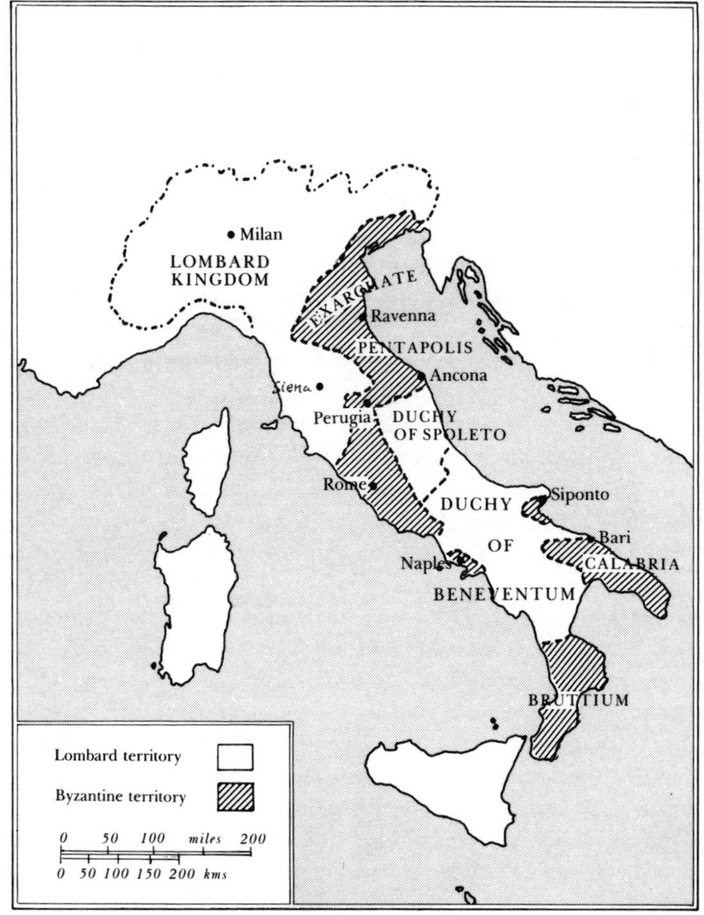

Italy at the time of the Lombards

Alboin was murdered in 572, and his successor Cleph suffered the same fate two years later – ambitious and power-hungry leaders coming to a sticky end is clearly a continuing theme in Italian history! There followed an interregnum of ten years during which the Lombards appear not to have had any overall leader, but by the end of the sixth century, under the young and romantic figure of Authari (584–90) and then Agilulf (590– 616), they controlled two-thirds of Italy. They clearly attempted to capture the whole of the peninsula, but essentially they lacked the resources to do so, being relatively few in number and often divided amongst themselves, to the extent that one of the Byzantines' main tactics against them seems to have been attempting to bribe some of their leaders. Additionally, the Byzantines, with their 'belt' of territory linking Ravenna and Rome, acted as an effective bulwark against Lombard expansion, often with the help of the native Italians who tended to regard the Greek empire as marginally preferable to the unsubtle pillaging of the barbarians. Thus the division of Italy into two parts was complete and became the political status quo in early medieval times.

It is important to note that the ability of the 'exarch' at Ravenna to repel the barbarians was very much dependent on the temporal power and support of the papacy, which can be seen as having developed into the 'third force' in the Italy of this period. The popes owned large amounts of land, and to a large extent enjoyed the support of the populace, providing as they did a rudimentary system of social security for the poor which they financed with the income from their estates. The eastern empire's hold on Italy was often tenuous, and the papacy to a large extent propped it up, fearing the militant paganism of the Lombards, exemplified by Authari's anti-Catholic edict of 590 (Authari died soon after – divine justice according to Gregory the Great!). The Church was thus largely responsible for administering Byzantine territory and for mustering resistance to the Lombards. It is probably legitimate to speculate that, had it not been for the papacy, Italy would have been reunited under Lombard rule during the sixth or seventh centuries.

The popes of this period were not exactly the paradigms of purity and holiness which we might expect from the encumbents of the position today, but many of them were remarkably interesting characters. None more so than Gregory the Great, a scholarly and astute Roman nobleman who reached the position in 590, and who negotiated with Agilulf to put an end to the Lombard siege of Rome in 594 – the prelude to a series of truces between the Byzantine exarchy and the Lombards which was to establish a reasonably stable equilibrium in Italy and give relative peace to the territory for about 130 years.

The Lombards established their capital at Pavia, and for much of their period in power the main Lombard kingdom in northern Italy and Tuscany was politically dominant over their duchies of Spoleto and Benevento, especially during the reign of Grimoald (662–71) and of Liutprand (712–44), probably the most significant of the Lombard kings. Pavia itself contained a variety of magnificent architectural features, reflecting its position as the pre-eminent Lombard city. These included the royal palace, several fine churches, and an interesting bath complex, one of the few which were operational in the seventh century. Unlike the Ostrogoths, the Lombards brought distinctly Germanic customs to Italy, although their administrative and political structures had a strong Roman flavour to them. We know a considerable amount about their ways because, in what may be seen as typically Germanic fashion, their customs were fully and systematically documented by Rothari in his Edict of 643. They were in essence organised around a series of fairly independent noble warriors, usually dukes or *gastaldi*, who controlled their locality, usually living in its most important city such as Milan, Brescia and Verona, and who owed some degree of allegiance only to the king. Lombard kings had often to be generous with patronage and estates in order to secure the support of their dukes. This resulted in a substantial devolution of power, and contributed to the growth in the independence and influence of the cities and the regions during this period – a foretaste of things to come in the Italy of later years. However, the central–southern duchies were generally more centralised, with the governments in Spoleto and Benevento maintaining a tight rein on their local gastalds. The large degree of local power in the main kingdom meant that there were frequent boundary disputes between the major cities, who usually turned to the king for mediation. For example, there were four disputes between Parma and Piacenza between 626 and 854, as well as an enduring one between Arezzo and Siena which is still reflected in modern rivalry between these cities.

The Lombards adopted the local Italian language, losing their own by about 700, and the local style of dress, shedding their traditional long hair and striped linens for Roman leggings and trousers. They mixed and intermarried with the local people, as their burials which have been discovered at Nocera Umbra, Castel Trosino (near Ascoli Piceno), Invillino (in the Friuli), Fiesole, Brescia and Cividale tend to testify. They thus fused almost completely with the local populace, leaving a permanent mark on the Italian people. It is, however, important to note that we are here discussing the invasion of what was essentially a ruling élite. The majority of the population of Italy was and remained Roman in origin, and there was thus a limit to the extent to which the Lombards, or for that matter any other invader, could change Italian ways: it was an evolutionary rather than a revolutionary set of influences. Lombard power over large parts of Italy lasted for nearly 200 years before they were finally overrun by the next major actors on the stage of the kingdom of Italy: the Franks.

CHARLEMAGNE AND THE FRANKS

The Franks were the most powerful military force of the time, and they had always been a major threat to the Lombard kingdom. As early as the reign of Authari they had very nearly succeeded in invading, only failing to do so by sheer chance. The Lombards in turn had usually attempted to placate them, King Liutprand, for example, helping them against the Arabs in Francia. What turned the threat into reality in the middle of the eighth century was the growing ambitions of the Lombards to eat into papal and Byzantine territory, coupled with a new relationship between the papacy and the Carolingian dynasty in Francia. The Lombards' gnawing desire for territorial expansion was to a large extent dictated by geographical imperatives: it was ridiculously illogical for the two areas of Lombard dominion in Italy to be separated by the strip of land between Ravenna and Rome. The military power of the Lombards had increased during the reign of Liutprand, who had in fact managed to conquer much of the Exarchate and who had also placed his own supporters in control of the duchies of Spoleto and Benevento. Now, in

752, King Aistulf, having completed the absorption of the two duchies into the Lombard kingdom, took Ravenna and set his sights on Rome. At this point Pope Stephen II appealed to the Franks for help. After the death of Charles Martel in 741, the popes had courted the Carolingian dynasty, realising the need for external help against the Lombards in the face of a declining willingness and ability on the part of the Byzantines to intervene in Italy. The Franks seized this mouth-watering opportunity and responded to the papal plea. Pepin III invaded in 755, defeated Aistulf, and handed the Exarchate over to the papacy before retreating back to Francia. When the Lombard king Desiderius again threatened Rome in 772, the new Frankish king Charlemagne invaded again and proceeded to conquer much of the peninsula in 773–4. Unlike his father Pepin, Charlemagne pressed home his advantage and, having confirmed the restoration of the Exarchate to the popes, himself took the Lombard crown. The Lombard kingdom of Italy had ended and the Carolingian kingdom now took its place.

In political terms, the century or so of Frankish dominance in northern and central Italy is mainly noteworthy for the re-creation of the Western Empire in the form of the Holy Roman Empire, and for the consolidation of the Papal States. The Church's control over the latter had been, as we have seen, established by Pepin and Charlemagne, but now it was legitimised by the sudden and rather convenient discovery of a document which has come to be known as the Donation of Constantine, by which the former Emperor of the East had supposedly made a gift of Italy to Pope Sylvester and his successors. The Holy Roman Empire was created on Christmas Day 800, when Pope Leo III (795–816) conferred the honorary title of Emperor on Charlemagne during one of the latter's few visits to Italy. The Empire, which can be regarded as a kind of union of Christian west Europe, with the Emperor holding political power and the Pope enjoying spiritual leadership, was to last for a thousand years, and its creation marks a critical point in Italian history, for it firmly tied the fate of the country to that of northern Europe.

Carolingian rule, however, had remarkably little effect either on daily life in Italy or on the political geography of the peninsula. This is hardly surprising when one considers that the Franks regarded Italy as a relatively insignificant corner of their empire, and never really took the task of governing it particularly seriously. Charlemagne even appointed a four-year-old, his son Pepin, as king in 781, and other minors, for example Bernard (812–17) and Lothar (817–55), were subsequently given the position. Even when the Frankish kings of Italy were adults, the position was regarded as very much the short straw of the Carolingian empire, and the kings invariably spent very little time in Italy. As a result the administration of the kingdom remained largely as it had been in Lombard times, with a central government in Pavia and a system of local officials centred around the dukes, gastalds and bishops in the major cities. It is true that the Lombard dukes were gradually replaced by Frankish and Aleman counts, but the only significant administrative development under the Franks was the use of *missi*, or king's messengers, who presided over local courts. Interestingly enough, the kingdom seems to have been run extremely efficiently during this period of absentee rulers, which may be a tribute to the system which the Lombards had established, but which also offers some intriguing parallels with modern Italy.

DECLINE OF THE KINGDOM

After Charlemagne's death in 814 the Carolingian empire, which had to a large extent been held together by his own personal charisma and ability, began to falter, and finally fell apart around 888. After Charlemagne the most significant Frankish emperor was undoubtedly Louis II, Lothar's son, who held the position for twenty years and fought notable battles against Arab invaders in the south before he died in 875, taking fleeting hopes of an Italy united under the Franks with him to his Milanese grave. After Louis II the kingdom entered a period of what could only be described as chaos and confusion, with local magnates as well as pretenders from abroad engaging in destructive civil wars to compete for the position of king of Italy and the title of emperor which usually went with it. If there is a discernible pattern to this period, it lies in the fact that the factions of the lay aristocracy who were engaged in the power struggles tended to favour either France or Germany, and most of the post-Carolingian kings can be clearly associated with one side or the other. For example, Guy of Spoleto (889–94) and the intriguingly named Charles the Bald (875–7) were supporters of France, while Berengar of Friuli (888–924) and the equally interestingly named Charles the Fat (879–87) were essentially pro-German.

The backcloth to this internecine struggle was the external threat which now came from the Arabs in the south and the Hungarians in the north. One of the enduring results of this was the growth in castle building, or *incastellamento*, to which nobles and their local communities resorted in order to defend themselves. This process was officially sanctioned by official charters, issued notably by Berengar during his reign, and it represents an important stage in the growth of the power of the localities and the cities which we will examine at length later. One interesting example, from the many castelli which were built in this period, is the one which was put up by the Deacon Audebert at Nogara near Verona, following the grant of a charter in 906.

Some semblance of order and central control was restored to the kingdom of Italy by a series of German emperors, notably the three Ottos: Otto I (962–73), Otto II (973–83) and, surprisingly enough, Otto III (983–1002), and Henry II (1004–24). They managed to repel the threat from the Hungarians by defeating them at the Battle of Lechfeld in 955, and established imperial control over the papacy by Pope John XII (955–64), a decidedly unsavoury character who had been basically foisted upon the Church by his father Alberic. The papacy, it is important to note, had by this time become no more than a quasi-hereditary aristocratic position which was held by the Roman nobility. It had thus lost any semblance of spiritual or religious credibility. Alberic's mother Marozia, to quote just one example, was notorious for her amorous dealings with the papacy. Nevertheless, despite the Germanic revival the kingdom of Italy was by now very much in a process of terminal decline and disintegration. Opposition to any central authority had been steadily on the increase, to the extent that Berengar and his successor Hugh had had continually to resort to force. During Berengar's reign the comital courts, an important symbol of central authority, had effectively ceased to function, and by about 990 the state had been forced to abandon its right to tax. The final blow came when the people of Pavia burned the royal palace in 1024. The symbol of the kingdom had now disappeared along with its authority and power.

What broke up the central state in the end was its own fundamental weaknesses, together with the inexorable growth of local identity and autonomy and the rise of a new Italian ruling class which went with it. As we have seen, Italy, because of its geographical and other features, had always been a collection of localities, each with its own particular character and traditions. The concept of a central state had been a phenomenon which was essentially a leftover surviving from Roman times. The strength of the Roman legacy was such that local aristocrats had been to some extent prepared to subordinate their local interests to central imperatives, and had thus structured their activities around the state. In return, the local aristocracies of course benefited from the patronage of kings eager to establish and consolidate their own positions. Now, however, the private activities and interests of powerful individuals, centred in their own localities, became so strong a force that the central state in a sense became irrelevant, and its power was consequently gradually eroded, to the point that, to all intents and purposes, it ceased to exist. The stage therefore passed from the centre to the locality, and from the eleventh century until the growth of nationalism and the economic transformations of the nineteenth century, the history of Italy becomes really the history of individual cities, localities and regions.

THE COUNTRYSIDE

We shall turn to this dramatic process of fragmentation shortly, but before we leave the kingdom of Italy two points need to be made. Firstly, it must be emphasised that the political history of the kingdom is really the history of a small group of aristocratic men, many originating from outside the peninsula. For the peasantry, who needless to say constituted the vast majority of the Italian population, the state was in many ways an almost complete irrelevance. They came into contact with it occasionally when they were forced to suffer its wars, and they sometimes feared it as a remote coercive force, but their day-to-day reality was largely untouched by it.

Life in the countryside was indeed very basic. There were often enormous local and regional differences in the pattern of Italian rural life. A substantial number of the peasantry were owner–cultivators, in the tradition of the Roman *coloni*, tending a small amount of land on a subsistence basis. The remainder were tenants of landlords of varying type and importance, ranging from the Church and nobility to small local landowners; they eked out a living from the land in return for a mixture of labour services, money rent and gifts in kind to the landlord, under what is known as the *sistema curtense*. Up to the period of *incastellamento*, which resulted in the growth of settlements based around fortified centres, the countryside was divided into *massae* or *fundi*, fragmented estates which were usually named after the original owner, and into villages, which were usually called *casalia*, *villae*, *loci* or *vici*. Much of the countryside at this time consisted of forests and marshes, although the period between 800 and 1100 is known to be one of widespread land reclamation and clearance. The main products of the countryside of course differed from region to region, but fundamentally they consisted of corn, wine, oil and some animals, usually pigs, cows and hens which were often given to the landlord as part of the rent. Additionally, most peasants tended a small fenced garden in which typically beans and fruit would be grown. Rixsolf, an eighth-century scribe, described the daily diet in the area around Lucca as consisting of one loaf of bread, one quarter amphora of wine, one quarter amphora of stew made from beans, wild-grain flour, fat or oil, and occasionally a little meat. Presumably this diet was eaten day in, day out over a whole lifetime. Agricultural techniques were primitive in the extreme, with ploughs infrequently used, the only real evidence of capitalisation the introduction of the water mill by the end of the millennium. In this context, whether the state was being run by Goths, Lombards, Franks or whoever must have been a sublime irrelevance to the great majority of the Italians of the time.

THE SOUTH

In addition, the discussion of early medieval Italy has so far concentrated on the centre–north, largely ignoring the south. This apparent bias is to an extent justified, since arguably the most significant developments of the period occurred in the Italian kingdom, and in any case there is a serious lack of documentation of events in the south. However, to complete the picture we need briefly to outline developments in this part of the peninsula. The history of the south around these times is, to put it mildly, complex and confused, and has been, perhaps a little unfairly, described by one historian as being one of 'intestinal struggles as sterile as they were obscure'. Politically, as we have seen, the south was under the control of the eastern empire after the Byzantine reconquest. This remained the case until the advent of the Lombards, who assumed control of a large part of the south, incorporating it into the duchy of Benevento. Much of the south, notably Sicily, the area around Naples, and what is now Calabria and Apulia, remained, however, in Byzantine hands, although Naples did enjoy a substantial degree of independence from Constantinople.

This somewhat tenuous status quo remained largely unchanged for over 250 years, until Sicily was conquered by Moorish invaders from Arabia. This conquest began in 827, when 10,000 Moors landed on the south coast of the island at Mazzara. By 843 most of Sicily was in Moorish hands, although it was not until 902 that the conquest was finally complete. The Moors used the island as a base for launching a series of concerted raids on the mainland, causing great panic and consternation, and sacking a variety of towns, such as Genoa in 934. Indeed, much of the history of the mainland during this period was conditioned by the Arab threat and the need to find an effective counter to it. Arab ambitions were eventually checked by the Frankish king Louis II and by an alliance of southern republics led by Pope Leo IV (847–55), who won a brilliant naval victory against them at Ostia in 849.

During roughly the last two centuries of the millennium one can for analytical purposes divide the south into four separate but interrelated parts, although the independent maritime republic of Amalfi flourished in the ninth century, rivalling Pisa, Genoa and Venice. Firstly there was Sicily, which remained under the control of the Saracens, who managed to develop a rather splendid civilisation which has fundamentally influenced the character of the island and its people every since. Byzantine rule persisted in the Captanate, which was formed in the tenth century from most of what is now Apulia and Calabria, and which was essentially characterised by a strong and efficient central government which survived the collapse of the northern kingdom by almost a century. It was based on the strong fiscal powers of the state, which ensured the funds required to administer a wide network of patronage; indeed, the state actually organised its constituent settlements into fiscal units, known as Kastra when they were fortified, or Khoria when they were not.

Next there was the duchy of Benevento, where the collapse of state power dates back as early as the ninth century. The state of Benevento was, not altogether surprisingly, modelled on that of the Italian kingdom under Liutprand and Aistulf, as was its local administration which was based on gastalds and, later, counts. Interestingly enough, the latter positions seem to have been filled by election rather than by heredity. The duchy issued its own independent coinage, and the dukes were extremely rich and powerful men who personally controlled much of the legal system. The relatively early collapse of Benevento can probably be put down to the geographical features of the duchy, which rendered outlying princes difficult to control and thus increased the degree of *de facto* local autonomy which they enjoyed.

Finally there was Rome and its immediate surrounds, if Rome can be legitimately seen as part of the south. Here society was dominated by the Church, which, as we have seen, had in turn come to be dominated by the local aristocracy. The city itself had become much smaller than in the heyday of empire but was still large enough to dominate the area around it, becoming the focal point for most of the nobility of Lazio, leaving the Church, which in any case owned most of the land, to control the countryside from monasteries such as Subiaco and Farsa, and from the large bishoprics such as those at Velletri and Tivoli. By the tenth century, however, with the rapid development of fortified communities throughout Lazio, the city and its environs had also succumbed to the quasi-anarchic process of devolution which was occurring in the rest of the peninsula. Life in the southern countryside was similar to that in northern rural areas, apart from having a greater proportion of tenancies of various sorts and therefore fewer owner-cultivators.

Cities and Communes

GROWTH OF THE CITIES

We can now turn to the rise of the cities and the devolution and localisation of effective power, which probably represents the dominant feature of Italian history in the last part of this early medieval period. Most of the important Italian cities of this period can be traced back to the Roman municipia, which in turn grew from settlements founded variously by the Etruscans, the Greeks, and by the Romans themselves. Some of the municipia, for example Luni and Brescello on the Po, had declined and disappeared. Others, such as Ventimiglia and Altino (Torcello and then Venice), had been relocated. Most, however, managed to survive the ravages of the Dark Ages, although the survival rate was greater in the north than in the south, where cities tended to be smaller and less numerous.

The typical Italian city in the later centuries of the millennium was architecturally modest, characterised by small churches and wooden private housing with a courtyard to the front and a garden to the rear. It of course had walls, usually dating back to Roman times, which defined its shape – usually square, with two main streets crossing in the centre at the forum and linking the city gates. As the state and the church gradually became the major forces in just about every city, so the forum was replaced as the city centre by a royal palace and was relegated to being the venue for the market or the commercial centre of the city. The cathedral was usually built on the edge of the old city, but it too developed into a focal point, with the area to the front (now typically Piazza del Duomo) becoming a place where citizens congregated and engaged in lively political discussion during the mornings and late afternoons, as they can often still be seen doing today. This layout can still be readily discerned in the historic centre of many modern Italian cities, for example Milan, Turin, Modena, Piacenza, Bologna, Florence, Verona and Lucca, to name but a few.

Towards the end of the millennium the cities developed in size and importance. There was a proliferation of church building, much of it sponsored, as a kind of medieval status symbol, by wealthy citizens who sometimes had the churches they built named after themselves. In Lucca alone there were fifty-seven churches by around the year 900. These citizens were usually either merchants or artisans. They shared the cities with the urban poor, many of whom had come to the city to escape the dangers and deprivations of rural life and were often dependent on handouts from the Church. Up to around the eleventh century the cities were essentially administrative centres which lived, one might say parasitically, from taxing the countryside. Such trade as there was consisted largely of the international variety, following the traditional salt-trade routes. It mainly consisted of luxury items to satisfy the consumption aspirations of the wealthy classes. The exception was Venice which was forced to develop its commerce at an earlier stage than other cities because it lacked any substantial agricultural environs on which to draw. By the late tenth century Venice was already established as a substantial trading power, enjoying significant commercial privileges from the eastern empire and controlling much of the Adriatic coast. Of the inland cities, Milan was the one which most rapidly developed its commerce during this period.

Thus at the end of the tenth century we have a pattern of urbanisation in Italy which is interesting enough to observe, but which is, at the same time, broadly in line with what is happening elsewhere in Europe. What happens next, however, is nothing short of remarkable, for during the eleventh and twelfth centuries a set of forces were set in motion which revolutionised the character of the Italian cities and propelled them into the very forefront of the history of the period.

ECONOMIC DEVELOPMENT

The historical conditions which enabled this to come about were, first of all, a dramatic increase in the size of the population of Italy, which is estimated to have doubled between the tenth and the fourteenth centuries. This led to an increase in the demand for and the price of both land and agricultural produce, and despite widespread land reclamation, it was accompanied by a large-scale demographic movement from the countryside to the cities, which therefore increased in size and consequently in political significance. Previously insignificant settlements such as Macerata in the Marche grew rapidly into towns, and the major cities such as Florence, Milan, Genoa, Pisa and Cremona expanded in a dramatic fashion.

Secondly, the period saw a very rapid expansion in commerce and the growth of merchant capitalism in Italy – a kind of medieval version of the 'economic miracle' of the post-1945 era. This process was fuelled by widespread trade – both local, in food, cheap textiles and artisan products, and, particularly in the case of the larger cities, the river towns and the seaports, international, in high-value goods such as spices and dyes. Hand in hand with this came the emergence of the banking and credit structures required to facilitate this expanding economic intercourse. By the end of the eleventh century Venice, Genoa and Pisa had become the masters of the Mediterranean, major centres of maritime trade as well as substantial naval powers. They expanded their trading spheres by putting themselves in the forefront of the struggle against the Saracens, and by supporting the Crusades and the Norman conquest of Sicily from the Arabs. In the south these processes were less marked; nevertheless, towns like Salerno, Gaeta and Amalfi still emerged as major traders. Inland towns such as Pavia, Milan, Piacenza, Lucca, Asti, Vercelli and Cremona, amongst others, are known to have traded extensively to the north, as far afield as Britain. (A small indication of the influence of the Italian merchant capitalism of this period is Lombard Street, one of the principal thoroughfares of the City of London, which was named after Lombard bankers.)

A NEW ARISTOCRACY

Finally, the enlarged cities and their flourishing economies precipitated rapid social change, spawning a new type of ruling class, more numerous and fiercely ambitious for greater wealth and power. The traditional ruling élite in the cities had consisted of the bishops and the agents of the state, the missi, gastalds, counts and other princes. Now these were joined or replaced by feudal magnates, the episcopal clergy, the main knights known as vavassors and captains, and all their associates and kinsmen. The division between the church and the laity became increasingly blurred, since the clergy were largely recruited from the nobility and effectively lived a lay life-style, residing in private houses and having wives or concubines. The optimism and prosperity of the new nobility of the period also led to an increase in their birth-rate, which of course in turn further increased their numbers.

The emergence of a new ruling class was not of course the only social development in the cities of this period. We also have the growth of the *cives*, an embryonic middle class of free men who prospered from commerce, money-lending, as well as from quality artisanship. In addition there developed the *popolino*, which we might now refer to as a working class, some free, some bound by varying degrees of servitude. They were, of course, the majority, and survived by labouring, working as servants, or by engaging in a variety of unskilled or semi-skilled activities; they were also often homeless, sleeping in the open air, but they naturally constituted an indispensible element in the growth of the cities. Nevertheless, it was the mushrooming nobility which provided the main impetus for the growth of local power in the eleventh century. Their growing numbers necessitated new sources of income, hence they looked to trade and commerce and to the mouth-watering estates and positions of the traditional church and aristocracy. Moreover, they possessed military capabilities, being brought up as horsemen and fighters.

ARISTOCRATIC COMMUNES

In the face of these forces the state, which was in any case weak and incapable of maintaining central control, collapsed, degenerating into no more than a theoretical presence, and turning Italy into just a geographical expression. Power was seized in the cities by the new élite, who either expelled or infiltrated the traditional aristocracy. They ruled by organising themselves into communes, which now became the dominant political force in the peninsula. The communes were essentially associations of men, initially the new *signori* or aristocracy, who were bound by an oath of allegiance and who collectively held public authority and ruled and administered their cities. The first ones emerged in the 1180s in Milan, Pisa, Lucca, Parma, Rome and Pavia, to be followed in the next decade by equivalents in Piacenza, Arezzo, Asti and Genoa, and then by Verona, Pistoia, Como, Siena, Bologna, Florence and many others in the early twelfth century. The communes emerged almost entirely in the north and centre of Italy, since in the south the Normans were at this time engaged in establishing a strong central state. They provide a truly fascinating study in the process of revolutionary change and political experiment, and have left behind them much for the visitor to relish.

The cities were governed through what is known as the consular system, an echo of classical times. This was based on consuls, whom the members of the commune chose from amongst themselves for a term of one year, investing in them powers of leadership which were backed by an oath of allegiance. There was a kind of rudimentary parliament in the form of the *concione*, or general assembly of all members of the commune, in which decisions were taken by the rather anarchic method of members shouting out yes or no. Truly important decisions were, however, taken by the assembled consuls, numbering anything between four and twenty, who were the commune's executive and judiciary. In practice, an élite of families would control the political life of a commune: the Giandonati, Fifanti and Abbati in Florence, the Della Torre, Soresino, Pusterla and Mandello in Milan, and the Gherardesca, Visconti and Gaetani in Pisa representing good examples.

This structure of government persisted until the strife-torn years of the 1190s and the early thirteenth century when, in response to the increasing threat from the *popolo* (see page 76), the aristocratic communes embraced the concept of a strong man, with more focused and potent executive powers, in charge of the government. These were the *podestà* selected from the nobility, albeit for relatively short terms of office. The cities during the time of the communes were almost invariably expansionist and militaristic in nature, fiercely parochial and concerned primarily with their own defence and aggrandisement. They gradually began to evolve into city-states by continually waging war on the feudal lords of the land around them, defeating and absorbing them. For much of the late eleventh and the twelfth centuries they succeeded in acting as compact units enjoying a good deal of internal harmony.

This harmony was consolidated by external threat since they, not altogether surprisingly, often fought with each other. Pisa and Genoa were at war between 1067 and 1085, Florence went to war with Siena in 1082 and then conquered Fiesole and attacked Lucca, Milan was in conflict with Pavia, Cremona and Lodi in 1107, to quote just a few examples. They also faced the constant menace of the armed threats from the old royal and imperial nobility, such as the Estensi who had designs on Ferrara and Padua, the Guidi, the Ubaldini and the Alberti who fought against Florence, and the Aldobrandeschi and Malaspina families who threatened the new order in Siena and Modena.

Matteo da Corriggia, Podesta of Perugia in 1278

The most serious challenge to the new city-states, however, and ultimately the factor which was to demonstrate their collective power, emerged from the Germanic central state in the form of the remarkable and much feared emperor Frederick I Barbarossa, or Redbeard. Barbarossa, a Hohenstaufen prince, was crowned emperor in 1155 and then set about attempting to restore central authority to the kingdom by putting what he must have regarded as the anarchic usurpers in the cities in their place. He crossed into Italy with a powerful German army in 1158 to smash the Milan commune, and subsequently claimed 'regalian' central power over the cities at a ceremony held at Roncaglia. When Milan rebelled against him in 1162 he ruthlessly burned it to the ground, and the situation briefly looked ominous for the leading city-states.

However, they responded with commendable unity and strength, forming the First Lombard League against him, which at its height in the late 1160s encompassed most of the cities of northern Italy, including Venice, Verona and Vicenza as well as the main cities of Piedmont, Lombardy and Emilia. Barbarossa marched against the League in 1174 but was soundly defeated at Legnano in 1176 and forced to agree to the Peace of Constance, which was ratified in 1183 and established legally the authority and position of the communes. Later in the century similar concessions were exacted from the Germans by the Tuscan communes, united in their own league, and thus the defeat of the state's counter-revolution was complete. A second Lombard League was formed to keep the Germans at bay in 1226.

TOWERS AMID CHAOS

Towards the end of the twelfth century the communes underwent a fundamental and profoundly significant series of developments which were eventually to challenge and then overthrow the nobility's monopoly of political power. The communes had always been highly competitive in nature, with much jostling for position and wealth, which is hardly surprising in such a period of rapid change. By the end of the century, however, this competitiveness had spilled over into bitter and often bloody internecine rivalry, which led to a substantial breakdown of law and order in many cities. Life became decidedly dangerous for the nobility, who responded by retreating into the comparative safety of tightly-knit, extended family clans, or *consorterie*.

A striking feature of these was that their members built towers, imposing edifices stretching eighty metres or more up above the crowded city streets, as fortresses and vantage points, but also as symbols of power and influence. Initially only the new aristocracy were allowed to build them, and the higher your tower the more status you commanded. The *consorterie* gradually entered into alliances with similar associations to form sworn societies, of anything between ten and forty people, which would control particular areas of a city. Access to the group tower or towers was restricted to members of the society, who sometimes had underground passages connecting their houses to the tower, or, more commonly, bridges from the upper storeys of their homes to a window in the tower. The society was, typically, a male-dominated organisation, with boys being initiated at the age of fifteen and girls being forbidden to inherit towers. Towers proliferated in most cities – Florence alone in 1180 contained about 100 of them – and they became a striking feature of the townscape, which was by now extremely crowded, with winding and narrow streets, small public squares, and two or three sets of city walls put up as development rendered previous ones redundant.

Medieval towers, as well as many of the other features described above, can be seen by the traveller in the 'centro storico' of many modern Italian cities. Pavia is one example. Perhaps the best-known tower is the Torre dell, Asinell which stretches ninety-seven metres up to the sky (and leans over two metres!) next to a smaller tower in the centre of Bologna, near the famous old university. San Gimignano, the 'city of the towers' between Siena and Florence, is full of many well-preserved towers which dominate the Tuscan countryside for miles around (fourteen out of an original seventy-two have survived).

The groups of *consorterie*, dominated by ambitious and ruthless nobles, gradually turned the various quarters of the cities into armed zones, competing with each other in a series of what amounted to local civil

The Towers of San Gimignano

wars. The different areas developed their own characteristics, fierce local loyalties and, according to Dante, even their own distinctive accents and ways of speech. This was the tragi-comic and logical conclusion of the very process of political disaggregation which had brought the city-states into existence.

POPULAR COMMUNES

At the same time the *cives*, the merchants and artisans of the cities, were organising themselves into guilds to protect their own interests against the rampant nobility. These guilds, as well as the popular neighbourhood societies which the nascent middle classes were organising to defend themselves against street violence, soon came into conflict with the nobility. The *popolo*, as it is now known, emerged in most of the cities (apart from the great trading states of Venice, Genoa and Pisa) between 1190 and 1225. They soon forcibly took a share of political power in the communes, and by late in the thirteenth century they had managed to wrest part or even all of the control of most cities from the nobility, sometimes expelling them in the process. In Milan they made their breakthrough into power in 1212 when they gained control of half of the offices of the commune, and similar events occurred in Cremona in 1210, Vicenza (1222), Verona (1227), Lucca and Modena (1229), Bologna (1231), Siena (1233), Florence (1244), and Perugia (1250), to quote a few examples. Even in the port of Genoa the popolo under Guglielmo Boccanegra gained a slice of power in 1257.

The end result was the creation of the popular commune. There are problems in placing a social class interpretation on this development since there was a great deal of mobility between the aristocracy and the popolo, and neither were compact units. Nevertheless, one could claim that the urban middle class in Italy had seized power from the aristocracy, and they had done so 500 years before the French Revolution! Although the popolo ultimately came to power by violence, they were invariably extremely well organised and disciplined, as one might perhaps expect from what we would now regard as the professional classes. For military purposes they divided themselves into armed companies, and administratively they relied on an amazingly intricate system of classification, dividing the cities into districts, parishes, neighbourhoods (in Siena, the *contrade* which now contest the famous annual *palio*), and even down to individual streets and houses. These qualities were reflected in the sophisticated way in which they organised the government of the communes. This was based on a written constitution, which was drafted by the notaries who of course formed part of their number, and it was remarkably democratic, certainly for the time. There was a large legislative assembly, the Council of the People, which made policy. The magistracy or executive consisted of a council of between eight and twelve men, usually known as the *anziani*, or elders, later to be replaced, much as had happened in the aristocratic communes, by the single strong man, the Captain of the People, for whom the anziani acted as advisers. The commune of the popolo also developed a large and sophisticated bureaucracy, including a court and a treasury, staffed of course by the professionals among its ranks.

This particular period of Italian history is truly rich in interest. It did not, however, last very long, and by the beginning of the fourteenth century it had largely burned itself out, leaving the city-states to move into their next phase: the oligarchies and dictatorships which was to be the background to the Renaissance. Why, then, did the popular commune, with its relatively democratic and advanced form of political organisation, eventually fall and give way to perhaps more predictable forms of government? The answer lies partly in the intrinsic weakness of the popolo, and partly in the historically irresistible power of the traditional aristocracy and the nouveaux riches, 'the organised resources of land and big money', as one historian has put it. It is important to note that the popolo was a heterogeneous and constantly changing set of people, an alliance of strange bedfellows: powerful bankers and traders as well as petty merchants and artisans – the poor were of course excluded. The bankers and traders essentially used the popolo to break the nobility's stranglehold on consular government; when they had achieved their aims, the more humble middle class were no longer needed – in fact they were often an embarrassment and a threat. Thus the rich and newly powerful middle class ditched them, undermining the popolo, and with it the popular commune. Most cities experienced a period of lawlessness and widespread serious violence, during which the urban merchant capitalists allied themselves with the more traditional nobility, from the fourteenth century onwards taking power and ruling the cities. Taking a wider perspective, the fall of the popolo can be seen as fairly predictable given the radical change for which they stood, in many ways far ahead of their time.

The legacy of the popular communes is indeed a profound one. They have been criticised by both conservative and radical historians, respectively for failing to secure law and order in the cities and for failing to develop a truly popular movement by including and organising the poor. Nevertheless, under the popolo the cities, as we have seen, were rapidly and often impressively developed, with substantial architectural projects which still delight modern visitors: the Palazzo del

The Palazzo Vecchio in Florence, built 1299–1314

Bargello and Palazzo Vecchio in Florence, the Palazzo dei Priori in Volterra, the Palazzo Pubblico in Siena, and the Palazzo del Capitano del Popolo and Palazzo dei Priori in Todi are good examples. The economy of the cities also flourished under the popular commune, perhaps predictably given the popolo's background in trade and industry. There is also evidence that the relaxed, friendly and congenial atmosphere which we now associate with many Italian cities, the 'Italian character' so to speak, originated at this time, despite the social unrest.

The popular communes also had a lasting effect on Italian political thought, on Italian literature, and on the very language of the country. Dante Alighieri (1265–1321) was 'popolano' and his 'dolce stil novo' (sweet new style), as exemplified in the *Divina Commedia*, was the basis of modern Italian. It was much influenced by the popolo and its attitudes, even though much of it was in fact a poetical reaction to the 'vulgar' language of the popolo.

Normans, Papacy and Empire: 1024–1303

Before we leave this period, it is necessary briefly to outline the more macro political developments in the peninsula as a whole during the eleventh, twelfth and thirteenth centuries. These provide the framework in which the city-states developed, the most significant and interesting of these being the rise and fall of the Normans in the south and Sicily, and the developments, both spiritual and political, which concerned the Catholic church and its relationship with the German emperors and, later, the French.

THE NORMANS

The Normans had begun settling in the south around the beginning of the eleventh century. They rapidly assimilated the Christianity and customs of the native population, and their prowess as mercenary warriors enabled them to accumulate territory, such as Aversa which was granted to them by the Duke of Naples in 1030. This permitted more immigrants to settle in the south. One of these was Tancred de Hauteville who with his twelve sons founded the Norman state in the south. One of his sons, Robert Guiscard, was primarily responsible for the capture of Calabria, using an early form of guerrilla warfare. His youngest son Roger initiated the conquest of Sicily, which was then completed by his own son who was crowned King Roger II in the cathedral at Palermo in 1130. The Normans initially faced opposition from the papacy, but overcame this by defeating Pope Leo IX (1049–1054) at the Battle of Civitate in 1053, after which their control of the south was accepted and legitimised by Pope Nicholas II in 1059.

The Normans proved themselves to be remarkably able and eclectic rulers of the south. Comparatively few in number, they nevertheless retained firm but reasonably harmonious control of their territory, and ran the kingdom of Sicily, as it was now called, efficiently. Their secret, so to speak, consisted of involving in the process of government the various races who made up the population of the south, Saracens, Italians, Greeks and Frenchmen, whilst at the same time allowing each to retain much of their individual characteristics and identity. Thus, for example, the Norman fleet was run by Greeks, and the fiscal system was based on the Arab model. Superimposed on all this was an absolutist central state based on a type of feudalism imported from Normandy, with princes of various sorts holding land and position on a grant from the king. The whole resulted in a state strong enough to prevent the type of disintegration which we have seen taking place in the rest of the peninsula, and also strong enough to withstand for the best part of a century challenge from both within and without, from the papacy and the empires of the East and the West. Indeed Roger II managed during his 24-year reign to conquer Malta and parts of Libya. Eclecticism is also evident in Norman architecture: the cathedral at Monreale, for example, overlooking Palermo, is a unique blend of Greek, Arabic, French and Roman influences. Decline eventually came as the result of a succession crisis, King William II leaving no legitimate male heir on his death in 1189. This enabled the German emperor Henry VI to impose imperial rule on the kingdom of Sicily, conquering it with the customary violence and cruelty.

PAPACY AND EMPIRE

Turning now to the papacy, we have seen how in the first part of this period the institution had been substantially corrupted, becoming the hereditary fief of the Roman aristocracy. During the eleventh century, however, the popes, beginning with the devout Leo IX who reached the position in 1049 with the help of the emperor Henry III, led a struggle to reform the Church. The aim was to purge Catholicism of some of its temporal links and to restore religious credibility to the papacy by ending such phenomena as married clergymen and the practice of simony. Additionally, the reformers strove to establish the central power of the papacy over the Church internationally by attempting to make bishops and other high religious officials in the whole of the western empire directly responsible to the popes, an ambition which must have been influenced by the legacy of the Roman empire of classical times. This led the popes into conflict with the western empire, which saw these developments as a challenge to its own political authority. A long and complex struggle between Papacy and Empire ensued.

A key issue in this struggle was the so-called investiture question, that is the question of who was to appoint church officials, including the pope himself. The establishment of the right of the cardinal bishops to elect the pope in 1059 proved a major step forward for the reformers, who then found a powerful champion in Hildebrand, a protégé of Leo IX, who was archdeacon of Rome before being elected Pope Gregory VII in 1073. After his investiture Gregory VII went on the offensive against Emperor Henry IV, issuing a decree forbidding lay investiture in 1075 and excommunicating him the following year. He then rubbed salt into Henry's wounds in 1077 by having him beg for absolution for three days in the winter cold of the courtyard of the castle of Canossa, where Gregory was staying as a guest of Countess Matilda of Tuscany. Henry IV, however, bounced back from this gross and undignified humiliation, having the German bishops elect an anti-pope, Archbishop Guibert of Ravenna, who became Clement III, and invading Rome in 1084 to enforce the deposition of Gregory VII and have the anti-pope invest him with the imperial crown. (Gregory died the following year in exile in Salerno.) Rome and its citizens, incidentally, suffered the usual fate of innocent bystanders of this period – the city was systematically sacked and pillaged both by the Germans and by the Normans who had come to Gregory's aid.

In the end this incident proved to be a mere temporary setback for the reformers of the Church. The prestige of the papacy was restored by Pope Urban II (1088–99), who helped mobilise the First Crusade against Islam, and in 1122 the reformers, now led by Pope Calixtus II (1119–24), won substantial concessions from Emperor Henry V under the Concordat of Worms, which settled the investiture issue largely in favour of the papacy. The power, both spiritual and political, of the Church grew after this victory, reaching its height during the papacy of Innocent II (1198–1216), who with great political and conspiratorial aptitude managed to create the Papal States. He played off the Hohenstaufen Philip of Swabia and Otto of Brunswick, the two contenders of the time for title of emperor, against each other, securing Otto's agreement to papal control of much of central-southern Italy in return for support for his candidature. When Otto reached the throne and predictably changed his mind, Innocent arranged for his ward Frederick, later Emperor Frederick II, to be elected king of Rome, in return for the latter's promise to respect papal control of the States and maintain the independence of the kingdom of Sicily.

On Innocent's death Frederick II, who turned out to be a man of many talents, known to his contemporaries as stupor mundi, the wonder of the world, attempted to extend his influence over as much of the peninsula as possible, and there followed thirty years of struggle between the emperor and Popes Honorius III (1216–27), Gregory IX (1227–41) and Innocent IV (1241–61). Frederick's death in 1250 precipitated the decline of imperial power in Italy; his eventual heir was his illegitimate son Manfred, who held the position of king of Sicily until a Frenchman, Urban IV, became pope (1261–4) and courted Charles of Anjou to take the imperial crown. The latter, despite some misgivings, exploited the opening and invaded, killing Manfred at the Battle of Benevento in 1266 to take control of the kingdom of Sicily. He then consolidated his position by defeating a Hohenstaufen counter-attack, led by Frederick II's sixteen-year-old grandson Conradin, at the Battle of Tagliacozzo in 1268, afterwards having the German prince beheaded in Naples. The death of Conradin represents a historical landmark since it effectively ended the Hohenstaufen dynasty and established France as the dominant foreign power in Italy. Powerful or not, the Angevins lost control of

Sicily to the Spanish in 1282, when the abuse of a woman on her way to church in Palermo sparked off anti-French riots, which were exploited by Peter of Aragon who captured the island with the help of his mighty fleet.

An interesting feature of this phase of Italian history is the emergence of an early type of party politics, in the form of the much-quoted division between Guelfs and Ghibellines. In essence, the Guelfs were the supporters of the papacy against the empire, while the Ghibellines supported imperial power, originally symbolised by Frederick II. This division, which it must be said mainly concerned the nobility, split Italy down the middle, with cities lining up with one side or the other according to how they perceived their interests might best be served. The period of Manfred's rule was one of Ghibelline ascendancy, while his fall represents a victory for the Guelfs, and so on. As often happens, the original causes became obscured by the passage of time but the divisions persisted, and the division between Guelfs and Ghibellines is an important characteristic of the political life of Italy in this period.

Needless to say, things were not always so simple. In Florence, for example, the Guelfs, who where firmly in control after the Battle of Benevento, were in turn split into two factions. there were the Whites, led by the Cerchi family, who were nobles willing to accommodate the aspirations of the popolo in the Florentine commune. Against them were pitted the so-called Blacks, hard-line, hawkish conservatives led by Corso Donati, who would have no truck with the popolo.

It was support for the Black faction in Florence which contributed to the fall of Pope Boniface VIII (1294–1303) and the last important development of this early medieval period: the fall of the medieval papacy. Boniface was another politically ambitious pope, in the tradition of Hildebrand, but he palpably lacked the latter's political skills, managing to alienate a wide cross-section of Italian opinion. Dante, a member of the White faction whom Boniface had exiled from Florence, places him in hell and is bitterly scathing of him in the *Divina Commedia*. The Florentine commune put him very firmly in his place by instructing him not to interfere in the internal affairs of the city. He also faced vehement opposition from the Ghibelline Colonna family, whose castle at Palestrina he destroyed; from the Franciscan monks, who considered him a heretic; and from the Spanish King Frederick of Sicily, whom he tried to expel from the island with the military help of the French under Charles of Valois. The latter's expedition ended in disaster and Boniface was forced by the Treaty of Caltabellotta in 1302 to recognise Frederick, as king. The French king, Philip IV, now took advantage of Boniface's weakness to send his representative Guillaume de Nogaret to Italy to mobilise the pope's enemies and have him arrested at Anagni in 1303. On Boniface's death in the same year, a Frenchman, Clement V from Gascony, was invested as pope, and he moved the seat of the papacy from Rome to Avignon, where it remained for over seventy years. Thus ended a complex, even confused, but always colourful phase of Italian history.

CHAPTER FOUR

Rinascimento

We now turn to what is frequently considered to be, along with classical Roman times, the greatest period of Italian history, the Rinascimento, or Renaissance. As in Roman times, the period was one in which the world looked to Italy for leadership, and in which the Italian people made a significant contribution to the development of civilisation. Unlike the Roman period, however, the leadership which Italy provided was artistic, philosophical and cultural rather than political. In Italy itself the architectural and artistic legacy of the period is widely evident, most notably of course in the great Renaissance city of Florence, with its stunning churches and palaces, and its famous art galleries such as the Uffizi, the Pitti, the Accademia and the Bargello, among others – all, unfortunately, these days buried under seemingly endless mounds of tourists. In this examination of the period we shall first of all outline the extremely complex political and other parameters against which the Renaissance occurred, and then examine the nature and importance of the phenomenon of the Renaissance itself.

At the beginning of the fourteenth century, then, Italy was the most divided and the most invaded of all the European countries. Power was shared by two parallel sets of forces. The, so to speak, 'official' central government was in the hands of the empire in the north, roughly around what is now Lombardy, the Veneto, Piedmont, Friuli and Tuscany. The papacy, now controlled from France, held much of central Italy, including the area around Rome, and what is now the Marche, Umbria, Emilia and Romagna. In the south, the mainland part of the kingdom of Sicily was controlled by the French Angevins, while the island itself was governed by the Aragonese from Spain. However, in the north and centre at least, the jurisdiction of the state was largely theoretical, and real political power was firmly established in the hands of the cities, who managed to resist all attempts, which it must be said were in any case at this time generally tentative and feeble, to establish central control. An unsuccessful attempt at such a move by Henry VII, a count from Luxemburg who reached the position of emperor, was a case in point. Despite support from Dante, who was acutely aware of the advantages of unity in the Italian peninsula, Henry was thwarted by tenacious resistance from Florence and other cities, eventually meeting his death in August 1313. Paradoxically, out of this melting-pot had emerged a people who, during the Middle Ages, had risen to the forefront of both commerce and legal affairs in Europe. Again we see an example of a major feature of Italian history, as well as a parallel with the modern country: progress and quality emerging from apparent chaos.

Despotism in the Cities

We have seen that the cities in the centre–north had developed a republican and quasi-democratic form of self-government, the commune, which had essentially gone through two distinctive phases, under the control first of the aristocracy and then of the popolo. Now the cities entered a further phase which was characterised by two developments: the passage of political power back into the hands of the élite among the aristocracy, and the consolidation by the major cities of their position as city-states. During the fourteenth century communal government in effect gradually disappeared from the scene in most cities, to be replaced by totalitarianism in the shape of hereditary dictatorships or oligarchies, tyranny as contemporaries referred to it. The most powerful cities flourished, gobbling up the less important and powerful cities and territories around them, and thus extending their influence over large geographical areas. All in all, concentration of power in social and geographic terms is a major theme of Italian history in the fourteenth and fifteenth centuries.

THE SIGNORI

The dictators in the cities were the signori, usually heads of major aristocratic families who managed to seize power in different cities in a variety of circumstances, and then set about establishing dynastic rule for their families. The transference of power from the communes to the signori was by no means a smooth process. Most cities experienced a power struggle between the various factions over an extended period of time, with widely differing, often colourful, local circumstances, as one would expect in such unstable and heterogeneous circumstances. Nor was the outcome universal: some of the great cities, as we shall see, either avoided dictatorship completely, or experienced it intermittently, responding to the crisis of the fourteenth century in a somewhat more republican fashion by restricting the membership of the ruling élite and becoming oligarchies. Nevertheless, by the fourteenth century the Della Scala family had managed to seize power in Verona, as had the Della Torre nobles in Milan, to quote just two examples from many.

How then, can we account for this widespread retreat from democracy in the cities? The historical circumstances which brought this about have been briefly discussed in the previous chapter, but some further consideration is required in order to understand better this important development. The immediate causes were clearly varied and complex, but with the benefit of hindsight some overall factors which make the process seem almost inevitable can be identified. First of all, in the late thirteenth and the fourteenth centuries the communes were inherently weak. Italy during this period experienced almost continuous warfare at the local level between the multitude of political factions which were jousting for power. The instability, confusion, and disruption of civil war, weakened the communes and provided the opportunity for factional leaders of the nobility to exploit their position as 'strong men' to seize absolute power. Furthermore, the resources of the communes were stretched, and their political and fiscal institutions were weakened by the economic crisis which struck Italy, and for that matter the rest of western Europe, at that time and which persisted at least until the late fifteenth century, providing one of the principal parameters of the Renaissance. During the fourteenth century the population, agricultural production and industrial output of Italy all fell, the decline being particularly serious in Florence and the rest of Tuscany. This resulted in a rapid increase in bankruptcies, and in food shortages which, coupled with the fearsome Black Death which ravaged the cities in 1348, led to widespread famine and poverty.

People tend to retreat into conservatism in times of economic hardship. Thus weakened, the communes were in any case unable to resist the advance of a powerful and numerous nobility, who were often embittered by exile and dispossession, and frequently strengthened by alliances with kindred spirits in other cities. As well as the oligarchic élites, therefore, the signori, themselves victors of secondary power struggles within the nobility, emerged to take complete power in many cities, sometimes tempestuously, often by meticulously building up their influence over a period of time. Two further points need to be made in this context. Firstly, the rise of the signori was considerably facilitated by the power vacuum which existed at the level of the state in the peninsula. After the struggle between the emperors and the popes had ended with the victory of the former and the exile to France of the papacy, the emperors largely ignored Italy, being solely interested in milking its resources in return for conferring titles on the local nobility; they left the stage clear for the signori to emerge without the shackles of central authority. Secondly, one must observe that dictatorship was nothing new to the communes: they had frequently resorted to it in times of crisis by conferring wide personal powers on captains of the people and others; the difference now was that there was no way back. The fascinating experiment of the cities with democracy, however flawed, was well and truly over.

In the cities where they took power, the signori exercised almost complete and unrestrained personal power. Their own characters, personalities and idiosyncrasies therefore became a key political factor. However, they were almost invariably very concerned with the legality and legitimacy of their regimes, probably as a result of their own sense of insecurity. As in other times and other places in history, the more dubious the regime, the greater was its claims to constitutional propriety. Thus the signori frequently maintained the major legislative bodies of the popular communes, for example the Council of 500 in Verona and the Council of 1200 in Milan. These were often packed with sycophants, and were used to rubber-stamp the faits accomplis presented to them by the signori, in an effort to bestow on them a modicum of superficial democratic legitimacy. As the confidence of the dictators increased, however, they felt increasingly able to dispense with this veneer and new institutions emerged. The position of Captain of the Popolo usually disappeared at an early stage, its powers naturally being taken by the signori, while the Podestà became the chief official of the signorial administration, or sometimes a leading magistrate. More politically important were the plethora of aides and advisers who tended to surround the signori, and who probably had significant influence over policy-making. Signorial rule brought peace and stability to some cities, notably Milan under the Visconti, Padua and Ferrara, but it would be wrong to regard this as a universal achievement, since in Romagna and Lombardy strife persisted under some of the less able signori.

OLIGARCHIES

Four cities resisted the signori consistently during the Renaissance: Venice, Florence, Siena, and Lucca. These became the great Renaissance republics, and came to be ruled by oligarchies. To these can be added Genoa, Perugia and Bologna, which oscillated between republican and dictatorial government, the last two finally succumbing to signory in the fifteenth century. It is worth briefly examining why these seven cities embraced oligarchy rather than one-person rule. As ever, the reasons were varied and complex. In Venice and Genoa, the great seaports and trading cities, the prosperity which came from commerce served to mollify social unrest, and thus led to the emergence of a relatively weak popular movement. The need for a strong popular movement was further obviated, especially in Venice which was the most stable of the oligarchies, by a strong police force and a relatively high degree of social mobility and of access to the ruling class. Ambitious people in Venice and Genoa could get on without having to resort to violence and revolution. Under these conditions, the crisis of the fourteenth and fifteenth centuries, when it came, was less pronounced in these two cities, and a modicum of democracy survived. In the remaining five cities, the popular commune had been particularly strong and successful, at least as far as territorial aggrandisement was concerned. This led to the establishment of a tradition of democracy, the legacy of which proved difficult to relinquish completely, even in times of crisis.

The size of the oligarchic élite in the seven cities varied, from about two per cent of the population in Venice to around twelve per cent in Bologna, although in practice only one per cent or so of citizens were actually involved actively in the process of government. In the large republics of Florence and Venice this effectively meant that power was in the hands of some 200 to 600 men. The workings of republican oligarchy were complicated, as well as extremely devious. Individuals and families schemed and 'operated' to secure key positions for themselves and to increase their own power, and there was much wheeling, dealing and behind-the-scenes fixing of situations and outcomes; the law, in particular, was ruthlessly manipulated for the ends of the élite, a state of affairs not without parallel in the contemporary world.

Key functions of government at all levels were typically carried out through very powerful small councils of citizens, the composition of which was meant to change constantly – at least in theory. Members of the ruling élite served on them for limited periods, ranging from two months to a year, in order to ensure that power was distributed equitably among the oligarchy. In practice, however, it was a very limited number of wealthy, influential, and conspiratorial men who dominated the councils and thus enjoyed almost complete power in the republics. In Venice and Florence, for example, high positions were filled exclusively from a select list of nominees who were screened by the councils themselves – a classic example of an élite perpetuating itself. In the 'good government' of Siena, the nine-man ruling council (*concistoro*) was also drawn from a very limited number of citizens, with documented cases of individuals serving on councils on as many as eight occasions.

Oligarchy and signory in the cities had, on balance, many common features. The central one was that they both represented a total return to rule by, of and for the rich, a phenomenon which had been to a limited extent ended, or at least threatened, by the popular communes. As a result the period of the Renaissance saw an even greater concentration of wealth in the hands of the few powerful nobles who controlled the city-states. The poor, needless to say, became poorer, while the interests of the majority were almost completely ignored. Paradoxically, we shall see that it was precisely this greater concentration of wealth which

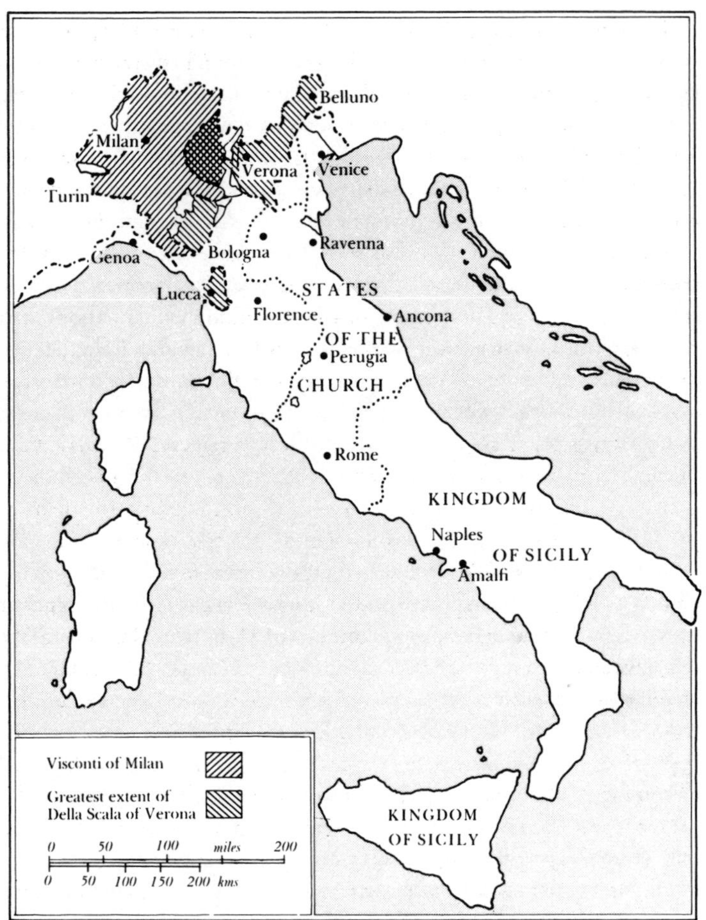

Italy in the mid-fourteenth century

created the conditions under which art could flourish.

By the latter half of the fourteenth century the territorial expansion of the major cities led to the geography and politics of Italy being, to all intents and purposes, dominated by five principal states, each with a population of between 800,000 and two million people. These were the republic of Venice, the Florentine republic, the duchy of Milan, the Papal States, and the kingdom of Naples, who balanced each other out, rendering further expansion by any one of them very difficult. This tentative status quo was formalised, following the Treaty of Lodi in 1454, by the creation of the Italian League in 1455, which brought a degree of stability to the peninsula in the years before the invasion by Charles VIII of France in 1494. This peace was, in retrospect, of much importance, providing as it did one of the essential parameters which made it possible for some of the greatest achievements of the Italian Renaissance to actually take place at all. The other, smaller Italian states, such as Genoa, Siena, Lucca, Mantua and Ferrara, maintained a degree of independence, but were essentially clients of the big five major states. We shall examine developments in each of the principal states in turn.

Venice

By the early Renaissance Venice had grown into a really major power, with the most impressive navy in the Mediterranean, a central role in world trade, as well as large amounts of territory both in north-east Italy and outside the peninsula. According to Doge Tomasso Mocenigo, in 1423 the Venetian fleet consisted of:

3000 small ships, with 17,000 crew;
300 large sailing ships, with 8000 crew;
45 galleys (25 merchants, 15 for war, 5 for passengers), with 11,000 crew.

This clearly represented impressive sea-power at the time, especially when one considers that there were another fifty or so galleys held in reserve in the arsenal, for wartime. Venetian trade stretched far into the east and the Mediterranean, and northwards as well, as far as Germany, Flanders, Scandinavia and England. At the zenith of its power, the city held large portions of Friuli and Lombardy, including the cities of Udine, Treviso, Padua, Vicenza, Verona, Brescia and Bergamo. Outside of Italy, the Venetian empire included the Dalmatian coast from Trieste to Albania, the coast of Morea, and much of the Aegean, including Crete, Corfu and Cyprus. The full extent of the Venetian economic and political miracle becomes evident when one considers that the city did not even exist in the year 400.

The origins of Venice's growth can be traced back to the beginning of the ninth century. The city had found itself in the middle of a bitter struggle between the Franks and the Byzantines, and it had been destroyed by the Frankish King Pepin despite heroic resistance by its citizens on the Rialto. It was rebuilt by the Doge Agnello Partecipazio and was then in the ideal position to exploit the peace between east and west which was ratified in 814, since it enjoyed reasonably good relations with both parties. The enterprising Venetians, proficient capitalists well before capitalism, were quick to seize this opportunity, making the city the bridge of communication between the two great empires. They built a large fleet to carry the spices, salt, cloth and slaves which formed the basis of their trade at the time, and developed an advanced financial system to oil the wheels of their economic machine. Over the next centuries their power grew relentlessly, accelerating as a result of the Crusades, which extended the city's sphere of influence and trade into the east. In particular, the Fourth Crusade, which led to the capture of Constantinople in 1204, laid the foundation of Venetian domination of the Levant. A treaty with the Turks in 1299 gave Venice the monopoly of the tourist trade to the Holy Land, by guaranteeing the safety of the pilgrims who were carried by Venetian ships – a very lucrative financial morsel. The privileged economic position which Venice enjoyed permitted it to be the wealthiest of the Italian renaissance states, and to weather relatively unscathed the general recession of the fourteenth and fifteenth centuries.

MARCO POLO

Like many imperial and trading powers, Venice spawned several intrepid venturers and explorers. The best known of these is Marco Polo, who was born into a merchant family in 1254. In 1260 his father and uncle set off on a ten-year business adventure which took them to the Crimea, the Volga, central Asia, and then to the court of Kublai Khan in China – further than any westerner had ever been. In 1271 the Polo brothers again set out for China, this time taking the seventeen-year-old Marco with them; they were away for twenty-five years. Their fabulous journey took them to Armenia, Georgia, Persia, Turkestan, Kangchow, Liongchiow, and then Peking, where Marco entered the imperial service of Kublai Khan himself. This permitted him to visit lands previously unexplored by Europeans, such as the far reaches of China, Indonesia, Malaya, Ceylon and Singapore. On his return, Marco was reportedly indistinguishable from a Tartar, with enormous drooping mustachios and oriental attire. At a banquet he is said to have ripped open his clothing, showering fabulous jewels over the table and the unsuspecting guests, which earned him the somewhat ironic nickname of Ser Marco il Milione (Sir Marco, the Millionaire). He was captured in battle and imprisoned by the Genoese, and enjoyed several further adventures before dying in 1324 in his beloved native city. Marco Polo in many ways typifies the Venetian character of the time: adventurous and daring in pursuit of profit, whilst financially extremely conservative and prudent – he was noted for his ruthless pursuit of interest on loans he had made both inside and outside his family circle.

By Marco Polo's time the city itself had developed into a splendid affair, fit to be the centre of such a powerful trading empire. It had, not surprisingly, a distinct oriental flavour, which is still evident in the modern city. Daily life consisted of play as well as work. Gambling with dice was very popular, although it was forbidden around Saint Mark's and the Doge's palace. More cruel and absurd were the annual beheading of ten pigs in the Piazza, the bull baiting, the dog chasing, and the organised street fights between youths of different neighbourhoods, which took place for the amusement of the citizens. Another feature of Renaissance life in Venice – as in the rest of Italy for that matter – was plague and pestilence, probably brought from the orient by the city's ships. There were no less than twenty-two outbreaks between 1361 and 1528 – one every seven or eight years – with the desperate effects that one may well imagine.

The main impediment to the expansion of Venice was Genoa, the other great Italian sea power, which in the fourteenth century controlled Corsica and Sardinia and traded extensively with north Africa. Extended rivalry between the two cities eventually resulted in the triumph of the Venetians, though not without several hiccups, and the decline of Genoa. This victory for Venice was in no small measure due to the stability of government and the communality of interests which, as we have seen, the city enjoyed during this period. The Venetians even managed to benefit from the foreign invasions of Italy at the end of the fifteenth and the beginning of the sixteenth centuries, temporarily gaining territory from Milan and in Apulia, while the independence of other city-states was seriously disrupted. Their aggressive, parochial, but successful approach earned them many enemies, as is evident from the war with the League of Cambrai in 1508–9. The League consisted of France, Spain, the Empire and the Papacy, as well as cities such as Mantua and Ferrara which had been damaged as a result of Venetian expansion. They initially managed to defeat the Venetians at the Battle of Agnadello in 1509, but were eventually forced to surrender virtually all the territory which they had gained.

Venice was at the apex of its power around the beginning of the sixteenth century, when the city made its most lasting contribution to the art of the Renaissance through the likes of Giovanni Bellini, Carpaccio, Titian and Giorgione. Subsequently, the Venetian monopoly over the spice trade was broken by the Portuguese discovery of the alternative ocean route to India – the beginning of the end of a great city, although much of the splendour continued until around the eighteenth century.

Florence

The growth of Florence into an influential city, and then a powerful state, can be traced back to the early Middle Ages, and was based essentially on two factors. Firstly, around the eleventh century the Florentines developed a major industrial sector, which was primarily directed at satisfying the growing demand from markets in the rest of Europe. Its most significant product was cloth, and in particular wool, which could be readily cleaned in the flowing waters of the River Arno and then exported by way of the port of Pisa. The Arte della Lana, or wool guild, produced a characteristic heavy, red cloth, and employed up to 6000 people at its height. Secondly, the Florentines (unlike, for example, the wool-producing cities of the Low Countries) developed a thriving commercial sector in parallel with their industry; their merchants were to be found trading throughout the vast international commercial network which the Italians had established in the Middle Ages, and their connections enabled them to become accepted as the European leaders in international banking and finance, with the Frescobaldi, Peruzzi and Bardi companies becoming major international banks. The Florentine gold florin, issued for the first time in 1252, quickly became accepted as one of the major European currencies.

During the fourteenth-century recession Florence suffered some particularly serious economic setbacks: production of cloth dropped from 80,000 bolts in 1338 to 20,000 in 1383, provoking a revolt of the *ciompi*, the workers in the industry; the population of the city plummeted from around 80,000 in 1338 to 55,000 in 1380, and 37,000 in 1427; while the price of grain increased by something like two-thirds during the half-century after 1338. Nevertheless, sufficient wealth remained, mainly concentrated in the hands of the ruling oligarchic élite, but also spread around the middle classes, to finance the great achievements of the artistic and architectural capital of the Renaissance.

THE MEDICI AND SAVONAROLA

The Florentine élite included several illustrious families. The Albizzi, the Capponi, the Pazzi, the Pitti, the Strozzi and the Uzzano were prominent in the fourteenth and fifteenth centuries. However, by far the most influential of the Florentine nobles at the time of the Renaissance were the Medici, and in particular Cosimo the Elder (1389–1464) and Lorenzo the Magnificent (1449–92), so named for his patronage of the arts and the contribution he made to the development of the city. He in effect took control of Florence in 1434 and then presided over its golden age during the following sixty years. The Medici, a family of bankers, exerted almost complete personal control over Florence during the bulk of the fifteenth century, despite the fact that the city was, in theory at least, a republican oligarchy in which supreme authority resided in the Signoria, consisting of the *gonfaloniere* of justice and eight *priori*. On the surface, the Medici maintained power by manipulating the elections to the Signoria, filling it with their own supporters, whose loyalty they had ensured by use of their vast financial resources. However, they fundamentally remained in power because a majority of the people who

Cosimo dei Medici

mattered considered their rule to be in the public interest. They courted popularity by their genuine love for, and large-scale patronage of, the city, and in particular its art. During the ascendancy of the Medici in the fifteenth century, Florence enjoyed a period of relative internal harmony and splendour, with daily pageants and festivals as well as much external prestige.

When the French invaded at the end of the fifteenth century, Florence, now under Piero de' Medici (1471–1503) intervened in defence of the threatened kingdom of Naples. When at first the war went badly, Piero was quickly deposed, to be replaced by one of the most prominent and influential figures of Renaissance Florence, the Dominican friar Girolamo Savonarola (1452–98). Savonarola can be seen as a kind of fanatical religious fundamentalist, who promoted prayer and piety, replaced the carnivals with religious processions, and turned Florence into an ally of the French. His forceful character and simple message had

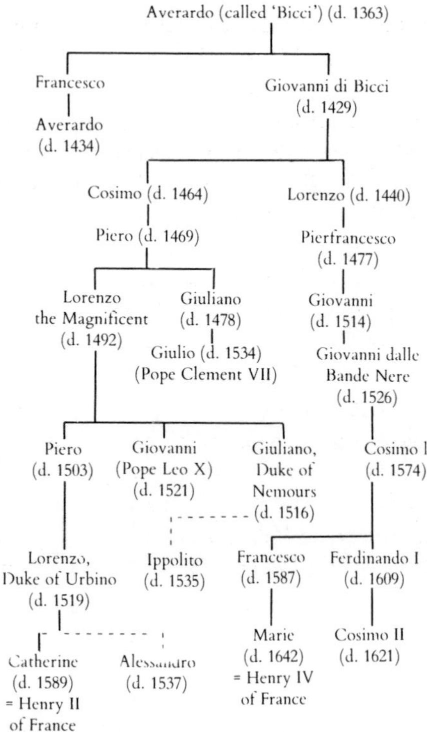

The Medici

a remarkable impact on Florentines of all persuasions, who flocked to contribute to the counter-revolution. Eventually the city turned against Savonarola as well, and he ended up being burned alive in the Piazza della Signoria in May 1498, ironically as a heretic.

By 1512, when French power in Italy had temporarily ended, the Medici had returned to power in Florence through Giovanni de' Medici (1475–1521). Giovanni extended the Medicean sphere of influence into the Papal States, becoming Pope Leo X in 1513. It was he who was Machiavelli's famous Prince (*Il Principe*), in the influential political work which has come to be regarded as a handbook for devious despots. One should not, however, that Machiavelli himself (1469–1527) was in fact a closet republican, who learned his strategies and techniques from Cesare Borgia and regarded signory as a necessary evil.

Apart from Medicean influence in the Papal States, the Florentine republic at its peak controlled large areas of Tuscany, including the cities of Pisa, Livorno, Piombino, Pistoia, Volterra, Arezzo, Cortona and Sansepolcro. Annexation by Florence usually meant exploitation by means of high taxes, as well as tight control over local industries to make sure they posed no competitive threat to Florentine production. On the credit side Florentine rule brought a modicum of stability, and, on occasions, economic development – for example, the Florentines facilitated growth in Pisa and Livorno as outlets for their foreign trade.

The city of Florence itself, of course, grew in splendour. We have seen how municipal and private architecture developed under the commune; hand in hand with this came the building of a number of impressive churches which still stand today, such as Santa Croce, Santa Maria Novella and, above all, the Duomo. The Duomo was begun in 1296 to a design by Arnolfo di Cambio as a replacement for the old church of Santa Reparata, and it took until 1434 to complete, employing the genius of generations of architects and artists, including Brunelleschi, who built the cupola, and Giotto, who provided the initial design for the campanile, the imposing bell-tower. The end result was the largest church in Christendom at the time, clearly visible for miles from the hills which rise above the city. The building activity also continued and indeed flourished under the republican oligarchy. Florentine painting and sculpture, of course, reached particularly impressive heights during the Renaissance. The artists of this period are household names which roll easily from the tongue: Cimabue, Giotto, Donatello, Fra Angelico, Uccello, Masaccio, Mantegna, Botticelli, Raphael, Titian, not to mention Michelangelo Buonarroti and the 'Renaissance genius' Leonardo da Vinci. (For a complete list, with dates, see p. 000.) Lorenzo Ghiberti's famous doors for the Baptistry were created in the first half of the fifteenth century; the east door, facing the Duomo, is the one Michelangelo later called the 'Gate to Paradise'. From the time of Dante, Florence was also a centre for poets and writers – Petrarch (1304–74) and

The City of Florence at the time of the Renaissance

Boccaccio (1313–75) in the fourteenth century, Machiavelli, the historian Guicciardini (1483–1540), the architect and art historian Vasari (1511–74). The two great poets of the sixteenth century both lived in Ferrara: Ariosto (1474–1533) and Torquato Tasso (1544–95).

Milan

The largest of the Italian land-locked cities, Milan flourished economically under its commune, before capitulating into signory during the thirteenth century, when the Della Torre family gradually came to control the leading positions of the executive council of the Credenza. Absolute power in Milan was thenceforth contested by the Della Torre and the other leading noble family, the Visconti.

THE VISCONTI

The latter eventually emerged as victors from this struggle when Ottone Visconti, who was Archbishop of Milan, managed to be appointed lord of the city in 1277. Ottone was succeeded by his great-nephew Matteo (1255–1322), and the Visconti came to be regarded as the natural rulers of Milan, producing a number of what might charitably be called colourful characters. Matteo managed to establish a family signory which was really more like a type of absolute monarchy than a form of despotism, and he also initiated the process of geographical expansion which was to turn Milan into a major state.

The most notorious of the Visconti, however, was Gian Galeazzo (1351–1402), who held power in the city from 1379 until his death. He was a devious, ruthless and wildly ambitious character, who succeeded in combining the various cities around Milan which the Visconti dominated into a centralised state under his own control. He furthermore turned family rule into total personal power by murdering his uncle, and potential rival, Bernabò. At the height of his power, the Milanese state incorporated large areas of territory, not only in Lombardy but also in the Veneto, Liguria, Emilia and Tuscany. The cities under his control included Genoa, Verona, Pavia, Cremona, Belluno, Bologna and, for a while, Pisa and Siena. He improved his international prestige and influence by a series of cynical marriage alliances with leading European families. Most notably, he married off his sister to Lionel, Duke of Clarence (second son of Edward III), and his daughter Valentina to Louis, Duke of Orleans. The latter move was, in time, to backfire on the Milanese since the French used the marriage as the basis of their claim to the city. In 1395 Gian Galeazzo's desire for formal recognition was satisfied when he was given the title of Duke of Milan by the emperor Wenceslaus.

Gian Galeazzo then set about attempting to extend his influence over the rest of Italy. For a while it seemed possible that he might even

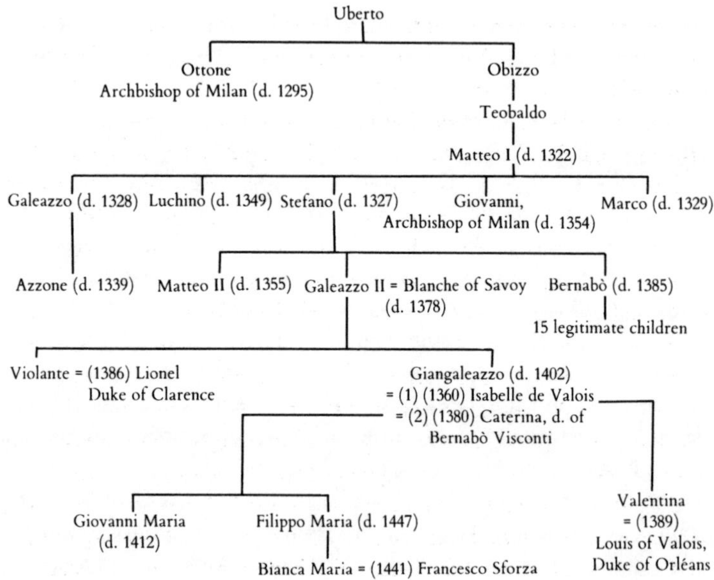

The Visconti

succeed in uniting much of the peninsula under his personal control. His armies pushed the Florentines, who strongly resisted his advance, back deep into their own territory, and they managed to cut off the city of Rome, placing them in a good position to make a major breakthrough. The armies on both sides were reinforced by mercenaries and adventurers, the *condottieri*, from various parts of Italy, and indeed of Europe. The use of condottieri had become a feature of the seemingly interminable warfare which blighted Italy during this period; in fact many of them, for example the infamous Braccio di Montone from Perugia, had developed into a force to be reckoned with in their own right, further complicating the already almost impenetrable maze of Italian renaissance power relations. However, as often happens, just at the key moment the hand of fate intervened – Gian Galeazzo suddenly and unexpectedly died of fever, and the political balance of fifteenth-century Italy was secured.

A megalomaniac he might have been, but Gian Galeazzo was also an efficient and able ruler. The cities which capitulated to him did so not solely out of fear but also because of the stability and sound government which he provided. His regime competently administered the basic functions of government, such as taxation and justice, and also pursued a coherent and moderately successful economic policy. For example, both land irrigation and communications were substantially improved with the construction of the Navigliaccio canal between Milan and Pavia. As a result dairy farming and commercial agriculture grew rapidly in the Milanese territories of the late fourteenth century, as did the Lombard textile industry. A particularly interesting development was the introduction and development of a silk industry, which by the middle of the fifteenth century employed some 15,000 people producing an elaborate silk cloth, laced with silver and gold. Architecture and the arts also flourished, with the famous and imposing Duomo of Milan and the Carthusian Certosa of Pavia being products of this period.

THE SFORZA

Gian Galeazzo's war with Florence severely stretched Milanese resources and provided an opportunity for another highly ambitious man. Francesco Sforza was a condottiere; born in 1401 from a relatively humble family of mercenaries, by his guile and opportunism he rose to be duke of Milan, and to secure a prominent position in the Milanese nobility for his heirs. His family name was Attendolo, but his father had acquired the name Sforza as a tribute to his toughness. Francesco had been a constant threat to the ruling Filippo Maria Visconti, who attempted to bribe him into compliance by tantalising him with the promise of the hand of his illegitimate daughter, Bianca Maria. The marriage did eventually take place, but not until 1441 when Filippo could stall no more. Between 1433 and 1447 Francesco contented himself with control of the March of Ancona, which he unceremoniously seized for himself. After this he set his sights much higher, besieging and capturing

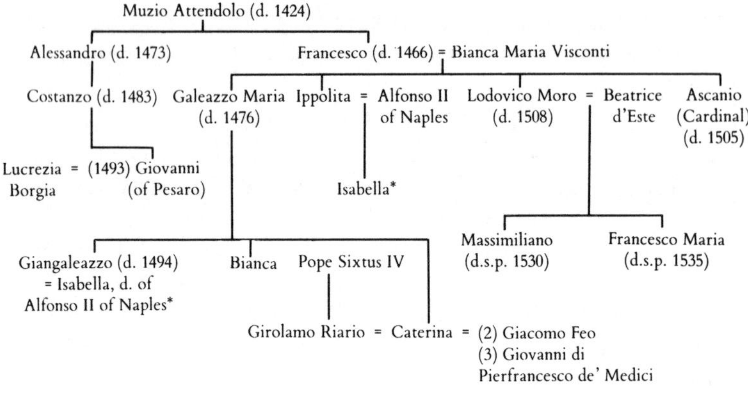

The Sforza

Milan itself and establishing his own personal rule in the duchy. Much to the relief of Cosimo de' Medici, he then accepted the status quo which was established by the Italian League.

In taking control of the city, Francesco Sforza overthrew the Ambrosian republic, which had been created in 1447 after Filippo Maria Visconti had died without leaving a legitimate heir. The republic in fact represented a brief and turbulent return by the Milanese to the vicissitudes of the commune, providing a politically exciting interlude between the signorie of the Visconti and the Sforza. The Sforza family ruled the duchy for most of the fifteenth century, continuing the solid economic policies of their predecessors. The most important of the Sforza nobles was Lodovico, who seized power by disposing of his nephew in rather suspicious circumstances, and generally proved himself to be a worthy upholder of the Visconti tradition of deviousness. It was he who encouraged the French invasion by Charles VIII, before ditching him once his purpose of keeping the Neapolitans in check had been achieved. Under Lodovico the court of Milan became a splendid affair with his wife Beatrice d'Este playing the 'hôtesse par excellence' and Leonardo da Vinci providing the artistic trappings. The party, however, eventually ended for the Sforza as well when their last duke, Francesco died heirless in 1535, leaving the city to the French.

The Papal States

DECADENCE ...

For the Papal States, the period was predominantly one of retrenchment and defensiveness in the face of internal division, followed by some degree of recovery and increasingly wider political ambition. From 1305 to 1376, while the papacy was in exile in Avignon, they were deprived of any effective central control. Left to their own devices, they degenerated into a quasi-anarchic collection of signories and city-states, the most notable of which were Ferrara, under the Este family, and Rimini under the Malatesta. An anachronistic and quaint survivor from this period is San Marino, which still maintains at least the veneer of independence from the modern Italian state. By this time, Rome itself had become a decaying and disjointed city, a mere shadow of its former self, with the ubiquitous ruins serving as a remainder of its glorious imperial past. The local feudal families, such as the Orsini and the Colonna, and their hired thugs vied with each other for supremacy in the midst of this melancholia.

The most significant attempt to restore some unity and direction to the Papal States during the absence of the popes was made by a certain Cola di Rienzo. Cola is one of the most striking figures of the whole Renaissance period, a surreal personage. Physically, he was incredibly fat, described as being akin to a buffalo when he was eventually suspended upside down by his feet after his predictably violent death. His character was extrovert in the extreme, with a very basic sense of humour. He was the son of a washerwoman and an innkeeper, who dreamed of a return to the Rome of the classical period, a vision which earned him the admiration of the poet Petrarch. He had bestowed on himself such grand titles as Tribune of the Roman Republic, Friend of the World, and Senator of Rome; in his delusion of grandeur he went so far as to invite the cities of Italy to participate in a parliament under his aegis, called on England and France to make peace, and even offered to act as mediator between the rival emperors, Louis of Bavaria and Charles of Luxemburg. Eventually he ran out of luck and was stabbed to death in a riot while on a mission to Rome from the pope in Avignon. His companion on this mission, Cardinal Gil Albornoz, had more success, recovering the key city of Bologna from the Visconti, and creating the basis of a central state through the Egidian Constitutions of 1357, which effectively divided the States into seven provinces, each controlled by a governor. This structure was to last for centuries, and provided Pope Gregory XI with the foundations of an organised state on his return to Rome in 1377.

No sooner had the popes returned to their traditional home than a further crisis befell the papacy – the great schism. Gregory XI's successor, Urban VI (1378–89), quickly alientated the cardinals who had chosen him, and they reacted by electing an alternative pope, Clement VII, who based himself at Avignon. Confusion turned to farce with the election of a third pope, and it was not until the selection of Martin V (1417–31) at Constance in 1417 that some semblance of rationality returned. In the meantime, the Papal States were again left abandoned and neglected, predictably sinking back into anarchy. The cities became easy prey for ambitious mercenary leaders, who often took full advantage; the most famous of them, Braccio di Montone, managed to become signore of Perugia, Assisi and Iesi from 1410 to 1424.

... AND RENAISSANCE

Recovery began with Martin V, who started to use the fiscal machinery set up by Albornoz to drain the periphery of resources, which were then diverted to Rome and used to rebuild the city and to restore central control by the popes over their territories. One of the consequences was that, while Rome embarked on a period of reconstruction and growth, the other cities of the Papal States, such as Perugia, Todi, Assisi, Spoleto and Ancona, stagnated and sometimes fell into decay. Subsequent Renaissance popes followed in Martin's footsteps. Eugenius IV (1431–47) was much influenced by Greek and Florentine scholars during a period of exile, and appointed Florentine humanists and artists to prominent

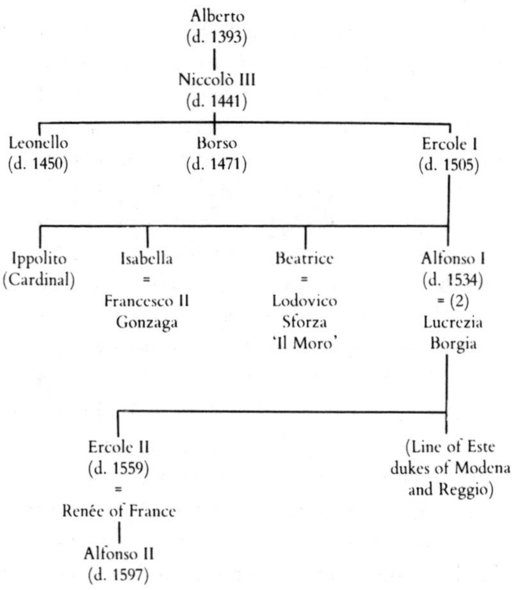

The Este of Ferrara

positions in the Vatican. Nicholas V (1447–55) was himself a humanist who studied at the university of Bologna, and he built up the Vatican library into an important intellectual resource, as well as employing Leon Battista Alberti to lay the foundations of the reconstruction of the city of Rome. He is remembered in the Vatican chapel, decorated by Fra Angelico, which carries his name. Aeneas Piccolomini, a scholar, diplomat and adventurer, became Pius II (1458–64) and is principally remembered for his activities in foreign policy, attempting to organise another crusade against Constantinople, before meeting his maker at Ancona on his way to the East. He too was honoured by a great painter, the Piccolomini library in Siena containing frescoes based on his life by Pinturicchio. Sixtus IV (1471–84), on the other hand, concentrated on matters nearer to home, consolidating papal control of the States by a mixture of diplomatic marriages and violence. He married his nephew Girolamo Riario to Caterina Sforza and installed him as ruler of Imola and Forlì, and tried to murder Lorenzo de' Medici whom he saw as a threat to his ambitions in Romagna. The only city which managed to resist him, and other Renaissance popes for that matter, was Ferrara, where the Este family remained firmly in control, confirming their status as one of the great Renaissance families. The bulk of Romagna was finally brought to heel by Alexander VI (1492–1503), who appointed his illegitimate son Cesare as its ruler. Alexander was a member of the notorious Borgia family, another of the great names of the Renaissance, who are remembered also for the antics of Cesare's sister Lucrezia.

JULIUS II

The greatest of the Renaissance popes was Giuliano della Rovere, who came to the papacy as Julius II in 1503. He further consolidated the Papal States as a powerful and united entity by finally defeating and bringing into the fold the important cities of Bologna and Perugia, and, by means of the League of Cambrai, recovering the cities of Romagna which had been lost to the Venetians. He furthermore strengthened the fiscal and administrative structures of the state, substantially increasing the tax revenues which financed the artistic and architectural accomplishments of the Renaissance in Rome. Julius II was also the first pope for a long time to nurture ambitions over the rest of Italy, wheeling and dealing to set up and then disband the League of Cambrai, and then in 1511 setting up the Holy League with Spain and Venice to drive the French out of the peninsula. His external exploits brought considerable prestige both to himself and to the Papal States.

The pontificate of Julius II changed the face of the Eternal City in a way which was more dramatic than anything seen since the days of the emperor Augustus. Under him and his predecessors Rome developed into a splendid and open city, with a population of around 100,000, and had become a major centre of the Renaissance. The best artists and scholars were liberally employed by the popes to work in the city. The new St Peter's church (1506–1626) was designed and founded by Bramante, who also designed the Tempietto of San Pietro in Montorio in Rome, on what was believed to be the site of St Peter's crucifixion; the Vatican galleries were built; Raphael directed the work on St Peter's and decorated the pope's apartments with frescoes; not to mention the work of Michelangelo who, of course, painted the ceiling of the Sistine Chapel and made the sculptures for Julius II's tomb in San Pietro in Vincoli, as well as designing the cupola of St Peter's and sculpting the Pietà. Julius died in 1513, leaving the papacy to the Medici.

The Kingdom of Naples

At the beginning of the fourteenth century, the old kingdom of Sicily was politically divided: the mainland of southern Italy was in the hands of the Angevins, while the Aragonese controlled the actual island of Sicily. The dominant political figure of the period in the south was Robert of Anjou, the king of the mainland part of Sicily, later to be referred to as the kingdom of Naples. Robert was a man of many abilities, who turned his court in Naples and the city's university into centres of cultural excellence, attracting scholars and artists, such as Giotto and Boccaccio, from all over Italy. He was much admired by both Petrarch and the same Boccaccio, and earned the title of 'Robert the wise' from his contemporaries. Robert's prowess also stretched to foreign affairs where he relentlessly championed the Guelf cause, intervening to repel every invasion of Italy by the empire. He came to be held in great esteem throughout Italy, being regarded as the dominant personage of his time, and was rewarded with various illustrious positions, including the lordship of five Tuscan cities and the title of Papal Vicar of Romagna. The kingdom of Sicily under Robert was a socially and economically compact and homogeneous state, its unity being basically due to the feudal institutions and power relations which had survived from Norman times. The monarchy, above all, was of a classically feudal nature, with the great majority of local communities in the hands of feudal barons.

Yet when one scratched beneath the surface, all was clearly not milk and honey in the kingdom, and its precarious economy rendered its political situation fundamentally unstable. Robert's reign proved to be a glittering lull before the storm. The kingdom was more sparsely populated than the rest of Italy, with far fewer, and much smaller, cities. Even the splendid capital city of Naples had a population of only about 30,000, who nevertheless managed to give it a strong cosmopolitan flavour, with the city divided into four segments, each populated by a different 'nation'. The kingdom was also extremely poor: its economy depended essentially on agriculture, and in particular corn, wine, wool, cheese, sugar, and saffron from Apulia. These were all exported in considerable quantities to the rest of Italy, but most of the traders and financiers in the kingdom were foreigners, and what was left after they had taken their share of the profits ended up in the pockets of the feudal lords. The peasantry were in general completely oppressed, living in abject poverty, much as they had done for centuries. So when the economic crisis of the fourteenth century came it hit Naples particularly strongly. The fall in agricultural prices, and the increase in competition which came with the crisis, decimated the agricultural sector, as did the dramatic fall in population which also occurred. There was no alternative resource to fall back on, and large areas of the south became depopulated and uncultivated. One-third of the villages were abandoned, in Sardinia a staggering 50% disappeared, while in Sicily the situation was broadly comparable.

The economic crisis precipitated a situation whereby, after Robert's death in 1343, the kingdom was effectively torn apart by political strife and feudal anarchy. He was succeeded by his depraved grand-daughter, Giovanna I, who murdered three husbands, in a style reminiscent of Henry VIII of England, before being imprisoned and given a taste of her own medicine by Charles of Durazzo, who then took the title of King Charles III for himself. Charles reigned for four years (1382–6), and was followed first by his son Ladislas (1386–1414), and then by his daughter Giovanna II (1414–35). The adventurous Ladislas enjoyed some notable military successes, holding the signory of Rome for ten years during the papal exile and nurturing further ambitions, thankfully unfulfilled, in the rest of Italy. Despite these diversions, the Durazzo dynasty presided over a period of almost continuous internal strife. Rival factions, notably the supporters of Louis II of Anjou and of Alfonso of Aragon, were involved in a bloody struggle for the right to succeed Giovanna. Furthermore, many barons, their revenues decimated and their outrageous life-styles threatened by the economic crisis, turned to warfare and outright banditry in an attempt to protect their personal interests, throwing the countryside into utter chaos. The situation in Sicily was in essence very similar after the death of Frederick III in 1377.

Eventually, the bitter struggle for succession ended with the victory of Alfonso of Aragon, who united the insular and mainland parts of the kingdom of Naples under his own leadership. He became known as 'Alfonso the Magnanimous', and during his period of absolute monarchy (1442–58) the kingdom regained some of its former prestige. The court of Naples became a centre of humanism, under leading scholars such as Pontano and Sannazaro, and the city underwent extensive development, with building projects such as the Triumphal Arch of Castel Nuovo, designed by Francesco Laurana (another Laurana, Luciano, was the architect of the Ducal Palace in Urbino). Alfonso was succeeded by his illegitimate son Ferrante (Ferdinand) on the mainland, and by his brother Giovanni in Sicily. Ferrante had to contend with an attempted invasion by René of Anjou, determined peasant revolts in Calabria between 1469–75, and mutiny by his feudal barons in 1486–7. He dealt with each of these, particularly the last two, with an iron fist, becoming notorious for his ruthlessness and cruelty. He died in 1494, by which time Charles VIII, of France egged on by southern Italian nobles exiled to his court, was preparing his invasion.

Charles' task was considerably facilitated by the support he received from Lodovico Sforza in Milan and from Savonarola in Florence. He was able literally to stroll unhindered into Naples, but quickly retreated back to France, leaving the kingdom of Naples to fall back into the hands of the Spanish. At first the Spanish made a treaty (1500) with Louis XII which partitioned the kingdom between the two powers. However, this was soon reneged on, the French were ejected, and the Spanish assumed full control of the south.

The Artistic and Cultural Renaissance

What of the Renaissance as an intellectual, cultural and artistic phenomenon? It is beyond the scope of this book to deal with this in any great detail; Nevertheless, no history of the Italian people could be complete without some reference to this fundamental development.

The first thing to emphasise about the Renaissance is that it did little to change the basic economic parameters in Italy, and was one of those periods in history in which cultural change was out of step with economic change. Nor, for that matter, did it significantly affect the lives of the vast majority of Italians, for it concerned but a tiny proportion of the population, and because of this, its status as a truly great epoch has sometimes been challenged. Nevertheless renaissance there was, and anybody who doubts it can never have experienced the excitement of walking from the railway station in Florence, along via de' Cerretani, to turn into Piazza del Duomo and be confronted by the façade of the Cathedral and Giotto's bell-tower; nor could such a person have stood in awe beneath Michelangelo's statue of David in the Galleria del Accademia in the same city. This Renaissance began in Italy in the fourteenth and fifteenth centuries and spread throughout the rest of Europe, lasting until the end of the eighteenth century. As such it represents one of Italy's greatest gifts to western civilisation.

What, then, was the precise nature of this 'cultural revolution'? It has been described as a change in the style of living, so completely did it pervade Italian society. In essence, one can see it as consisting of two features: the ascent of humanism as the dominant intellectual force; and the concomitant evolution of a new form of art.

HUMANISM

Humanism originated from the increased demand for intellectuals, which arose from the mushrooming courts of the aristocracy, and from the need for educated people to deal with the complex tasks involved in administering the cities and the states, as well as in conducting diplomatic relations between them. The curricula of the universities were inadequate to meet these demands, providing little except teaching of the Aristotelian, encyclopaedic tradition. Consequently, new, private, schools emerged, developing a new type of education, to meet the changing demands of the intellectual labour market. The most famous of these Schools was the Casa Gioiosa in Mantua, run by Vittorino da Feltre. Humanist education was based on the study of classical Roman and Greek literature, and its teachings were heavily weighted in favour of the 'humanities'. The principal theme was the role of man in society, or, more accurately, the role of privileged men in society. The Roman and Greek poets were studied for what they could reveal about contemporary life, as well as for their own sake. Important areas of interest included those of rhetoric, history, and ethics. The value of rhetoric, in particular, was emphasised to the point that eloquence became an obsession and a way of life for the leading humanists, from Petrarch and Salutati to Valla and Vegio.

The pursuit of humanism required the expenditure of considerable resources, in terms of both time and money, with a complete education engaging the youth of the period in full-time study up to the age of seventeen. It was thus restricted to the offspring of the élite. Not surprisingly, therefore, the humanists made what has been called 'an alliance with power'; they concentrated in detail on the dominant groups of the classical period, and they frequently took care to praise their own rulers and patrons. They tended to validate wealth while simultaneously emphasising the duties and responsibilities which come in its wake, and attacking the excesses of money. At the same time they often scorned the mass of the population for their ignorance. Politics was praised, and the importance and desirability of public life and office was particularly emphasised. The 'dignity of man' is a modern slogan which dates from the time of the humanists. From a contemporary viewpoint, the problem with the humanists is their narrow definition of the word 'man', which excluded the great majority of the population; nevertheless, from a broader historical perspective the movement was indeed influential, and it has left a truly lasting impression, even on contemporary culture and civilisation. Modern scientific criteria, including the idea of objectivity in research, for example, can be traced back to their work. It is, additionally, difficult to imagine how the subsequent development of west European culture could possibly have taken place without the rediscovery of the classical heritage for which the humanists were responsible.

Leading humanists were appointed to the aristocratic courts, and to administrative, academic and advisory posts in all the leading cities, and several of them reached positions of great power and influence in government. Many classical texts were diligently restored and copied and the first libraries were founded, including the Vatican library, the Marciana library in Venice, and the library at San Marco in Florence, which was the work of Niccolò Niccoli. The development of printing hastened the spread of ideas, as did the tireless travels of leading humanists such as Lorenzo Valla and Leon Battista Alberti. The cities of Italy were suddenly vibrant with architects, town-planners, geographers, cartographers, artists, scientists and innovators. Perhaps the greatest humanist, 'Renaissance man' personified, was Leonardo da Vinci (1456–1519), who, apart from being a great painter, was also a highly original and accomplished scientist and inventor. It is interesting to note that Leonardo was coming up with designs for such modern developments as contact lenses as early as the fifteenth century!

ART

The ideas and social experience of humanism found a figurative expression in Renaissance art. There is no need in this context to dwell on the qualities and greatness of Italian Renaissance art; suffice it to say that, from a technical and emotional point of view, it is revolutionary in nature. Yet it would be wrong to concentrate solely, as many art historians have done, on the artist and the artistic experience per se, in a vacuum, for in order to understand the true nature of the art of the Renaissance one must understand the economic and social context in which it was created. The salient point here is the relationship between art and the money and power which rendered it possible. The artists of the period were basically craftsmen, at best from the middle classes. It is true that some of them, for example Lorenzo Ghiberti and Verrocchio, ended up being rich and prosperous; it is also true that others, such as Leonardo, Raphael and Titian, lived their lives in the style of gentlemen. However, virtually none of them came from the nobility – an exception was Brunelleschi, who was a member of the Florentine élite. Most of the art of the period, therefore, did not appear spontaneously, and was not created for sale on an open market, but in fact depended on commissions for its existence. Leading artists needed to earn a living and travelled extensively for work, moving about the country to find finance for their services.

Patronage, therefore, was a key factor in the art of the Renaissance.

It took several forms and came from a variety of sources, most of them associated with the urban ruling groups. Architecture, because of its scale and cost, was the exclusive domain of the popes, princes, rich oligarchs, and wealthy businessmen. As such, the layout of cities and expenditures on such items as the renovation of churches tended to involve not only pure aesthetics, but also a statement of the power relationships within the community, with aspiring tyrants using patronage to build up their own personal popularity. The patronage of painting was naturally more broadly spread, although it was often carried out for similar reasons. Rich and powerful individuals would commission paintings for their private chapels, tombs and houses. Many of them must have loved painting for its own sake, but many also used it as a kind of status symbol, as an expression of their own worthiness and piety, or simply to glorify themselves or their office. A good example of the latter is the work which Michelangelo and Raphael carried out for the popes Julius II and Leo X. This tendency to achieve aggrandisement through art can also be clearly identified in the career of Lorenzo 'the Magnificent' de' Medici, who made no bones about courting popularity through his sponsorship of the arts. The relationship between patron and artist was a mutually advantageous one: the patron provided the money which the artist needed to live, while the artist provided the prestige and kudos which the patron craved. Art, as one historian has put it, was in alliance with power. A corollary of this is that Renaissance art changed with the changing tastes and aspirations of its patrons, which tended to be predominantly conservative and based on somewhat stodgy religious propaganda up to the middle of the fifteenth century, but thereafter became more adventurous and imaginative.

Apart from individuals, patronage also came from corporate bodies such as governments, guilds of merchants, and religious confraternities. Michelangelo's David was sculpted on commission from the government of Florence, while the administration of Venice, for example, paid Giovanni Bellini to paint the hall of the Great Council. A third, and clearly less significant, source of patronage emanated from the more humble commissions of the bourgeoisie and the petty clergy, who tended to pay artists to produce less grandiose, but often still high-quality pieces of work, such as the decorations which can be found on the wedding chests of the period. Whatever its socio-political background, much Renaissance art and architecture is still highly moving and impressive, a major delight for the visitor in Italy to experience.

CHAPTER FIVE

A Pawn in the Game: Centuries of Foreign Domination

The Italy which we find at the beginning of the sixteenth century was indeed one of great contrasts: individual wealth and courtly splendour amid abject poverty, especially in the countryside; and political fragmentation and disunity. All this in the context of a situation where overall control was exercised by five large states. At least, however, most of the country was in Italian hands, that is if we define 'Italian' in a broad sense, and if we ignore the situation in much of the south. Additionally, of course, the country, or at least a part of it, was enjoying the intellectual and artistic atmosphere of the Renaissance. In the course of the sixteenth century, however, these last two factors were to change: the independence of the Italian states came to an end, and with this lost autonomy the Renaissance as a cultural phenomenon to a large extent disappeared. The splendour of Italy's cultural influence was exported, to be taken up in other parts of Europe, while politically the peninsula came to be dominated by foreigners. An extended period of subjection and stagnation ensued, a phase of Italian history which was to last something like 300 years, before a reawakening of Italian national identity led to the unification of the peninsula and the creation of the modern Italian state, at the time of the Risorgimento.

The End of the Renaissance

THE SACK OF ROME

The sack of Rome in 1527 is usually considered to be the symbolic end of the Renaissance. The sack of the eternal city was, in truth, largely a chance event, precipitated by the coincidence of a number of random factors. However, one can also regard it as the culmination of a number of developments which were propelling Italy inexorably into a new, and mainly dark, era, in which it was to be to a large extent at the mercy of the interests and vicissitudes of foreign powers.

The background was the struggle between the Empire and France for control of Italy. In 1519, on the death of his grandfather, the Emperor Maximilian, Charles of Habsburg had been elected emperor of the Holy Roman Empire. Already king of Spain and ruler of the Low Countries and the Habsburg lands, as Charles V he proved to be a resolute and reserved man, with a powerful sense of purpose and large ambitions. He believed that the control of Italy and a harmonious relationship with the papacy were the essential prerequisites for legitimising mastery over the whole of Europe. In addition, control of the duchy of Milan would ensure a convenient and strategically important link between the Spanish and German parts of the empire. Naples, Sicily, and Sardinia were, as we have seen, already under imperial domination; the main obstacle to Charles V's ambitions was the French who, under François I, had captured Milan and threatened his hold over the remainder of Europe. A 30-year struggle between the Empire and France ensued, most of which was fought out in Italy. In 1521 Charles' troops ejected the French from Milan, setting up Francesco Sforza as a puppet ruler, and the Battle of Pavia in 1525, at which François was taken prisoner, seemed to seal the Spanish domination of Italy. But Charles' position in the peninsula was then challenged for a while by the League of Cognac, created by France in alliance with the major Italian states, including Pope Clement VII (Giulio de' Medici, 1523–34), who saw their independence imperilled by the ambitions and power of the Emperor.

In response, Charles sent an army to sort out these potential usurpers of his influence. It eventually arrived at the gates of Rome, where its leader, Constable of Bourbon, was killed. This disorganised, unruly, and now leaderless rabble proceeded mercilessly to sack and pillage the great city, to the disbelief and horror of the world. An inestimable number of important works of art were destroyed, and the event was seen by contemporaries as an omen from God, who was punishing the Italians for their degeneracy and their departure from fundamental religious ideals.

A basic change in the intellectual atmosphere followed, and although the city of Rome subsequently grew in splendour, with the completion of St Peter's and the great baroque churches, and although Michelangelo was still alive and working, the Renaissance in Italy went into irreversible decline. The shock waves from the sack of Rome were felt in Florence, where the Medici were ousted in a resurgence of the republican religious fundamentalism which had characterised the age of Savonarola.

THE SETTLEMENT OF BOLOGNA

Eventually the struggle for Italy turned in favour of Charles V, largely as a result of the defection from the French ranks of Genoa, under Andrea Doria. François renounced his rights to Italy for the time being by the Treaties of Cambrai and Barcelona, and Charles V was crowned Holy Roman Emperor by Pope Clement VII in the church of San Petronio in Bologna, during the congress which was held in the city in 1529–30. At this congress the pattern of Spanish imperial rule of Italy was established. Milan was restored to the Sforza, in the shape of Francesco II; Genoa was left in the power of Andrea Doria; the control of the popes over the Papal States was confirmed; the rule of the Este family in Ferrara and Modena was officially accepted; the Gonzaga dynasty had their control of Mantua confirmed; while the hold of the Empire on Naples and the south was recognised by Clement VII. With the partial exception of the Papal territories, all these states were effectively puppets, or at least clients, of the Holy Roman Empire, with their connections frequently cemented by convenient marriages.

The one exception was the republic of Florence. However, the compliance of the Medicean Pope Clement VII was soon rewarded. Imperial troops besieged the recalcitrant city, which put up a legendary and heroic defence of its independence, with the help of the fortifications which were erected under the direction of Michelangelo; gallantry, however, was not enough, and the Florentine republic fell. It was handed back to the Medici, Alessandro being the new ruler, and client. He was followed by Cosimo II (1537–74), one of the ablest rulers of the sixteenth century, and by Ferdinando I (1587–1609). Thus Italy came to be dominated by the Spanish, even though ostensibly it remained largely in the hands of Italians.

Italy under the Spanish

This status quo remained substantially unchanged until 1559, despite a series of Franco–Spanish wars, mainly over the duchy of Milan where, after the heirless death of Francesco Sforza in 1535, the Spanish exercised more direct rule. The only alterations to the political geography of the country were the absorption by Florence of the republic of Siena in 1555, and the creation of the duchy of Parma and Piacenza in 1545, under the control of Pier Luigi Farnese, the son of Pope Paul III (1534–49), who had been responsible for persuading Charles V to create the new state (a classical piece of nepotism!). Spanish rule was finally cemented in 1559 with the Treaty of Câteau-Cambrésis, which put an end to the Franco–Spanish war, froze the Italian status quo into place, and (perhaps most important from a long-term perspective) reinstated Emanuele Filiberto to the duchy of Savoy after nearly twenty years of French occupation. He and his heirs, beginning with the influential Carlo Emanuele I, were to build up a strong state based on the French model of absolute monarchy, and ensure that Piedmont became a powerful force in Italian history in years to come.

Italy Under Spanish Control

The Spanish domination of Italy was to last for a century and a half, until 1713. It was predominantly a period of political, social and intellectual stagnation – a prolonged period of darkness and retrenchment to follow the splendour and openness of the previous two centuries. Italy moved from being a major actor in key areas of the international scene, to occupying a marginal role on the edge of European affairs.

COUNTER-REFORMATION

The first significant development was the religious counter-reformation, which consisted of a reactionary, paranoic and often vicious return to what were perceived as basic Catholic religious values. This development can be traced back to the failure of the Regensberg Conference in 1541–2, which had been set up to attempt a reconciliation between Catholicism and Protestantism. An ugly Inquisition followed, as a result of which many intellectuals fled the country. Heretics were mercilessly persecuted by zealous Spanish and Italian bishops, led in turn by Popes Paul III (1534–49), who presided over the opening of the Council of Trent in 1545, Julius III (1550–5), Paul IV (1555–9) and Pius IV (1559–65). The infamous 'Index of Prohibited Books' was established in 1558, banning works by, amongst others, Boccaccio, Machiavelli and even Dante – how far Italy had regressed in a few decades! The advent of the counter-reformation was officially sealed by 'Professio fidei tridentinae', which closed the Council of Trent in 1563. The Inquisition had well and truly arrived in Italy.

Among the intellectuals who suffered at the hands of this attack on the freedom of worship and thought was the great mathematician, philosopher and astronomer Galileo Galilei (1564–1642), who was tried and imprisoned in 1633 for daring to propound innovatory ideas about the nature of the universe, including the preposterous one that the earth is round. At least he died in freedom: Giordano Bruno (1548–1600) and Tommaso Campanella (1568–1639) fared much worse. The former was burned at the stake in the Piazza del Campo dei Fiori in Rome in

The burning of a heretic at the stake

February 1600 for the crime of living his life in an eccentric and intellectually innovatory fashion. The later spent much of his life rotting in gaol for the similar crime of being a free and different mind, who threatened the fundamental bigotry and insecurity of the Inquisition. Astrology was one of his unthinkable pursuits.

These are but a few visible examples of the kind of hypocrisy which played a major part in bringing to an end the intellectual development which had occurred in the Renaissance. Less obvious, but probably in the long run more influential, was the creation of the Jesuits as 'ideologically sound' replacements for the humanists in the teaching sphere. The only state which to an extent managed to resist the extreme Catholicism of the counter-reformation was Venice which, for most of this period, managed to avoid adopting the Index, and won notable victories in the course of the Interdict dispute in 1605–6 when it stood up to Pope Paul V (1605–21), who had placed the city under an Interdict, by expelling the Jesuits from the city and asserting its own sovereignty in religious affairs.

Yet, paradoxically as ever, the years of Spanish rule were also years of notable achievement by individuals in various spheres. This was the period of the Mannerists – painters such as Bronzino and Parmigianino, Tintoretto and El Greco, and sculptors such as Benvenuto Cellini; of Gianlorenzo Bernini (1598–1680), who was responsible for the Piazza Navona and Piazza San Pietro in Rome, and for many fine sculptures such as his 'Ecstasy of St Teresa' in the Cornaro chapel of Santa Maria della Vittoria; of composers such as Palestrina (1525–94) and Monteverdi (1567–1643); and of the influential medical researcher Marcello Malpighi (1628–94). These, along with Galileo, Bruno and Campanella, were the exceptions which confirmed the rule, people who flourished in spite of the Inquisition.

RISE AND FALL OF THE ECONOMY

Ironically, the latter part of the sixteenth century was a period of economic expansion and optimism in Italy – the 'St Martin's Summer' of the Italian economy, as it has been called. The growth of maritime trade and the great voyages of discovery had given an impetus to the European economy as a whole, as had the 'price revolution', the reflationary impetus given to the economy by imports of large quantities of silver from America. This period was characterised by widespread, and frequently uncontrolled, speculation. It brought a building boom in many cities, especially in Rome with its new churches, palaces and villas, in Naples, in Milan, and in Venice, with the development of St Mark's Square in the form with which we are familiar today. Industrial growth accelerated, particularly in the silk and luxury goods sectors, and in printing. There was also an expansion of the banking and financial sectors, notably in Genoa. Prosperity is often reflected in population growth, and the Italy of this period was no exception: in the territory of Naples, taxation statistics suggest an overall increase in population of around 60% between 1532 and 1599, and in Calabria in particular the number of households doubled between 1505 and 1561 – from 50,669 to 105, 493; the population of the city of Milan grew from 80,000 in 1542 to 112,000 in 1592, while the population of Rome had reached 115,000 by the mid-sixteenth century, and that of Venice and Naples 175,00 and 200,000 respectively by roughly the same time. Nor, apparently, did the great plague of 1676–7 significantly reduce the population of the peninsula.

Recession, however, was around the corner. Around the very end of the sixteenth century, the Italian economy went into a decline which was to persist for the whole of the next century. Needless to say, the causes were complex. Firstly, the crisis in Italy was part of a wider European problem: partly precipitated by the Thirty Years War between France and the Empire, it was exacerbated by Italy's position as part of the Spanish sphere of influence, and by its being on the periphery of European affairs. This resulted both in a large-scale fiscal drain into the Spanish treasury, and in serious damage to Italy's traditionally strong trading position as the Dutch, the French and the English gradually took over trade routes in which the Italians had previously enjoyed a monopoly. In the industrial sphere too, the Italians were now faced with stiff competition from northern Europe in sectors which they had formerly dominated, and proved themselves palpably incapable of responding in any appropriate fashion to this new threat. Part of the reason for this can be found in the behaviour of the wealthy, who reacted to the crisis in a classically defensive fashion, attempting to protect their own interests by sinking the available capital into real-estate, thereby starving the productive part of the economy of investment.

Whatever its causes, economic decline was evident for all to see. For example, the annual Venetian production of woollen cloth fell from 29,000 rolls to only 2000 in the course of the seventeenth century, whilst Florentine output of the same product dropped from 20,000 rolls to 5000 in the first half of the century. The turnover of freight in the port of Genoa fell from 9 million tons per annum to around 3 million, which was typical of what happened to Italian shipping as a whole, while the city's silk industry was decimated. The situation in other industries and in other towns was generally similar. Typically for a period of recession, prices of course fell and the population of Italy remained stagnant, at a time when it might have been expected to increase. The situation was not helped either by a succession of natural calamities: there were outbreaks of plague – such as the one in 1630 described by Manzoni in his *I Promessi Sposi* (which is required reading for all modern Italian schoolchildren) – and an earthquake hit Sicily in 1693. There were exceptions in the economic gloom: the flourishing farming industries of Lombardy and Emilia, which in the course of the seventeenth century developed new products such as hemp, and the growing port of Livorno are two examples.

The most widespread and visible consequences of the recession of the seventeenth century were famine, pauperism and vagrancy. However, there were also a number of longer-term developments which were precipitated by the crisis, and which proved to be of considerable significance. The revolt in the south is considered later (pp. 127–28). The recession drove large numbers of Italians, both desperate peasants and, significantly, members of the baronial class, mainly in the south and in the Papal States, to see little alternative but to espouse a life of banditry and brigandage. In the late sixteenth century, in the Papal States, there emerged brigand leaders as diverse as Alfonso Piccolomini (the Duke of Montemarciano near Ancona), and Marco Sciarra, a man of much humbler origin who became a kind of Robin Hood figure, robbing the rich to give to the poor. Brigandage in the Papal States persisted, and indeed grew in importance despite ruthless attempts by the authorities, and in particular Sixtus V (1585–90), to suppress it: between 1590 and

1595 alone, 5000 men were executed. In Naples the situation was comparable, and in the late sixteenth century the viceroy, Pedro of Toledo, condemned as many as 18,000 people to death in an attempt to halt its spread – with only limited success as the movement developed on a massive scale, plunging the countryside into anarchy.

A further result of the recession, which also contributed to its severity, was the retrenchment of the capital-owning aristocracy into property. During the late sixteenth century the newly enriched middle classes who had emerged were rapidly absorbed into the various local élites, and economic expansion had had little effect on the social structure of Italy. The gap between the privileged and the poor, between the cities and the countryside, persisted substantially unchanged as it had done for centuries. So too did the fierce local identity, which remained a factor keeping Italy fragmented and disunited. Now, with the recession, the monied classes were determined to keep what they had got, and saw land and houses as the best way to achieve this objective. Thus, in the cities, great baroque buildings appeared, while everywhere large estates were created – the beginning of the latifundia – and great villas were built in which the landowners could reside in splendour while all around them suffered the ravages of a disintegrating economy. In Tuscany the Medici and others built up their vast estates; in Venice the aristocracy built grand villas in the countryside around the city, 322 in all by the end of the seventeenth century, such as the Villa Foscari at Malcontenta, built by Palladio (1508–80) in 1574, and the Villa Badoer at Rovigo – many of these followed the baroque style. Sicily was the location of the villa of the Palagonia family at Bagheria, near Palermo, a veritable monument to conspicuous consumption.

This retreat into property might have bequeathed some great architectural achievements, but it also had the effect, already described, of damaging the productive sector of the economy, and freezing into place a feudal system which was to endure for many years, and which to an extent still persists in Italy today, particularly in Tuscany, Umbria, and other rural parts of the centre–south of the country.

DIRECT SPANISH RULE AND REVOLT IN THE SOUTH

The parts of the country which were directly ruled by Spain predictably fared the worst. Naples and Sicily were governed by a series of viceroys, the first of whom, Don Pedro of Toledo, set about exacting systematic retribution on those who had supported France. Under the Spanish, there was no substantial change in the way the area was ruled; it remained in essence an absolute monarchy supported by the power of the barons. Those barons who had, so to speak, backed the right horse in the war emerged with a degree of independence as well as substantial privileges; it was they who controlled the main organs of state: the Parliament at Naples, the Council of State, and the Regia Camera Sommari.

The major feature of Spanish rule in the south, however, was the way in which the territory was used as a milch-cow, sucked dry of every conceivable resource in order to help finance both Spain's continuous warfare with France, and the conspicuous consumption and courtly excesses of the likes of the Duke of Olivares. Thus the Spanish would regularly indulge in a form of press-ganging, snatching unsuspecting southern peasants from their fields and homes, to take them in chains to fight for their oppressors on various distant fronts. The territory was bled by crippling taxation – direct taxes, indirect taxes, extraordinary taxes, and anything else which the viceroys and their lackeys could dream up. A particularly insidious practice was that of selling the right to levy taxes to unscrupulous local speculators, such as the notorious Bartolomeo D'Aquino, who could then pillage the poor inhabitants with even more zeal than the Spanish themselves.

In the face of all this exploitation and inhumanity, something had to snap. There were warning signs at the end of the sixteenth century, when revolts broke out – one led by Tommaso Campanella in Calabria in 1599, for instance. This was put down, and Campanella himself was imprisoned, but the big eruption occurred in July 1647, when the people of Naples took to the streets in response to the imposition of a new tax on, of all things, fruit. The revolt quickly spread to the provinces and the countryside, and soon the Spanish had a revolution on their hands. As one might imagine, the revolutionaries were a motley bunch, confused and divided, consisting of a mixture of desperate members of the sub-proletariat as well as the more moderate bourgeoisie. Led by Giulio Genoino, and then Gennaro Annese, and spurred on by the French, they won notable successes. In October 1647 they declared a republic, putting the fear of Christ into the southern barons who had naturally lined themselves with the Spanish establishment. Inevitably, the revolution was crushed by the Spanish in the course of 1648, and the vengeance which followed was of unparalleled severity and heartlessness. The very soul was burned and carved out of the southern peasantry, beating them into a spirit of resigned submission towards the baronial classes which to an extent persists to this day, and is arguably one of the fundamental causes of the contemporary economic and social duality between the south (Il Mezzogiorno) and the north of the country.

Milan, the other state which was directly ruled by the Spanish, fared a little better, at least in economic terms. It was, none the less, constantly in the front line of the Franco–Spanish conflict, with Valtellina and Monferrato being particularly exposed to the ravages of warfare. The Lombard aristocracy, however, was much more paternalistic in its attitude towards the peasantry, following the example of the energetic and industrious Carlo Borromeo, Archbishop of Milan from 1565 to 1584. The lives of the Lombard peasantry were, accordingly, a little less unpleasant.

THE QUASI-INDEPENDENT STATES

Of the states which enjoyed a degree of independence in this period, albeit often illusory, Venice was by far the most interesting, tolerant and lively. It managed to preserve its splendour and power throughout the sixteenth century, and it fared better than others in the economic crisis of the seventeenth century. Nevertheless, this could not disguise a process of overall Venetian decline. It lost much of its influence in the Mediterranean to the Dutch and the French; in the Adriatic it was threatened, on the one hand, by Slavonic pirates, who were supported by the Habsburgs, and on the other by the Turks. At home the Venetians were, of course, threatened by the Spanish. They were forced into fighting a series of wars, which seriously undermined the state financially and culminated in a twenty-year war with Turkey, which ended in the loss of the Isle of Candia (Crete) in 1669 and drove Venice into the Holy League with the Habsburgs, and a step nearer the end of the republic.

Nevertheless, the Venetians enjoyed a greater degree of pluralism and intellectual liberty than any other Italian state, resisting the counter-Reformation as no one else had done, and nurturing notable intellectuals and artists, such as Pietro Aretino, Paolo Paruta and Francesco Sansovino, son of the Florentine Jacopo who had designed St Mark's Square. It was the Venetians who were in the vanguard of the anti-Spanish movements of the period. Led by Doge Leonardo Donaa and Paolo Sarpi, they managed to 'win' the Interdict dispute, as well as forcing the Habsburgs to abandon their support for the Slavonic pirates. Unfortunately, they were effectively isolated, and thus had limited power on the international stage, being in no position to match the great powers of the time.

Savoy, under Carlo Emanuele I, also fared relatively well, as did Genoa, which grew rich on banking although the efficacy of its political structures unfortunately failed to match its financial prowess. For Florence, on the other hand, this was truly a period of regression. Here, the state was run as a signory by the Medici, who controlled the executive, the Pratica Segreta which after 1580 was housed in Giorgio Vasari's new Uffizi. The city-state of Florence became the Grand Duchy of Tuscany in 1569, but the new lofty title could not hide the process of stagnation which had taken hold. The Duchy, and in particular the city itself, were no longer major industrial and financial entities. Florence became a haven for bureaucrats and landlords, a service-based city along the lines of the one which exists today. During this period it experienced hardly any architectural development, as is emphasised by the almost total lack of baroque churches within its walls. The situation was broadly similar in other Tuscan cities, the only exception being the port of Livorno which flourished as a result of its strategically convenient location.

The intellectual and artistic life of the duchy, so open and enlightened in previous centuries, now mirrored its economy. Even allowing that the Renaissance was a difficult act to follow, one cannot escape from the fact that it became largely unexciting and complacent, inward-looking and closed to external influence. The Florentine Accademia della Crusca was responsible for fostering the same provincialism and devotion to the city which Paruta and Jacopo Sansovino were advocating in Venice, which Di Costanzo was nurturing in Naples, and which is so evident in the Commedia dell'Arte, with its locally inspired masks and characters. Paradoxically, during this period of intellectual slumber Florence managed to spawn some great personages, such as Galileo Galilei and Giorgio Vasari.

Finally, Rome and the Papal States, the centre of the counter-reformation, also entered a period of decline, despite absorbing the states of Ferrara in 1598, of Urbino in 1631, and of Castro in 1649. The city of Rome grew in architectural stature, many of its new buildings unfortunately being constructed from masonery which had been stripped from the monuments of the classical era, several of which were thus destroyed or severely damaged. It developed into a cosmopolitan city, with intriguing imbalances in the composition of its population – there were many more men than women, probably because of the city's position as a religious centre, and there was a large transient population of pilgrims and tourists. One of the results was the emergence of widespread prostitution in the city. Rome lived essentially as a parasite on the surrounding area, funding its conspicuous consumption from the onerous taxation of the rest of the papal States, some parts of which, partly as a result, went into secular decline. A case in point is the farm land around Rome and in the Maremma around Tarquinia, which was ruined by being transformed into pastures to produce the lamb and goat's cheese which the Romans craved, and which they still consume in vast quantities today.

The Spanish domination of Italy had persisted for so long, partly because of the strength and power of the Spanish themselves, but also because of the tacit support of the Italian nobility who, especially at the time of Philip II, had been prepared to accept it as the best way of preserving peace, stability, and their own position. During the seventeenth century, however, the power of Spain declined. Their great Armada had been defeated by the English, and they were increasingly under threat from the France of Louis XIV, who lost no opportunity to embarrass the Habsburgs in the Italian peninsula. By the latter half of the seventeenth century Spain was no longer a great power, and the Italians were subjected to the worst of both worlds: exploitation and subjugation to the whims and imperatives of a foreigner, but with no protection in return. Northern Italy in fact increasingly became the battlefield of Europe. Eventually, the Spanish War of Succession, which was sparked off by the death of Charles II in 1700 and raged for thirteen years, led to the complete fall from grace of the Spanish, and to the end of their control of Italy. The Peace of Utrecht of 1713 formalised this change, and effectively reduced Italy to a pawn in the game of international diplomacy. Overall control of Italy now passed to the Austrian Habsburgs.

The Eighteenth Century: Utrecht to Napoleon

The political geography of eighteenth-century Italy was initially established at Utrecht. The principal aim of the Peace of 1713 was, however, to establish a balance of power between the major powers in Europe, and not to deal specifically with the needs and problems of the Italians. Italy was therefore roughtly carved up among these major powers, with little or no regard to the traditions and aspirations of the people whose lives were involved, nor, seemingly, to any inherent logic. Thus the new emperor Charles VI, Archduke Charles of Austria, was given most of the former Spanish possessions in Italy: Milan, Mantua, Naples, and Sardinia. The Piedmontese under Victor Amadeus II, who by this time had become a united and powerful state which had significantly influenced the Franco-Spanish wars, were given some Milanese territory around Alessandria. They also found themselves with the duchy of Montferrat and the island of Sicily – once again the two parts of the kingdom of Naples were separated.

The Utrecht partition did not prove stable and was altered at the margin throughout the first half of the eighteenth century. The first upset occurred in 1720, when the house of Savoy was forced to exchange Sicily, which passed to Austria, for Sardinia. In 1734 Naples and Sicily returned into Spanish hands when Don Carlos, the son of Philip V of Spain and Elisabetta Farnese, captured the state with his army and installed himself as King Charles III. In 1737 the last of the Medici, Giovanni Gastone, died, and the Grand Duchy of Tuscany fell into the hands of Francis of Lorraine, who then gave it to his son Leopold in 1745. Then at Aix-la-Chapelle in 17489 the Piedmontese reacquired Nice and

Savoy. These territorial arrangements persisted more or less unchanged until 1796, when Napoleon Bonaparte invaded Italy, and after his defeat were once more restored by the Congress of Vienna in 1815.

The period of the Utrecht settlement was one of peace in Italy – remarkable in the light of what had gone on before, and indeed what was to happen in the first half of the nineteenth century. It was also a period which saw widespread social degradation, attempts at a degree of reform in some parts of the peninsula, and some intellectual development in the context of the enlightenment.

SOCIAL POLARISATION

Italian society in the eighteenth century was truly a deeply divided one, even more so than in the rest of Europe, which also experienced serious social polarisation during this period. The aristocracies of the various Italian states effectively owned everything, and lived lives of ostentatious luxury and splendour in the cities and in their estates in the countryside which they had accumulated, particularly during the course of the economic decline of the previous century. In Lombardy, for example, the nobility, excluding the Church, owned over 40% of the land; in Venetia this proportion was around 50%; while in Tuscany the vast estates of the Medici, Della Gherardesca and Ferroni families dominated the countryside. The remainder of the population, the vast majority of course, by contrast had almost nothing, living for the most part in great urban or rural poverty and squalor. The nobility enjoyed tax exemptions and other fiscal privileges, while at the same time exerting traditional feudal rights over the rest of the population, exacting tithes, tolls and a plethora of other levies to augment their income and wealth. This hangover from feudal times was particularly prevalent in the rural south, although it also existed widely in the north.

It is important to note two factors in this context. Firstly, aristocratic wealth and power was being increasingly concentrated in the hands of fewer and fewer families. In Naples fifteen (out of a total of 1500) titled families owned around three-quarters of all feudal lands; in the Agro Romano around Rome thirteen families owned 61% of the land; while in Mantua 142 families owned one-third of the whole territory. Secondly, the Church had emerged in this period as a major repository of privilege and wealth; in mid-eighteenth-century Lombardy, for example, it owned around 22% of the land; in the Agro Romano in 1783 sixty-four ecclesiastical bodies owned 37% of the land; and in Naples the Church held something like one-third of the territory.

The aristocracy were to all intents and purposes above the law, enjoying, and frequently exercising, absolute and terrifying power over the lives of their vassals, who could be imprisoned, evicted or even murdered at the whim of the lord. They neglected their duties towards the rural economy, spending their wealth on conspicuous and ostentatious consumption while ignoring investment on infrastructure and capital projects in the countryside. They were also frequently absentee landlords, prefering to live in the cities where they could enjoy the advantages of courtly life, and using their villas in the country as occasional abodes. Absenteeism by nobility and churchmen led to the emergence of a new system of land management and tenure, as estates were rented out to middlemen who then administered them. Thus, for example, in Tuscany there emerged the *fattorie*, organised agricultural settlements and units, which were divided into several small farms, or *poderi*, of usually fewer than ten hectares. Throughout the centre–north of the country, the *poderi* or *cascine* were worked by peasant families of *coloni*, who paid rent in the form of money, or *mezzadri* (share-croppers), who paid rent in kind. In the south there were the *latifondi*, with the widespread use of hired labour to work in the grain fields and sheep farms.

During the eighteenth century, the population of Italy increased from 13 million to around 17 million, in line with the trend in the rest of Europe. This increased the demand for food, and in turn led to the emergence of new systems of land tenure, with the stewards or administrators of the noble lands taking on greater responsibilities and powers – an embryonic agrarian middle class was emerging along with the beginnings of rural capitalism. For the peasantry, however, the situation worsened. Abject poverty, exploitation, ignorance, illiteracy and the lack of any real power to affect their own destinies were already established features of their life; now the peasants were increasingly squeezed both by the stewards and by the *fermiers*, the state tax-farmers, and many were driven from the relative security of being *coloni* or *mezzadri* into the far more precarious position of hired labourers. Many fell heavily into debt, with the infamous *contratto alla voce* becoming a way of life in the south. This consisted of merchants giving exploitative loans of wheat to peasants, which were repayable in kind at harvest time when prices were much lower. The situation in the countryside was brought to a head by the famine of 1764–6, which mainly affected southern Italy. The price of food increased while wages remained static, and the plight of the peasants worsened accordingly. As a result the latter part of the century saw the emergence of emigration and of begging as mass social phenomena in the fragmented and isolated Italian countryside. The exodus grew to the extent that the kingdom of Naples actually experienced labour shortages late in the century, and all states passed laws in ineffective attempts to stem the outflow of people.

Life in the cities was marginally better, but was nevertheless characterised by fundamentally similar inequalities and poverty. The rich lived in their palaces and enjoyed active courtly and cultural lives. In decadent Venice, for example, they warmed to the carnival and the comic plays of Carlo Goldoni (1707–93) – and indeed the music of Vivaldi (1675–1741) – while the proletariat scratched out a very basic existence. At least in the cities the government could control the worst excesses of the aristocracy, and could also fix prices and distribute alms, while some limited employment was available servicing the nobility and in the guilds. The population of the cities grew less rapidly than that of the countryside. The cities dominated and often exploited the countryside, but at the same time there was little communication between the two. The economy of the cities was generally stagnant, the exceptions being the ports, which grew in response to increases in trade as Italy became integrated into the European economic and political scene. Several became free ports: Livorno had shown the way in 1675, and Trieste in 1713; Messina followed in 1728, and then Ancona in 1732, and to an extent these flourishing coastal towns began to challenge the predominance of the traditionally influential cities.

A perhaps predictable consequence of all this social inequality and injustice was crime which grew to alarming proportions during the eighteenth century. In the Papal States, which had a population of around three million, there were no fewer than 13,000 recorded murders in the eleven-year pontificate of Clement XIII (1758–69). In Venice, between 1741–62, 73,000 executions or life sentences in the galleys were meted out. In an attempt to stem the tide the Venetians instigated a tragi-comic system of itinerant instant justice: a judge, a lawyer, a priest and a hangman would tour the city and its surroundings, backed by a group of policemen, pouncing on any criminal they came across and hanging him on the spot.

Enlightenment and Reform

Another natural consequence of the injustices inherent in the Italian society of the eighteenth century was a desire for reform. The impetus was provided by the intellectuals of the enlightenment. This in essence was the first mass cultural movement of modern Europe. It spread to Italy from France, with the help of the expanding book trade as well as the diffusion of the threatre – La Scala was opened in Milan in 1778, and the Fenice in Venice in 1790, for example. It united Italian intellectuals into a relatively cohesive force, which informed the literate sections of the population of the latest ideas and developments in the natural sciences, the social sciences and the humanities, and fuelled the calls for change from the emerging force of public opinion, by means of publications such as the Milanese review *Il Caffè*. A particularly significant feature was the development of the new social science of economics, advocating free trade, industrial development and improvements in agricultural methods. It commanded the attentions of some of the major Italian thinkers of the period: the great Neapolitan Antonio Genovesi (1713–69), from 1754 the first European university professor of political economy; Ferdinando Galiani (1728–87); Cesare Beccaria (1738–94), the visionary criminologist and advocate of the abolition of capital punishment; Pietro Verri (1728–97), the editor of *Il Caffè*; and the Venetian monk Gian Maria Ortes. Perhaps the greatest of the Italian enlightenment intellectuals, however, was the historian Ludovico Antonio Muratori (1672–1750), who looked back to the Middle Ages for inspiration for his very articulate condemnations of contemporary injustices and the abuses of the Church and the upper classes. The eighteenth-century enlightenment also gave Italy major literary figures such as Goldoni, Vittorio Alfieri (1749–1803), and the satirist Abbot Giuseppe Parini (1729–99). The movement spread rapidly, with a little help from French agents, and from the masonic lodges which had been founded in Italy by itinerant English aristocrats.

The often covert agitation on the part of the reform movement fell on deaf ears in much of the peninsula. What reform there was came from the basically benevolent Habsburg and Bourbon despots who controlled Milan, Tuscany and Naples. In Lombardy the need for change was arguably not as pressing as elsewhere: there was little feudalism in the state, and in the second half of the eighteenth century agricultural productivity increased considerably, in response both to the introduction of new techniques, some of which were pioneered by enlightenment intellectuals themselves, and to considerable investment by the state and by the relatively progressive landlords. The cultivation of mulberry trees, for instance, permitted the development of silk as a cash crop for export, and generally the state was emerging as the spearhead of the Italian economy – a position it has enjoyed ever since. Nevertheless, economic progress had not led to analagous social and political development, and the old structures with their rigidities and iniquities remained. The Church, in particular, constituted a huge and corrupt vested interest, with nearly 600 monasteries to service the spiritual needs of a population of only one million. The peasants were clearly the worst-off section of the population, but the impetus for change came, as it would in France, from the bourgeoisie. In Lombardy these consisted of a limited number of small landowners, of the tax farmers based predominantly in the cities, and, naturally, the intellectuals.

The nettle of reform was grasped by the absolute Habsburg monarchs of Lombardy, Maria Theresa and Joseph II. The task of modernising the social structures of the state to bring them in line with its economic structures was an imposing one, and what was achieved took half a century to complete, employing the talents of the leading figures of the Italian enlightenment – such people as Verri, Beccaria and Parini. By 1760, a land register was established, and was used as the basis for shifting the burden of taxation from people onto property and land. One of the indirect results was that it facilitated the progress of Lombard agriculture by encouraging the development of intensive agriculture, rather than the extensive variety which had hitherto predominated in the state. The bulk of the reform programme was carried out during the thirty years between 1760 and 1790. The programme was impressively comprehensive: local government was restructured; the financial system was overhauled, with the creation of a fiscal bureaucracy to replace the tax farmers, the reform of indirect taxation, and some monetary and trading changes. The privileges of the Church were attacked, particularly in the sphere of education with the suppression of the Jesuit order; conscription was abolished; and the University of Pavia was expanded. Additionally infrastructural projects such as road and hospital building were undertaken; and reform of the labour market was attempted, with the abolition of the guilds.

After 1780, with the accession of Joseph II, the pace of change accelerated, but its direction altered in a critical way. Reform now tended to centralise power in the hands of the despot, by taking powers from the local Lombard citizens and vesting it in Austrian officials. Things in the state changed but no real breakthrough was achieved; the despots of Lombardy may have been enlightened, but they were still fundamentally despots, with no vested interest in change beyond a certain point.

Eighteenth-century Tuscany, whose agricultural sector was far more backward than that of Lombardy, was in the hands first of Maria Theresa's husband Francis II, and then of Joseph II's brother Leopold. All the family were steeped in the ideas of the enlightenment, and reform was therefore also on the agenda in the Grand Duchy. Francis, however, was a largely absentee monarch; as a consequence the pace of reform was rather slow, even though some important measures to liberalise trade in corn and to diminish the power of the Church were enacted. On Leopold's accession, though, the velocity of reform increased considerably. The principal objective was economic change, and between 1766 and 1773 the internal and external trade in corn was liberalised, and the market for land was similarly deregulated. Economic reform was supplemented by administrative and fiscal improvements, both of which featured a considerable degree of decentralisation. Perhaps the most significant of the fiscal reforms was the introduction, in principle at least, of equality in taxation for all citizens. In alliance with the Bishop of Prato, Scipione de' Ricci, and other Jansenists, Leopold also tackled clerical privilege, with limited success it must be said since his proposals were altogether too radical for the ecclesiastical establishment, who forced him to abandon them in the late 1780s. Despite this particular setback, however, Leopold did in fact manage to force through several more important reforms: the abolition of the guilds, land reclamation in Val di Chiana, the introduction of vaccination, and, perhaps most remarkable, the abolition of torture and the death penalty.

Like his relatives in Milan, Leopold only really succeeded in changing matters at the margin in his kingdom. The basic nature of the state as a despotism, albeit an enlightened one, of course did not change, nor did the essential power relations between the various groups and classes in the state. Nor, with the wisdom of hindsight, could one reasonably expect them to have done. We must not forget that the Italy of the enlightenment, certainly in relation to some of its European neighbours, was in many ways a relatively backward country, ruled by what were often absentee despotic kings, and at a time when the French Revolution had yet to happen. Perhaps what was really remarkable was that so much change had actually taken place at all. Certainly life did improve for some in the states which experienced the concrete effects of the enlightenment, which is surely more than can be said for conditions in the remaining states which did not. Venice, for example, continued under the Doges on its journey into what is now regarded as its splendidly decadent twilight. The Papal States and Piedmont and Sardinia remained stagnant and immobile in their backwardness, the Piedmontese under Vittorio Amadeo III, who came to the throne in 1773, being more interested in building up their military forces than in the niceties of social reform.

Reform on the Habsburg model also took place in Modena, where the ruling Este nobles were linked by family ties to the Viennese court. However, the main other part of Italy which experienced change was the south, under the Bourbons. Bourbon reform was unquestionably the most needed, for the situation in the kingdom of Naples was clearly more serious than anywhere else. It was here that the feudal excesses of the aristocracy were the most glaring, and it was also here that the poverty and ignorance of the peasantry was at its most abject and ecclesiastical abuses at their most preposterous. For example, the kingdom supported the consumption and the fiscal privileges of something like 100,000 priests and monks of various sorts, who were backed by a veritable array of bishops, archbishops and abbots. In the city of Naples all the usual confusion, corruption and privilege were supplemented by legal anarchy, with ten different codes of law in daily use, and literally tens of thousands of lawyers kept busy sorting out the mess.

Bourbon reform in the south therefore clearly faced serious obstacles from deeply-entrenched vested interests. The approach which was adopted was, accordingly, considerably more circumspect than in the Habsburg centre–north, and perhaps predictably considerably less was achieved. The bulk of what change there was came under the direction of the viceroy, the Marquis di Tanucci, but when, on his retirement in 1776, King Ferdinand took over the direction of the state, his interests really lay elsewhere (principally in hunting on his estates and pursuing his own pleasures) and the impetus for change gradually ebbed away.

Out of Lethargy: Italy and the French Revolution

The relatively uneventful course of the eighteenth century in Italy was rudely interrupted by events in France. The revolution of 1789 was followed in 1793 by the outbreak of war between France and Austria and Piedmont. The French Army of Italy was under the command of a Corsican, a certain Napoleon Bonaparte, who in 1796 broke through the Piedmontese defences and plunged Italy into nearly twenty years of upheaval and turmoil.

THE EVENTS

The developments of this period read a little like a spaghetti western: plenty of changes of scene and lots of blood and gore. The bare events are as follows. In late 1796 Napoleon swept triumphantly from Piedmont into Milan, Bologna and Verona, where a popular rising led to the occupation of Venetia. By early 1797 the various northern Italian cities were scurrying around busily organising themselves into republics: Bologna, Ferrara, Mantua and Reggio Emilia formed themselves into the Cispadane Republic, while Milan, Brescia and surrounding cities became the Transpadane Republic; they then amalgamated as the Cisalpine Republic. Genoa meanwhile became the Ligurian Republic. The Peace of Campo Formio with Austria in October 1797 sealed France's hold over the whole of northern Italy, apart from Venice which went to the Austrians. Thus ended the long period of proud independence and liberty of this formerly magnificent, but by now rather squalid, city of lagoons and Doges. Napoleon now departed for pastures new in Egypt, passing the control of Italy to General Berthier. In his absence, republicanism spread like wildfire: Rome and Tuscany became respectively the Roman and Etruscan Republics; Piedmont was absorbed directly into France, after the abdication and flight to Sardinia of Carlo Emanuele IV. In the south, Ferdinand of Naples was routed by the French under Championnet while attempting to capture Rome (under the instigation of the British ambassador Sir William Hamilton, the husband of Nelson's famous lover Lady Hamilton). Ferdinand fled to Sicily on the British fleet with his wife Maria Carolina and as much of his money as he could grab. Naples was left to become the Parthenopean Republic.

The new republican structure proved to be extremely short-lived. In 1799 a combination of the Austrian and Russian armies, and of mobs of Italian peasants stirred into a frenzy by clergymen, drove the French out of all the peninsula apart from Genoa, with all the ritualistic violence which one would expect. The bloodshed and sheer inhumanity were, perhaps predictably, worst in the south, where Ferdinand's sidekick, Cardinal Ruffo, organised what was essentially a hoard of lowlife, known by the somewhat ironic name of 'The Army of the Sacred Faith' and including the infamous Fra Diavolo, to lay waste to the city of Naples. The republican forces were tricked into surrender with promises of safe conduct, only for their leader Admiral Caracciolo to end up swinging from the yard-arm of Nelson's flagship, and for large numbers of his followers to be subjected to Ferdinand and Maria Carolina's predictable and immensely ugly revenge. The reaper was once again kept busy in Naples.

The pendulum swung back soon enough. By the end of 1800 Napoleon was back in Italy, defeating the Austrians at Marengo, and recapturing most of the north except for a part of Venetia. The Treaty of Luneville in 1801 formalised this new situation. This time Napoleon was having no nonsense: he needed the country's resources, and in particular its people for cannon-fodder. He assumed direct control of the north of the peninsula, dividing it into three parts, and eventually created the Italian republic, with himself as president and Eugene Beauharnais as viceroy. When the Corsican became emperor, his Italian possessions became the kingdom of Italy – there are no prizes for guessing who was King! By 1810 the kingdom had absorbed Venice, the Tyrol and Ancona. In the south, Ferdinand was in 1806 once again off to Sicily in exile, with Napoleon's brother Joseph Bonaparte taking over, to be succeeded in turn by Marshal Murat, as King Joachim of Naples, Tuscany and the Papal States were in turn gobbled up by the French empire. Needless to say, this particular political arrangement lasted only as long as Napoleon. After his fall, the Congress of Vienna in 1815 restored the old order.

THE LEGACY

Some Italian historians, probably blinkered by nationalism, have interpreted the Napoleonic period as having had a negative influence on the course of Italian history, claiming that it interrupted the process of enlightenment reform, and thus delayed the modernisation of the peninsula. A more objective analysis would soon discredit this view, however. By the time of the French Revolution, the enlightenment reforms had more or less petered out everywhere, with the possible exception of Lombardy. In any case, in much of the territory reform was simply not taking place at all.

An alternative, and perhaps more realistic, approach would be that the comings and goings of the Napoleonic years in fact had a generally positive effect on the historical development of Italy. To begin with, Napoleon brought several obvious but important improvements to the lives of the Italians: the Code Napoleon introduced the revolutionary concept of equality of all before the law; new schools, roads and other public projects were undertaken; the financial and administrative system was overhauled. But the real importance of the Napoleonic period for the Italians was more subtle than this. Firstly, Napoleon shook the states out of centuries of lethargy and immobility, demonstrating to the Italians of the future how easily and rapidly a long-established status quo could in fact be overturned. Secondly, the possibility of a united Italy was brought onto the political agenda. The French kingdom of Italy broke down traditional geographical boundaries, and provided a model for future nationalists, being often subsequently regarded as a prototype for a unified Italy. The Italian flag, the *tricolore* with the green of freedom and the red and white of Bologna, dates back to the days of the Cisalpine Republic, for example.

Perhaps most crucially, this period laid the foundations of a nationalistic Italian middle class. These people would, in future years, be in a position to influence the new force of public opinion, having been exposed to new models of political organisation and activity. At first, these young idealists had surfaced as Italian Jacobins – Luigi Zamboni, for example, had organised a revolt in Bologna before being executed in 1795 at the age of twenty-three, and the 22-year-old Emanuele de Deo was active in Naples before being hanged in 1794. Then, as Napoleonic rule became established, the nascent middle class were able to find new outlets for their talents in the reformed administrations, in journalism (the writer Ugo Foscolo (1778–1827) followed this particular path), in academic life, and especially in the French army, where they also acquired military skills. What a change from the situation before the French Revolution, when such youth had been predominantly forced into careers in the Church!

Another feature was the emergence of secret societies, through which the impetus for change was channelled: the Adelfia in the north, the Guelfia in the Papal States and Romagna and, above all, the Carbonari in the south. They originated from the masonic lodges, and although their cellular organisation and the aura of mystery which surrounded them may make them seem slightly surreal to the modern observer, they were to prove important vehicles for developing nationalistic sentiment. This sentiment was further fuelled by widespread resentment at the cavalier way in which Italy and the Italians were being treated, as pawns of little significance whose fate was very much at the mercy of the whims of foreigners. One thing is for sure: the years of submission to foreign dominance were nearing an end, and the movement towards nationhood was under way. Italy would never be the same again.

CHAPTER SIX

Risorgimento and Unification

The nineteenth century was to prove momentous for the Italian people, with the unification of the country, and the establishment of the modern state of Italy, roughly on the lines with which we are familiar today. The *risorgimento* (reawakening) is the term which is usually used to refer to the development of a national consciousness and movement in Italy. There is some dispute over exactly when this process began, and therefore how far back one has to delve in order to discover its roots. Arguably, it began with the Napoleonic period, or even the enlightenment, but here we shall take the post-Napoleonic settlement as the start of the risorgimento. Yet after the Congress of Vienna in 1815 the chances of unification were slim in the extreme: they very idea of an Italian nation must have seemed remote, and in the main not even particularly desirable, to most Italians. Italy might have existed as a geographical expression, but that was as far as it went.

The Vienna settlement had in essence restored the pre-Napoleonic establishment in Italy, a veritable turn of the clock back to the eighteenth century. The aim of the Congress, like that of most peace settlements, was basically to make sure that the losing party, in this case France, could never again threaten the winners. As far as Italy was concerned, this meant making Austria the dominant power in the peninsula, and it further entailed removing all traces of nationalism and liberalism from the collection of states into which the peninsula was again divided. So Ferdinand continued his comings and goings, returning as king of Naples and Sicily, the Kingdom of the Two Sicilies as it was now known. Vittorio Emanuele I crossed the sea from his refuge in Sardinia to take control of Piedmont, a kingdom which now also included Genoa.

Tuscany was restored to Ferdinand III of Habsburg–Lorraine, the son of the previous ruler, while the duchy of Parma was given to Napoleon's wife Marie Louise, whose ideological loyalty was now controlled by her Austrian lover, the one-eyed General Neipperg. All of the Papal States were given back to the popes, and finally the Austrians were granted Lombardy, Venetia, and the right to keep garrisons in Piacenza, Ferrara and the Comacchio.

Of the great powers of this period, the British were the least hostile to the idea of Italian nationalism, the Whigs in fact questioning the Vienna settlement on the grounds that it ignored the aspirations of the Italians. The Austrians predictably, for they had their own ideas for the peninsula, were the most opposed to the concept of Italian independence or national identity. 'Italy does not exist,' stated the Austrian chancellor, Prince Metternich, and the main newspaper in Vienna removed its 'Italian' section, henceforth referring only to the separate states. As for France, it was still licking its wounds and Italy was clearly not high on its agenda. Much would have to change, therefore, for Italy to have any chance of becoming an independent political entity: the international situation, the power of the entrenched vested interests of despots and popes, and, last but not least, the consciousness of the Italian people themselves. That all this did change in a relatively short time, and that the Italian nation was in fact created, is in many ways remarkable. However, the risorgimento and the unification of Italy should not be seen, as some nationalistic views have implied, as an historical inevitability, driven on by irrepressible forces. It was rather a series of random, even chance, events which happily ended up creating the historical and to a large extent culturally logical and coherent entity which we have today.

The Early Risorgimento: Failed Revolution in 1820–1 and 1831–2

In the immediate aftermath of the Congress of Vienna no such change appeared to be on the horizon. Many of the major states in fact embarked upon a policy of reaction, partly in order to strengthen the position of the restored rulers. The Papal States took steps to return to religious fundamentalism, reviving the Jesuit order as well as restoring several monasteries. The rest, particularly Piedmont and the two Sicilies, followed a similar course, although the Austrian territories and Tuscany did hold out against the Jesuit restoration. The international situation was also most unpromising. Metternich's policy was one of staunchly preserving the status quo in Europe, regardless of the fundamental changes, in particular the growth of nationalism, which were taking place at the time throughout the continent. In this he relied on the support of the Quadruple Alliance between Austria, Britain, Russia and Prussia, which worked through the Congress System – a kind of nineteenth-century political and diplomatic cartel which organised a series of regular liaisons to sort out the major issues which arose in Europe and its environs. In this scenario, the Italian states were of course no more than very minor and powerless actors. Metternich was prepared to use violence to achieve his objectives, and in addition could deploy a formidable system of espionage and a network of secret police to nip any sedition in the bud.

Opposition to the established order inside Italy did exist but, as ever, the dissidents were divided and confused, and in any case there were not very many of them. One small but significant source of opposition came from a group of extreme and impulsive revolutionaries, who were well-meaning but naïve idealists with little social analysis or tactical sense, and who were prepared to conspire and agitate regardless of the cost or of the probability of success. The best-known of these were the Buonarroti, and as a group they were advocates of change in the broadest sense, Italian unity not being high on their list of priorities, at least in the early years of the risorgimento. Opposition of a more moderate kind came from a group of intellectuals who supported the French constitution of 1814, which allowed for a limited degree of suffrage within the context of a two-chamber legislature. The most colourful and romantic source of opposition, however, came from the so-called 'radicals', who advocated the adoption of the Spanish constitution of 1812, in which power was held by one legislative chamber at least partly elected by universal suffrage. The best-known of the radicals were the Carbonari, the secret society based in Naples, whose strange ritualistic practices reflected their freemasonic origins.

The years immediately after 1815 were fundamentally characterised by these secret societies, their numbers swelled by men demobbed from the Napoleonic armies: the Federati, the Adelfi, the Bersaglieri Americani, the Spillo Nero, the Latinisti, as well as the Carbonari. Their activities give the period a conspiratorial feel which adds considerably to the fascination surrounding the risorgimento. Tactically naïve and ideologically confused these predominantly middle-class adventurers might have been, but by their espousal of hopeless causes they kept Italy from retreating into the political void of the eighteenth century.

In any event, two major outbreaks of sedition and revolt resulted from their activities. The first of these began in 1820, although there had been a prelude in the form of an uprising in Macerata, in what is now the Marche, in 1817. The 1820 rebellion originated in Naples, the stronghold of the Carbonari, and then spread to Sicily and Piedmont. The Neapolitan revolutionaries, led by General Pepe, were predominantly middle-class or aristocratic; seizing the opportunity presented to them by revolts in Spain, they forced King Ferdinand to accept the 1812 Spanish constitution. In Sicily the revolution was more popular in nature, based as it was largely on the *maestranze*, which were organisations of artisans. Here too the adoption of the 1812 Spanish constitution was the main objective.

In principle, the two groups of revolutionaries from the same state would seem to have had many things in common. Their differences, however, outweighed the points on which they agreed. The Neapolitan insurgents wanted Sicily to be subject to control from the mainland and therefore gave their support to Ferdinand when he set about reconquering the island. They thus contributed, in the long run, to their own demise, and provide a good case-study of the conflicts between local interests and wider consciousness which had always been a characteristic of Italy, and which in the nineteenth century constituted a major obstacle to any idea of unification. The Sicilian revolutionaries, who in any case were divided amongst themselves, were duly put down, but as things turned out the fate of all the southern revolutionaries was sealed by external developments.

Austria, Russia and Prussia had agreed in principle at the Congress of Troppau in 1820 to intervene in the internal affairs of other states if they felt the European balance of power was under threat. At the Congress of Laibach (Ljubljana) in 1821 the perfidious King Ferdinand, having obtained permission to attend the Congress from the new Neapolitan parliament by guaranteeing his good faith, with customary deceit asked the great powers for his own reinstatement. The Congress duly obliged, and an Austrian army was despatched to enforce its decision. The Carbonari urged the Neapolitans to resist, but the rhetoric of defiance was not enough and the forces of General Pepe were defeated by the Austrians at Rieti in March 1821, the city itself capitulating tamely soon after. Ferdinand returned to Naples safely in the slipstream of the Austrian army, and set about exacting a terrible revenge on his subjects yet again, this time with the help of the feared prince of Canosa. The cowardly, unprincipled and cruel figure of Ferdinand hangs like a gruesome nightmare over the history of the south in the late eighteenth and early nineteenth centuries; his death in 1825 was certainly not mourned by the majority of his subjects.

In Piedmont the mainly aristocratic revolutionaries of 1821, led by Santorre di Santarosa, forced the king to abdicate in favour of his brother, Carlo Felice, and the heir to the throne, Carlo Alberto, the regent, to introduce the Spanish constitution. The revolt, for it would be an exaggeration to call it a revolution, had very little popular support and lasted but a short time. Its failure has several parallels with the end of the southern revolt: here too the rebels were naïve and divided, and here as well an appeal by the threatened monarch brought a swift response from the Austrian military, who put an end to the disruption in May 1821. As in Naples, the majority of the largely ignorant and illiterate population welcomed the restoration of the previous order – the risorgimento was clearly still a long way from capturing the imagination of the masses. Unlike Naples, however, bloodshed in Piedmont was very limited, with only two recorded fatalities. Metternich's secret police made sure that no repeat of the Piedmontese revolt took place in nearby Lombardy, while the popes (Pius VII, 1800–23; Leo X, 1823–9) pre-empted any trouble in the Papal States by a policy of control and repression – a case of getting one's retaliation in first!

Throughout the 1820s a combination of the presence of the Austrian garrisons and of vigilance on the part of the Italian rulers was sufficient to ensure that no major disturbances occurred. In February 1831, however, parts of Italy were once again in ferment. Once again revolutionary activity abroad, this time the July revolution of 1830 in France which brought Louis Philippe to the throne, was the immediate catalyst. The revolts were centred on Modena and Parma, and in the Papal States, especially the city of Bologna. In Modena it was organised by a young lawyer, Henry Misley, who had enlisted the tacit support of the rather shifty local ruler, Archduke Francis IV, who saw in the situation some potential for personal advancement. As was the case ten years before, the revolts had very little popular base, and predominantly involved upper and middle class people in the municipalities. In Modena it was a cosy little affair, with some of the plotters living two doors away from Archduke Francis. This time the army was not involved. The greatest disruption occurred in the Papal States, where a reactionary pope, Gregory XVI (1831–46), had just been elected, and at one stage most of the territory was in revolt. At first there seemed to be some hope on the crucial international front, since it was considered possible that the French might intervene on the side of the revolutionaries and against Austria; in the event, the Austrians suppressed the revolt without too much fuss. The new regime in France then put pressure on Austria to mollify its intransigent position in Italy, and the Austrian troops were in fact withdrawn from the Papal States. Left to his own devices, the pope was palpably incapable of controlling the situation in his own state and the Austrians duly returned in January 1832; they were to occupy Bologna until 1838. The French, for their part, attempted to save face by sending troops to Ancona, which they then occupied until late in the decade. The risorgimento was back to square one, defeated and still without much direction or popular support.

The Road to 1848

On the surface at least, little changed in Italy between the revolts of the early 1830s and the next big upheaval, which was to occur, as elsewhere in Europe, in 1848. The international situation was broadly static troubled only by a few trade disputes, such as the one around 1840 between Britain, whose foreign policy was at this time under the control of Palmerston, and Naples over sulphur, a key raw material for the growing industrialisation which was sweeping across much of Europe. In Italy most of the states remained largely in a condition of apparent immobility, but beneath the surface things were moving.

CARLO ALBERTO

In the first place, a subtle transformation was very gradually taking place in Piedmont. Carlo Alberto, whom we remember from his vacillations as regent during the 1821 revolts, had acceded to the throne in 1831, in succession to his uncle Carlo Felice. Carlo Alberto is one of the really mysterious figures of the risorgimento. During the early part of his reign he to all intents and purposes played the role of a Catholic reactionary, refusing an amnesty for the prisoners of 1821, suppressing conspiracies, supporting the Jesuits, championing Catholicism, and strictly enforcing

Carlo Alberto of Piedmont

censorship to the extent that progressives such as Mazzini, Cavour and Garibaldi were forced to flee from Piedmont. He was also an economic liberal, and in foreign affairs he was at first a staunch ally of the Austrians, in line with the traditional Piedmontese position of wheeling and dealing between the major powers in order to preserve and if possible expand Piedmontese influence. Yet this same monarch was to fight wars against the very same Austrians in 1848–9 in support of rebels in Lombardy, and Piedmont was to be the state which ultimately led Italy to independence and unity. What could possibly account for such a transformation? In the absence of significant evidence to the contrary, several level-headed historians have concluded that the most convincing explanation for this apparently schizophrenic behaviour probably lies in the romantic notion that deep down Carlo Alberto was a closet revolutionary or nationalist, who kept a low profile until he perceived that the time was right for action. Implausible perhaps, but then the risorgimento is a period of great romantic appeal, as we shall see with Garibaldi and others. Carlo Alberto's private, almost mystical character, Hamlet-like according to Mazzini, gives a degree of credence to this view.

MAZZINI

The years which preceded 1848 were also notable for the growth of the risorgimento as a substantial intellectual and literary phenomenon. The major figure was Giuseppe Mazzini (1805–72), who is often seen as the father of the Italian nation. Mazzini was born in Genoa and showed considerable literary promise before deciding to concentrate his talents on political activity. He was forced to flee to France in 1831, after getting himself involved in a conspiracy organised by the Carbonari. From 1837 he used London as the base for his activities (an example to be followed by other visionaries including, of course, Karl Marx). His great contribution to the risorgimento was to bring the idea of a united Italy on to the political agenda, and therefore to give the risorgimento, or at least some of the people involved in it, a degree of direction and vision – something which the ideologically confused revolutionaries of 1820–1 and 1831–2 had clearly lacked. Like Buonarroti, his precursor in advocating Italian unity, Mazzini's preferred form of government for

Giuseppe Mazzini

the new, independent state was a republic. He perceived the role of a unified Italy as being one of providing cultural leadership for the rest of Europe, and he was not interested in the idea of the state of his dreams pursuing a policy of expansion or imperialism. He envisaged achieving his objectives by means of a popular insurrection, which was to be fomented by the use of propaganda which should be addressed not only to the literate middle classes, but also to the mass of the people. This last point was probably a little unrealistic, given the lack of sophistication and illiteracy of the majority of the population, particularly the peasantry, but Mazzini's approach was clearly different in spirit from that of his predecessors, and indeed most of his contemporaries. His favourite motto, 'Pensiero ed Azione' (Thought and Action), admirably encapsulates his position.

The vehicle which Mazzini set up to work towards his objectives was

Giovine Italia (Young Italy), a society limited to those under the age of forty, which he founded in Marseilles in early 1831. The propaganda work which he and his followers undertook, typified by his open letter to Carlo Alberto in 1831 appealing to him to lead a great nationalist move against Austria, and by numerous public meetings and press pieces, led to the rapid expansion of Giovine Italia to a size never approached by previous secret societies. His claims of 50,000 affiliates are almost certainly exaggerated, but in Milan alone in the mid-1830s, for example, Giovine Italia did have upwards of 3000 members. In an immediate sense the Mazzinians achieved very little: their networks were broken up, and many of them were forced into exile – one of these was Garibaldi, who went off to South America. Mazzini himself, as we have seen, fled to London, where by all accounts his dashing, romantic, guitar-playing and cultured persona was a great success with the middle-class women of the city. A suggestive, if futile, gesture by his followers was the attempted coup in Calabria carried out by the fratelli Bandiera and their associates. All nineteen plotters were killed, but the incident has been immortalised in Italian nationalistic folklore.

Mazzini's role in the risorgimento, and indeed his position as an internationally important historical figure, has been the subject of some debate. He is unquestionably a major personage in Italian nationalistic consciousness – every Italian child is taught at school to look up to him as a romantic and significant figure, second only to Garibaldi – and he has been regarded as an inspiration, a figure of respect, and even a role-model, by politicians ranging from Lloyd George to Gandhi. Most historians see his role in the risorgimento as being one of considerable importance, in the long run if not in the 1830s and 1840s. There are, however, some interpretations, principally Marxist, which perceive of his role as a minor prelude to the more popular risings of 1848.

GIOBERTI AND THE MODERATES

If Mazzini was the most influential figure at this stage of the risorgimento he was certainly not the only one of note, for this was also the period in which the so-called moderates emerged to challenge his hold on the hearts and minds of progressive Italians. The foundations of this essentially liberal Catholic, but also unitarian, movement can be traced back to the reviews *Il Conciliatore* and *Antologia*, which were suppressed in the 1830s. It also owed much to the work of Silvio Pellico (1789–1845), a devout and anti-revolutionary Catholic, who was imprisoned by the Austrians and wrote the very influential book *Le Mie Prigioni* (My Prisons) during his captivity; and to Alessandro Manzoni (1785–1873), author of the romantic historical novel *I Promessi Sposi* (The Betrothed) which has become a classic of Italian literature. All of these basically espoused Catholicism, reform and an Italian identity, criticised foreign rule, and rejected violence and revolution as means of effecting change.

The movement gathered support in the years after 1840, the impetus for its rise being provided by the work of an exiled Piedmontese abbot, Vincenzo Gioberti (1801–52), who wrote *Il Primato Morale e Civile degli Italiani* (The Moral and Civil Supremacy of the Italians, usually referred to as the *Primato*), a rather long-winded book which was published in Brussels in 1843. Gioberti had been a fellow-traveller with Mazzini, but now he chose to mix his fervent Catholicism with his nationalism, and proposed an Italian federation along neo-Guelf lines, with the pope as head of state, a cabinet composed of the state princes, and Piedmont as the 'warrior province'. The book caused quite a stir when it appeared and it was then supplemented by Cesare Balbo's (1789–1853) *Le Speranze d'Italia* (Italy's Hopes), published in 1844 in which the author attempted to tackle the international impediments to a federal Italy by suggesting that Austria might be compensated for its Italian losses by being allowed some gains in the Balkans. He also saw Piedmont as the natural leader of such a federation, thus reflecting the views of the 'Albertisti', who saw a monarchy under Carlo Alberto as the logical political structure for the new Italy.

A prerequisite for a federal Italy would be internal reform as well as external movement, and Gioberti tackled this issue in his *Prolegomeni del Primato* (Preliminary Discourse on the *Primato*), which attacked the existing abuses in the Italian states and advocated such a policy of internal change. The flesh was put on the bones of these outlines by Massimo D'Azeglio (1798–1866) in his contribution *Programma per l'Opinione Nazionale Italiana* (Programme for Italian National Opinion), which became a sort of manifesto for the Moderate Party. Legal reforms, the introduction of a jury system, freedom of the press, free-trade, and an internal customs union on the lines of the German Zollverein were the main proposals. Another major exponent of the moderate view point was Carlo Cattaneo, the editor of the journal *Il Politecnico*, which was lauched in 1839. Eight years later another review was founded in Piedmont, with the participation of Cavour: *Il Risorgimento*, a title to remember!

In the main, the moderates were basically a close-knit clique of upper-middle-class and aristocratic people, mostly from Piedmont or Lombardy and related by family ties or friendship. They were not at all in touch with the mass of the people. Although they propounded their fair share of utopian nonsense they nevertheless cannot be dismissed for this since they did succeed in keeping up the momentum of the risorgimento when it might have flagged. Many of them worked hard to make possible the leading role which Piedmont was to play in the process of unification; they also provided important examples of change by their personal example. Scientific congresses and other meetings were organised on a national scale to foster a collective identity, and individual moderates were responsible for important projects in land reclamation and railways, as well as for commercial ventures such as the Gorgonzola cheese industry and the Ricasoli Chianti vineyards at Brolio.

Where Manzoni was the greatest novelist of the nineteenth century in Italy, the outstanding poet was Giacomo Leopardi (1798–1837), whose lyrical poetry was tinged with both patriotism and pessimism. In music, too, this was a golden age, and no more so than in opera. In Italy opera was popular with all classes rather than a diversion for the rich as elsewhere, and the first half of the eighteenth century had seen the beginning of its great period with Bellini (1801–35) – *La Sonnambula* and *Norma* were both first performed in 1831; Donizetti (1797–1848) – *L'Elisir d'Amore* appeared in 1832 and *Lucia di Lammermoor* in 1836; and Rossini (1792–1868), who had conducted the first performance of his *Il Barbiere di Seviglia* in Rome in 1816. Composers were able to express a national feeling through their music: Rossini's *Gugliemo Tell* (1829) had a patriotic theme, as did an early work by Giuseppe Verdi (1813–1901), *I Lombardi all Prima Crociata* (The Lombards at the First Crusade, 1843). Whenever a popular theme was struck the applause would stop the performance until it was repeated. It would be sung in the streets, and a current cry was 'Viva VERDI' – 'Viva Vittorio Emanuele, Re D'Italia'. Verdi went on to write a string of world-famous operas, including *Rigoletto* (1851), *La Traviata* (1853) and *Aida* (1871). He was to be a member of the first national parliament between 1861–5 (during which he wrote *La Forza del Destino*).

Thus by the mid 1840s a consistent national movement had developed in Italy, at least among the middle and upper classes and the intelligentsia. There was, of course, no concerted or generally agreed position on how a united country could be brought about, or even on what its political structure should look like once it had been created: federalists, monarchists and Mazzinian republicans all had differing views of the way forward. Nor did the movement enjoy any great support among the mass of the people. Nevertheless, progress was being made. The diffusion of the movement and the creation of some sort of national consciousness were facilitated by developments which had taken place in communications and in the economies of the industrial states. The single most significant change was the advent of the railways: the Florence–Pisa, Turin–Genoa, Turin–Moncalieri and Milan–Venice lines were all completed during the 1840s. Before the railways had come the banks, then the factories, and then the big machines, particularly in the textile sector. Foreign trade expanded as well. Capitalism had not arrived in Italy to the same extent as elsewhere in Europe, but it had arrived, and things were never to be the same again.

With capitalism came more pronounced cyclical fluctuations, increased competition, the transformation of a proportion of the peasant population into day labourers, increasing disparities and inequalities between sectors and regions, as well as growth of intensive cultivation and land reclamation. In passing, one must note that the deforestation which took place in the south as part of these developments disturbed the ecological balance of the area, and is to an extent responsible for the problems which southern agriculture and the economy of the region have suffered ever since. Nevertheless, the arrival of capitalism with its new social structures also created conditions in which there was alienation among the mass of the people, and a certain amount of potential for their organisation and politicisation. In fact, around 1847 there was evidence of growing unrest and agitation amongst the workers and the peasants (partly as a result of the poor harvest of that year), and a good deal of paranoia about Communism surfaced for the first time among the Italian upper classes. The situation in the Italian states was ripe for something to happen. In 1848 it did.

1848: A Missed Opportunity?

The general atmosphere of political excitement and expectation increased in pitch with the election of Pius IX to the papacy in June 1846. He was a progressive and a reformer who held a certain amount of sympathy for Gioberti's ideas. And why not, since the position of head of a new federal Italian state was clearly a tempting proposition for the papacy? In any case, he proceeded to free political prisoners and to instigate important changes in the Papal States. Movement in one state forced the hand of the others. Piedmont and Tuscany were the most receptive to reform, and indeed these two states agreed in principle to form a customs union with the Papal States. In the end this measure did not materialise, but it was on the agenda of the national movement, and its very consideration by the powers that be served to fuel more excitement.

On the international scene, not a lot had altered. Austria, still under Metternich, was as intransigent as ever, and reinforced its garrisons in Italy when its intelligence network reported that something was afoot. In England there was a certain amount of sympathy for the cause of Italian nationalism, but the over-riding preoccupation of the government was to support Austria in order to preserve the Vienna settlement and to keep Russia under control. France clearly had less of a vested interest in keeping the 1815 restoration unchanged, but equally was not prepared to fight Austria over a largely marginal issue.

By the end of 1847 some kind of trouble was more or less inevitable, and it began, perhaps predictably, in the south, where Ferdinand II had resisted all demands for change. A wide cross-section of the population of Palermo rose in rebellion and took control of the city, forcing the king in January 1848 to grant them a constitution. Significantly, Ferdinand was unable to obtain help from the Austrians, partly because of geographic factors, but also because they were too busy dealing with their own increasingly precarious domestic situation. The Palermo rising provided the catalyst for a full-scale rebellion throughout virtually the whole of Italy. By March Tuscany, Piedmont–Sardinia and the Papal States had obtained at least the promise of a constitution. The climate of revolt spread to much of the rest of Europe, including Vienna, and Metternich himself was forced to flee the country. The temporary removal of the Austrian protective umbrella resulted in revolts in both Venice, under the moderate republican Daniele Manin, and in Milan, where Cattaneo was one of the leaders. Modena and Parma overthrew their despots, and the die was well and truly cast when Carlo Alberto, urged on by his subjects, declared war on Austria, and at the same time virtually annexed Lombardy, Venice, Parma and Modena into the Piedmontese state. Both Tuscany and Naples supported Carlo Alberto, in principle if not in concrete terms, and whole of Italy was in a state of ferment and revolt.

The revolutionaries were soon brought down to earth, however. Austria managed to shake itself out of its paralysis, and Marshal Radetzky defeated the Piedmontese at Custoza in July. Carlo Alberto was forced to sign an armistice, ending what has come to be known as the First War of Independence and relinquishing all the territory he had seized. None the less, rebellion continued elsewhere. Tuscany finally capitulated in February 1849. The Venetians declared a republic (the republic of San Marco), with Manin as president, and resisted the Austrians, through a long siege and with considerable heroism, until August 1849. In Naples Ferdinand actually restored himself and then recaptured Sicily. In Piedmont Carlo Alberto once again took up arms against the Austrians in March 1849, only to be summarily defeated at the Battle of Novara; he then abdicated in favour of his son Vittorio Emanuele II. The most inspiring happenings of 1848–9, however, took place in Rome, where Pius IX had got cold feet as far back as April 1848. He was forced to leave the city, and in February 1849 a republic was declared based on universal suffrage and under the leadership of a triumvirate which included Mazzini – his only direct experience of goverment. Radicals and progressives of various sorts flocked to the city; Garibaldi organised its defences. It was the stuff of which legends are made, but by July 1849 the Austrian and French armies in tandem had recaptured the city and ended the revolt – amid scenes of great fervour and heroism, it should be added. Garibaldi fled to Tuscany and lived to fight another day.

Thus ended the 1848–9 revolutions in Italy. A rapid evaluation of their impact gives us an ambiguous set of conclusions. Their immediate cause had been the economic crisis of 1847, though they had been permitted to develop into a serious challenge to the established order by the temporary incapacitation of Austria and France. However, the revolutions were also to a large extent fomented by the growing national and independence movement, built around the Mazzinians and the liberal Catholic moderates, who even managed to collaborate on some occasions. There was unquestionably more direction and greater purpose than there had been earlier in the century; significantly, the revolts also captured the imagination of a far broader range of people and enjoyed a much greater degree of popular support, with the cities frequently becoming involved and often fighting bravely for their independence. However, the popular base of the revolutions must not be overestimated; the majority of the peasantry still supported the restorations. One important precedent was co-operation, to a limited extent at least, between the various states in the face of external threat; to this extent, the risorgimento had taken steps forward.

On the other hand, the revolutionaries had revealed considerable divisions amongst themselves, and had also displayed a serious lack of tactical sense and of realism. The national movement was still critically flawed: 1848 was a unique opportunity and the nationalists were clearly not ready to accept it. In fact the revolutions to an extent left the risorgimento weakened, since Gioberti's ideas of the pope leading an Italian federation had been discredited. Even with a relative progressive such as Pius IX at the helm, the papacy had clearly demonstrated itself to be incapable or unwilling to provide political leadership for Italy. Above all, 1848–9 had shown how vulnerable internal events continued to be in face of the external situation: no matter what the nationalists did, Austria would sooner or later intervene to restore the old status quo. This would clearly have to change if Italy was to free itself from the yoke of foreign domination. (An interesting postscript to the events of 1848 is provided by the expression 'fare un quarantotto' (to do a forty-eight), which has passed into the Italian language as a synonym for disorganisation and chaos – a fitting epitaph for a succession of important events which, for all the excitement they generated, basically constituted a setback for the risorgimento.)

Unification: 1849–70

Yet out of the ashes of 1848 grew a united Italy. The succession of events which brought unification about has all the ingredients of an improbable historical novel: heroism, intrigue, conspiracy, force of character and diplomatic brilliance all played their part, as did large doses of fate and sheer chance. The central characters in this amazing but true story were an ambitious king, an outstanding diplomat, and a brave and resourceful, if also headstrong, guerrilla leader: Vittorio Emanuele II, Cavour and Garibaldi respectively.

CAVOUR AND VITTORIO EMANUELE

The aftermath of 1848 in most of the Italian states was a bleak one. Austria resumed its control of Lombardy and Venetia, which were now ruled with an iron fist. The Grand Duke was restored in Tuscany but the presence of Austrian troops rendered him no more than a puppet ruler. Austria also maintained its troops stationed in Parma, Modena and the Romagna. Pius IX returned to Rome; now chastened and a little angry, he jettisoned all his previous liberal and progressive tendencies, with the help of Austrian troops establishing a tight reactionary regime in the Papal States. As for the Two Sicilies, Ferdinand II demonstrated some of his grandfather's propensity for revenge and reaction, with a massive repression which led Gladstone to describe the state as the 'negation of God'.

The one exception to this picture of despondency was Piedmont, which had critically managed to maintain its constitution, and therefore much of its independence. That it succeeded in doing so has been traditionally attributed to Vittorio Emanuele's firmness and ability in the peace negotiations with Radetzky. This view grossly overestimates his power at the time. In truth, Piedmont was allowed to keep its

Vittorio Emanuele II

constitution only because it suited Austria's interests. Austria needed an independent and moderate Piedmont to protect her own international strategic interests, and the only way Piedmont could remain both independent and moderate was by supporting the king against the Piedmontese radicals. In order to maintain his position, Vittorio Emanuele needed the constitution which he had himself frequently criticised, and so it remained.

The constitution was in fact a very conservative affair, which had been based on the 1814 French model and had been introduced by Carlo Alberto. It consisted of a monarch, backed by a parliament of two chambers: the senate, comprising dignitaries who were appointed by the king, and the chamber of deputies, who were elected by literate male taxpayers over the age of twenty-one – only just over 2% of the population were enfranchised. There was also a council of ministers, presided over by the prime minister. Conservative or not, it was the only constitution in Italy, and it won the support of most of the Italian middle classes, pushing the Mazzinian and Giobertian models, which had been discredited by the events of 1848, into the background. Gioberti himself abandoned his position in 1851, while Mazzini's agitations never again quite had their previous impact, despite the continued expenditure of much energy, and occasional escapades such as the futile attempt to start a revolution at Sapri in 1857, which claimed the life of one of the major figures of the risorgimento in Carlo Pisacane. The Piedmontese constitution was to become the constitution of the united Italian state.

The independence of Piedmont permitted the emergence of Camillo di Cavour, who succeeded Massimo D'Azeglio as prime minister in 1852 and kept the position, almost without interruption, until his death in 1861. Born in 1810 into an aristocratic Piedmontese family, Cavour gave up a military career to study, farm and travel, before establishing himself as an important liberal and moderate political figure in the 1840s. He proved himself to be a real manipulator, with a strong conspiratorial sense, often resorting to what one might term 'unconventional methods', such as deceiving his colleagues, using emergency powers to introduce delicate measures, and bribing newspapers, in order to achieve his objectives. He was also, however, an outstanding parliamentarian, a great supporter of monarchy and the constitution, an opponent of revolutionary tactics, and a believer in public opinion. On the domestic front he was a resourceful and effective politician, amongst other things improving the state's finances, promoting economic growth, building railways, reorganising the army, and reforming the operation of the law.

But it was in foreign affairs that Cavour was to reveal the statesmanship, and indeed true genius, which would firmly establish him as one of the major diplomatic and political figures of modern European history. His genius lay essentially in his eclecticism and in his brilliance at exploiting situations. Under him Italy was to be unified, but it is important to note that unification was not the final outcome of some carefully conceived long-term plan. Cavour did have a desire for Italian independence, but his main objective lay in expanding the influence of the state of Piedmont. To this end he courted the support of France against Austria, the chief impediment to the achievement of his plans. Thus, early in his period of office he concluded trade agreements with

Camillo de Cavour

France which favoured the established power, and then in 1855 he sent Piedmontese troops to fight with France and Britain in the Crimean War against Russia. The troops, under La Marmora, did not exactly distinguish themselves in battle, but the gesture earned Cavour a seat at the Congress of Paris, which concluded the peace in 1856. There he had a direct and private channel of communication with Napoleon III of France, and even induced Lord Clarendon of England to bring up what had become known as the 'Italian question', and roundly denounce the governments of the Two Sicilies and the Papal States. Italy was again high on the international political agenda. Some historians have interpreted Cavour's manoeuvres as part of some cunning plot, since the troops were in fact sent against both public and parliamentary opinion. However, Cavour had little option but to do so. He was pressurised both from abroad, by the allies' need for manpower and their desire to get others to do their fighting for them, and internally, by Vittorio Emanuele's ambition and desire for glory. Had he not sent the troops in, the king would probably have removed him in favour of somebody more compliant and right-wing.

The Crimean War not only propelled Cavour and Italy into the international limelight but also precipitated a diplomatic scenario in which Italian unity became a feasible proposition. The Vienna settlement had been well and truly torn apart, and it was now possible for France to ally itself with Piedmont against Austria. The alliance materialised during a momentous meeting between Napoleon III and Cavour at Plombières on 21 July 1858. Napoleon's motives are to an extent confusing, but he regarded the independence and liberty of Italy as part of the historical mission of his dynasty, and he also saw in the situation an inviting opportunity to enhance his own and France's position. In any event he was stirred into action when the Italian revolutionary Felice Orsini attempted to assassinate him in January 1858. At Plombières he and Cavour secretly planned a war with Austria. The tactics were to isolate Austria diplomatically and induce her to start a war with Piedmont, in which France would intervene on Piedmont's side. Two armies of one million Italians and two million Frenchmen respectively would then drive the Austrians out of Italy and force a surrender by marching on Vienna. Vittorio Emanuele II would be the king of a new Piedmontese state which would comprise most of northern Italy, and would effectively control the whole of the peninsula, even though the pope and the south would remain independent. The fate of central Italy was left uncertain. Napoleon would obtain Nice and Savoy for his trouble, and his cousin would marry Vittorio Emanuele's daughter Clotilda. The last condition was slipped into the deal by Napoleon during an afternoon carriage ride with Cavour through the countryside around Plombières.

It is important to note that, at this stage, neither Cavour nor Napoleon had unification in mind. Cavour frequently dismissed the idea, while Napoleon saw a large united Italian state as a potential threat for France. Jerome Napoleon duly married Princess Clotilda in January 1859, while Cavour proceeded to build up the Piedmontese armed forces, amongst other things recruiting a force of volunteers from all the Italian states, under the command of a certain Giuseppe Garibaldi. He also organised a pro-Piedmontese propaganda campaign throughout Italy by means of the National Society under La Farina. Unfortunately the Austrians were not very obliging as far as providing the new allies with an excuse for war: as a result of reforms in their territories, they felt reasonably comfortable of their position in Italy. Cavour had begun to despair, and Napoleon had just about given up the whole idea, when in April 1859 Austria finally took the bait by handing the Piedmontese an ultimatum to disarm within three days. They did not, and the Second War of Independence began. It lasted for two months, during which the allies defeated the Austrians at the Battles of Magenta and Solferino. The Italian puppet princes in Tuscany, Parma and Modena fled, and Cavour sent in commissioners to take over the states.

At this point Napoleon, having taken substantial casualties and concerned about international repercussions, had second thoughts: instead of sweeping the Austrians completely out of Italy he sued for peace, which was concluded at Villafranca on 11 July. Lombardy was to end up in Piedmontese hands, being handed over via France; the princes would return to Tuscany, Parma and Modena; and Italy would be a federation under the pope. But the Austrians continued to hold Venetia, and would retain considerable power in Italy as a whole. Cavour was disgusted: Piedmontese gains were limited, especially since Austria continued to hold the major Lombard fortresses, and in any case he had not been consulted. He resigned.

During his absence from office, Bettino Ricasoli held firm in Tuscany and demanded unity with Piedmont. So did Romagna, Modena and Parma, where Luigi Farini had taken a strong grip. Napoleon's initial hostility rendered these annexations impossible, but as the year wore on the French position relaxed a little, partly as a result of British pressure. Cavour returned to office in January 1860 more radical than before and quickly set about exploiting the new situation to the full. He cunningly arranged for plebiscites in Nice, Savoy and the central states, knowing full well that the outcomes were a foregone conclusion. Nice and Savoy duly voted to become part of France, while Tuscany and Emilia elected to join the enlarged Piedmontese state. This might well have been as far as matters went, with the peninsula split in three and dominated by a large kingdom of northern and central Italy. That it was not, and that the whole of Italy was united under one flag, was from this point largely due to Garibaldi.

GARIBALDI E I MILLE

The intrepid exploits of Garibaldi and his followers represent one of the more remarkable episodes of modern times. The adjective amazing is frequently misused, but in the case of Garibaldi himself it really is warranted. The story of his life is one of endless incident, adventure and not a little heroism, in the pursuit of seemingly lost causes. It is little wonder that this romantic guerrilla leader is almost worshipped as a hero figure by the children (and many of the adults, for that matter) of contemporary Italy. Born in Nice on 4 July 1807, he spent his formative years as a merchant seaman. He met Mazzini in Marseilles at the end of 1833, joined Giovine Italia, and by June 1834 had managed to get himself condemned to death, fortunately in absentia, after having been involved in an insurrection in Genoa. In 1835 he fled to Rio de Janeiro, were he fought as a corsair for the republic of the Rio Grande against Brazil. A series of South American adventures followed, in which he fought naval battles as commander of the Uruguayan navy, was shipwrecked, suffered serious injury, was captured and tortured, and, on a more mundane level, worked as a salesman in Montevideo. He also married his first wife Anita and had three children. Garibaldi maintained his fierce Italian patriotism, however, and with his followers, the first Garibaldini, returned to Italy in spring 1848 on learning of the outbreak of revolution. The next year saw him as a general of the Milanese provisional government, and then invited to Rome to be first a deputy in the Roman parliament and subsequently, as we have seen, the chief defender of the Roman republic. In this period he was also wounded in battle in the abdomen and his beloved Anita died of exhaustion. Following the defeat of the revolts, a further period of travel took him to New York, where he worked as a candlemaker, to China and Australia as a merchant seaman, and then in February 1854 to London. In 1855 he moved permanently back to Italy, settling as a farmer on the island of Caprera off Sardinia. When war broke out again in 1859, he collected around him

Giuseppe Garibaldi

a group of volunteers, the nucleus of 'I Mille' (the thousand), and was made a Piedmontese major-general, playing a leading role in the war. He then moved to the army of central Italy and launched a subscription for 'a million rifles' for the unification of Italy.

By the time Cavour returned to power in early 1860 Garibaldi was a free agent, having resigned from the Tuscan army. He had gathered around him his famous 'thousand' and, stung by the secession of his native Nice to France, set sail for Sicily to support the uprisings on the island and smash apart the impasse which followed the Peace of Villafranca. It is important to note that he set out on this mission without Cavour's support: Cavour was naturally suspicious of any Mazzini-style revolutionary activity, and was really forced to stand aside by the enthusiasm of Vittorio Emanuele and by the weight of Piedmontese public opinion. There was little love lost between Cavour and Garibaldi, a fact which was to have an important impact on subsequent events.

With his small band of adventurers, which included his trusted lieutenants Francesco Crispi, a future prime minister of Italy, and Nino Bixio, he landed at Marsala on 11 May. Victory on the island was swift and complete. The ground had been prepared by Mazzini's agent Nicola Fabrizi, and by Crispi. Thus when the Garibaldini had defeated a Neapolitan army of twice their size at Calatafimi and were marching on Palermo, they were reinforced by 3000 Sicilians under La Masa. Garibaldi entered Palermo on 27 May, the population rising to fight side by side with him, and by 6 June the 12,000-strong Neapolitan garrison had surrendered. After the Battle of Milazzo on 20 July Sicily was his. Garibaldi had shown something of his ruthlessness and a little political acumen, as well as great military abilities. At first he sided with the peasants who were in revolt, and then, when it suited him, he turned his back on them to win the support of the landowners.

Cavour, somewhat embarrassed and worried about Napoleon's reaction to all this, now urged immediate annexation of the territories which had been captured. He sent La Farina to Sicily to arrange this but Garibaldi, who understood little about diplomacy and probably cared less, sent him packing. He was in any case still angry about the fate of Nice and, fortunately for Italy, decided to follow his guerrilla instincts and cross over to the mainland. Napoleon was at first alarmed by events, but he was prevented from intervening by the British. (Incidentally, Garibaldi's volunteers included a legion of British volunteers, who fought alongside the Garibaldini for the freedom of Italy.) On 19 August Nino Bixio's divison landed at Melito, and thereafter Garibaldi's progress through the south was as swift and triumphant as had been his capture of Sicily. By 30 August Calabria had been liberated, and on 7 September Garibaldi entered Naples and then set off towards Rome. His progress was challenged by the remains of the Neapolitan army at Volturno. He was eventually victorious, but success was costly and it delayed the advance on Rome.

THE KINGDOM OF ITALY

At this point Cavour decided to act, in an attempt to keep control of a situation which was fast being wrenched from him by the dramatic exploits of the guerrilla leader. He had not really considered it possible that Garibaldi's motley bunch could defeat the cream of the Neapolitan army, and he had hedged his bets by negotiating with both Napoleon and King Francis II of the Two Sicilies (who had succeeded his father Ferdinand II in 1859). However, the Piedmontese army, with Vittorio Emanuele at its head, was now dispatched down the Adriatic coast to capture the rest of the Papal States, except for Rome. The two Italian armies linked up, and on 8 November Garibaldi handed over southern Italy to Vittorio Emanuele, proclaiming him king of Italy before departing for Caprera, flatly refusing all offers of reward.

Cavour organised plebiscites to confirm the annexations, and then legitimised the new state by holding elections to the first Italian national parliament. It met on 18 February 1861 and declared Vittorio Emanuele king of the new country. Even though it did not include Venice and Rome, this outcome was truly astounding. Nobody had planned or even desired it. Not Cavour. Not the people of the south who acclaimed Garibaldi without really understanding what he was doing. Not even Mazzini, who only accepted it on sufferance, being unhappy about the monarchic structure of the new state. The pope, of course, abhorred the idea. Austria did too, but was powerless to intervene. The French in the end reluctantly accepted the situation, mollified by fears of the international situation and also by Cavour's clever scaremongering about the possibility of a republican outcome. The only support for Garibaldi's venture had come from Vittorio Emanuele, and to an extent from the British, who nevertheless had their own reservations about the whole matter. Yet Italy was created, and its creation was achieved by the force of character of Garibaldi, who brushed aside almost single-handedly the huge constraints imposed by political probabilities and by diplomacy.

On 6 June Cavour suddenly collapsed and died. Palmerston's tribute to him provides a fitting epitaph: 'Italy, present and future, will regard him as one of the greatest patriots that has ever adorned the history of any nation. I know no country that owes so much to any of its sons, as Italy owes to him.' A cliché perhaps, but with more than a grain of truth in it.

Garibaldi's astonishing thirst for action led him into yet more daring adventures. He was elected to the Italian parliament, and actually turned down an offer by President Abraham Lincoln to command the Union Army, before getting back to the business of trying to complete the Italian jigsaw by capturing Rome and Venice. With the new order now established, he had no chance of achieving this 'alla Garibaldina'. He was wounded in the heel at Aspromonte in the deep south in August 1862 while attempting to reach Rome, and was badly beaten by the French at Mentana in 1867 while attempting to invade the Papal States. He was frequently an embarrassment to the Piedmontese establishment, who were palpably incapable of controlling him, even by imprisonment and banishment to Caprera. He lived to see the completion of his dream of a totally united Italy, and saw action in France, served in the Italian parliament again, and married his third wife, Francesca Armosino, with whom he had two more daughters, before finally dying on Caprera on 2 June 1882. The Garibaldini, although formally disbanded, continued under his sons as a kind of band of itinerant freedom fighters, championing various causes in Greece, France, Poland and South Africa, where they fought with the Boers. Many interesting mementoes of the great man, and of the period as a whole, can be found at the Museo del Risorgimento in Rome, the museums of the same name in Milan and Turin, and the Instituto Mazziniano in Genoa.

International developments finally delivered Venetia to Italy in 1866, after a disastrously incompetent Italian intervention in the Austro–Prussian war, the so-called Third War of Independence. In Rome Pius IX took a firm stand, refusing to have anything to do with the new secular Italian state. In 1864 he published a 'Syllabus of Modern Errors' (*Syllabus Errorum*) laying out his position, and the promulgation of the Doctrine of Papal Infallibility in 1870 demonstrated that he could not possibly be wrong. Acceptance of the temporal power of the pope now became a matter of faith, dissent being against the will of God. Meanwhile, in the real world, the pope's position actually depended on the presence of the French garrison. When this was withdrawn to fight in the Franco–Prussian war, the Italian army marched unhindered into Rome on 20 September 1870. The eternal city was incorporated into the Italian state after the customary plebiscite, and every Italian city now has a 'Via Ventisettembre' to commemorate the event. The papacy was isolated

The Unification of Italy 1859–1870

inside the Vatican which, with San Giovanni in Laterano and the pope's summer residence in Castelgandolfo, remained in the pope's hands. The temporal power of the Church in Italy was legally abolished, and in return the Vatican was allowed the vestiges of a state – for example, the right to run its own postal service and later print its own stamps. The pope was given a grant from the state, which he refused to accept. He excommunicated all who had been involved and voluntarily shut himself up in his state. No pontiff was to emerge for nearly sixty years, until the advent of Fascism. The new Italian state was complete.

CHAPTER SEVEN

The Liberal State and Fascism

The newly united Italian state was, of course, greeted with great celebrations. But after the party was over, what? Unification was an immensely significant watershed in the history of the Italian people, but it was only a start. The fundamental problems were still there, and they had to an extent become even more pressing, since the creation of the Kingdom of Italy had raised expectations of a new and better future, expectations which were to prove difficult to fulfil. What, then, were these problems which the Italian state was forced to confront? In essence, they consisted firstly of the relative backwardness of the country, and secondly its deep division. The new Italy was split between north and south; between the cities and the countryside; between regions, and indeed between different cities and localities within each region; between Catholics and lay people; between the ruling élite and the mass of the people; between the different ideological positions of various groups of the population. As well as developing the country, a major task of the new state was, therefore, to extend 'legal' unification, that is the creation of a common set of institutions, to provide 'real' social, political and economic integration, and to get the Italian people to accept and support the state, and feel a communality of purpose and interest with it. The achievement, of 'hegemony', as Antonio Gramsci described it. In the context of Italy this was no mean task for, as we have seen, its history had been one of separate development and strong local identity. 'We have made Italy; now we must make Italians ... To make Italy out of Italians, one must not be in a hurry,' as Massimo D'Azeglio put it. The task was to prove so difficult that the Italian 'Liberal' state ultimately failed, opening the way to Fascism in the 1920s.

Early Years of the Liberal State, 1861–87

SOCIAL AND ECONOMIC STATE OF THE KINGDOM

The backwardness of the kingdom was manifest. A snapshot of life in post-unification Italy would reveal a picture of a society which was predominantly rural and agricultural, with 60% of the population working, or more accurately existing, on the land. The state of agriculture was therefore a key factor, and it was indeed in a state. A fifteen-volume parliamentary report by Senator Jacini in the 1880s paints a picture of an agricultural sector which had only marginally progressed since the Middle Ages, and which was characterised by enormous differences and divisions between and even within regions: differences in the fertility of the soil, in the structure of land tenure, in capitalisation, in the sophistication of the techniques which were employed, and in the wages which were paid.

The most advanced farming was, predictably, to be found in the north. In the plains at least the soil was good and farms were run along capitalist lines, with large units, professional managers, advanced techniques, and relatively acceptable wages for the many day labourers. Even here, however, there were serious problems, emanating basically from foreign competition and cyclical fluctuations, since the products of the area were dependent on European, even world, markets. There were problems, too, in the hill areas of the north: the infertility of the land and the paucity of technique meant that the small peasant landowners who were predominant scratched out a meagre existence, and were forced into seasonal migration for work to make ends meet. In central Italy, most peasants were share-croppers (*mezzadri*), typically handing over half of their production to the landlord in rent. The problem here, apart from obvious considerations of justice and equity, was that the system was not at all conducive to capitalisation: the peasants did not have the money to invest in the land, the landlords did not have the incentive to provide it. However, the *mezzadri* were in a sense the lucky ones, since below them were the landless labourers – 110,000 in Tuscany alone in 1881 – who relied exclusively on haphazard employment for their existence.

As we move further south, so the picture becomes more and more bleak. The area around Rome, the Agro Romano, was dominated by latifundia, the main landowners being the Church and a few old aristocrats. The land was neglected, only 10% of it being under cultivation, usually by managers who rented the land and worked it with hired labour. Further south, the land around the Adriatic coast was malarial and poorly irrigated, and so the peasants tended to retreat to the hillsides to eke out a living. Inland, this area was characterised by endless stretches of uncultivated latifundia, dominating a land scorched by the sun and ecologically devastated by the deforestation which had taken place earlier in the century. There was also some share-cropping, mainly in the Abruzzi, Molise, Campania and in Sicily, as well as a little subsistence owner-cultivation. There were some advanced areas, mainly along the Tyrrhenian coast, but these were very much the exception to the rule. The general picture in the agricultural south was one of ignorance, illiteracy and poverty amongst the peasants, of absenteeism and cynical exploitation by the landlords, and of a chronic scarcity of investment which became more serious as one moved away from the markets of the north.

The general plight of the peasants makes sorry reading. Their diet was extremely basic, much as it had been in the Middle Ages. Stomachs were filled by bread or polenta, supplemented by some beans, lard, oil and a few vegetables. Meat, poultry and eggs were consumed only on special occasions, since they were either out of the economic reach of the peasants, or the landlords were careful to demand them as part of rent in share-cropping contracts. Housing consisted largely of mud huts, with straw roofs and no flooring. The more fortunate peasants shared their accommodation with their animals – the poorest had no animals – if they were really well-off in the characteristic *case coloniche* in which humans occupied the first floor and animals the ground floor. Most people who kept animals lived with them in one room. Hygiene was non-existent; disease and physical deformity of all sorts were commonplace – malaria alone killed something like 2500 people each year. In the south the peasants were so poor that they did not even have the resources to bury their dead, who were thrown over cliffs, left to be eaten by crows and dogs, or piled up in crypts and left to decompose and infect those still alive with terrible diseases. Was it any surprise that the southern peasants were in an almost continuous state of revolt throughout the nineteenth century? What did they have to lose? To complete this picture of desolation, it should be noted that the main product of the countryside was corn, which was badly hit in the 1880s by falling prices and foreign competition. All in all, the countryside was on the verge of collapse.

Conditions in the towns were better, but there were still great problems. Most people were either labourers or artisans. The Industrial Revolution had yet to reach Italy, which in this respect was far behind other European countries. There were few factories, mainly small in size; industrial production was centred on textiles – silk, cotton and wool – although food processing, metallurgy, engineering and chemicals were emerging, albeit very slowly. It is important to note that the public works of the period, financed by burdensome taxation, failed to provide the 'engine of growth' which might have been expected from them. As with everything else, the north was more advanced, with most of the industry which did exist concentrated there. The south had to contend with crippling handicaps: remoteness from the main European markets, lack of capital, an almost total absence of both entrepreneurial spirit and ability and skilled labour.

In this context, it seems almost churlish to think about the social structure, but this was inevitably very traditional and conservative, based as it was on the extended family, which was also the predominant economic unit. Society was basically patriarchal, and most women were regarded as items of property whose role in life was to service the needs of the family, and to remain faithful to their husbands. Even at this stage many women also had an economic role. In the countryside they frequently shouldered their share of the burden of working in the fields. In the cities they were, surprisingly, often involved in the labour market: a survey in 1876 revealed that 230,000 out of a total of 382,000 industrial factory workers in Italy (about 60%) were women, an extremely high proportion by European standards. Among the middle classes women dominated the teaching profession, but teaching and factory work apart, there were few employment opportunities for women. Some worked as telegraph operators or domestic servants, while others were forced into prostitution which was rife at the time, particularly in Naples.

Juxtaposed to the social and economic desolation were the privileged classes, the élite of the new kingdom. There were nearly 8000 noble families in the country at this time, owning most of the land and living as parasites from the meagre resources of the kingdom; by and large they put little back, lacking the skills, the motivation and the vision to do so. One might have expected the impetus for change to come, as elsewhere in Europe, from the middle classes: in Italy, however, the middle classes were simply not up to the task at this time. The upper middle class consisted of around 200,000 medium-sized landowners, rentiers and entrepreneurs, together with about 100,000 'professionals' such as lawyers, teachers and doctors. The petty bourgeois were more numerous, with something like 100,000 private-sector white-collar workers and 250,000 non-manual state employees and bureaucrats. There were some businesspeople and entrepreneurs in their midst, but in general the Italian bourgeoisie were small-minded, conservative and ill-educated, with little enterprise and even less interest in matters economic. Like the aristocracy, they were in essence parasitic. Their primary objective was to live as well as possible from unearned income, or failing that a nice state sinecure, while putting as little as possible back into the society which supported them. Hardly the stuff of which a young nation had need.

GOVERNMENT OF THE 'RIGHT', 1861–1876

The political reaction to this difficult state of affairs was in the hands of the king and of the new parliament, which first met in Turin in February 1861, and was then transferred to Rome when the city was incorporated into the kingdom in 1870. It can hardly be regarded as democratically elected in the modern sense: the initial 443 members were chosen by 300,000 out of a population of twenty million. Catholics were forbidden by the pope from voting or standing for election. The parliament came to be split into two parties, the 'left' and the 'right'. The Right was based on a block of Piedmontese deputies, whose ranks were swollen by supporters from the rest of Italy. The Left, on the other hand, consisted mainly of Mazzinian former republicans and a varied collection of Garibaldini. For the first fifteen years of the kingdom, the restricted electorate consistently returned the Right to power. Not that this led to stability, for during this period there were eight different prime ministers, who tried to fill the political void left by Cavour, and as many as thirteen different governments. The king and parliament were supported by the army, of around 215,000 conscripts and two million reserves, which gobbled up 25% of all public expenditure, and by the police. The latter was dominated by the Carabinieri, paramilitary police who were highly efficient at what they did but became extremely unpopular with the bulk of the population because of their distinctly illiberal attitudes and activities, especially towards the poorest people. Particularly unpopular were the practices of widespread 'cautions', the stigma of which could ruin a person's life, and above all of 'enforced domicile', by which 'undesirable' elements could be randomly forced away to the islands or to the mountains to live. This latter affected between 3000 and 5000 people each year.

The Right's attempt to 'create Italy' and to tackle the country's problems of backwardness led them to institute a number of important measures. At an early stage they organised the administration of the kingdom, dividing Italy into fifty-nine provinces, each, as in France, governed by a prefect, with a *sindaco* (mayor) in each town. A common legal system was introduced, on the Piedmontese model, as were common systems of coinage and weights and measures. The secret police were abolished and freedom of the press introduced. Railways and roads were built to link the extremities of the kingdom. A particularly important measure was an attempt to introduce a common education system: some movement in this area was essential in order to 'make Italy', for not only was there widespread illiteracy in the country, but the vast majority of the population spoke only their own regional dialect, and people from different parts of the country could usually not understand each other – a situation which to an extent still persists today. The measures which were taken to foster basic and standardised education were very sketchy, however, and they were frequently ignored. Compulsory primary education was not introduced until 1877, and then only for two years; the rate of truancy in the south has been estimated to have been over 80%.

On the economic front, large-scale public works were undertaken, internal tariff barriers removed, and the large rural estates tackled.

Feudal rights were abolished, inheritance laws introduced to fragment large land-holdings, and Church and demesne lands sold off at auction by state agencies. The landless peasants, however, bought little of the land; they were generally penniless, and additionally they were often intimidated by the presence at the auctions of the local dignitaries, and by the threat of excommunication for those who purchased ecclesiastical land. Most of the land was bought by the old nobility, and by a new group of rural middle-class small landowners. Thus, although important changes in land tenure did take place, they did not normally affect the poorest. Indeed, the situation in the south became so desperate that brigandage became a widespread social phenomenon, only put down by a bloody five-year campaign by the army. With hindsight, the most enduring contribution of the governments of the Right was in presiding over the completion of the process of unification, and in laying the foundations of the new state. They are also remembered for passing in 1871 the Law of Guarantees, which defined the relations between Church and state and made the clergy subject to civil law.

DEPRETIS AND TRASFORMISMO, 1876–1887

In 1876 the Left came to power under Agostino Depretis (1813–87) and remained there for about thirty years. With the advent of Depretis, the previous two-party system in parliament effectively fell to pieces. The Left were not at all a homogeneous group: many of them had a strong individualistic streak, were prepared to adopt 'unconventional' methods in their dealings, and were generally not prepared to tow strict party lines, tending to split into factions. The method which Depretis adopted to preserve a majority in the face of all this fragmentation has come to be known as 'trasformismo'. The system, if this is the appropriate way to describe it, was essentially based on bribery. Individual, or individual groups of, deputies were induced to vote for the government by a variety of 'incentives', ranging from seats in the cabinet, through being awarded public honours, to the allocation of public works to their constituencies. 'Eclectic democracy', one might charitably term it. Trasformismo has been severely criticised on the grounds that it facilitated, or even precipitated, a decline in standards of morality, but it nevertheless ensured stable government, keeping Depretis more or less continuously in power until his death in 1887, and it endured as a means of parliamentary operation well after he passed away. Not that the stability which Depretis ensured was used to achieve very much. His governments had few or no policies, and his only real achievement on the domestic front was the electoral reform of 1882 which increased the electorate to more than two million, 7% of the population. The majority of new voters were from the urban middle classes; the south fared badly in comparison, thus adding another dimension to the evolving dualism of Italy.

The social and economic consequences of the Depretis period were inevitably negative. The problems which we have seen existed badly needed to be tackled. They were not, and in consequence the situation deteriorated. Emigration was often the only escape from poverty, and it increased with a vengeance. During the late 1870s some 80,000 people emigrated each year to the rest of Europe and around 20,000 to America. By the late 1880s European emigration had increased to 100,000 per annum, while transatlantic migration had soared to a staggering 200,000. At first most migrants came from the north, but the exodus from the south increased rapidly, and in the years to come the Mezzogiorno became the primary source of emigration, as economic growth came to be concentrated in the north.

Ironically, one of the most significant developments in foreign policy in this period occurred during one of Depretis' absences from power. The Congress of Berlin, at which Italy for the first time sat as a major European power, took place in 1878 in the premiership of Benedetto Cairoli. The experience proved to be a profoundly disappointing one, for the Italian representative, Count Corti, totally failed to gain any support for Italy's claim to the Trentino. This was followed by further setbacks as France seized Tunis, over which the Italians nurtured ambitions, and where many Italians had settled. These developments were partly responsible for Italy joining the Triple Alliance with Bismarck's Germany and Austria in 1882, a development which was to condition Italian foreign policy until the First World War. Frustration over the seizure of Tunis was also partially and indirectly responsible for Italian nationalism being channelled into a new direction: colonialism.

Crispi and the Crisis of the State, 1887–1900

On the death of Depretis, Francesco Crispi (1819–1901) became prime minister. He came to the position with a good pedigree, having been a republican and a Mazzinian, and also one of Garibaldi's leading associates in Sicily during the risorgimento. Once in power, however, he proved to be a volatile, temperamental, easily-influenced, and profoundly undemocratic leader. The principle features of his regime were support for Germany, colonial ambition, support for the new landowning and industrial middle classes, intolerance of opposition, and distinct dictatorial tendencies. No wonder the Fascists were to look back on him as a kindred spirit.

Crispi did bring a new energy to the static Italian political scene. He served for two terms as prime minister, from August 1887 to February 1891, and from December 1893 to March 1896, when he was forced from office at the age of seventy-seven. At home, his first administration at least is remembered for its reforms. Taking for himself the position of minister for the interior, which in his quest for personal power he held along with the premiership and the ministry of foreign affairs, Crispi reformed local govenment, which had by now become a source of power to rival Rome. Local suffrage was extended, and elected mayors were introduced in most towns. He also set up the ministry of posts and telegraphs, which still survives to this day, reformed the civil service, introduced new sanitary laws, and a new penal code. The essential thrust of his actions was to strengthen the executive at the expense of the legislature, and to increase the authoritarianism of the state which was more and more in his own hands.

The most significant domestic developments during Crispi's period in office, however, were occurring outside parliament and formal politics, although they were to an extent precipitated by the tone which Crispi had given to the political scene. Opposition to the state was mounting, the new ideas of socialism were on the march. In the early 1880s opposition to the state, although unquestionably present, tended to be fragmented and directionless. There were the anarchists in the south, who from time to time indulged in romantically appealing but futile adventures such as marching into remote villages to burn official records and declare the bemused peasants freed from their oppressors. These

Bakuninian insurgents, appealing in their innocent idealism, usually ended up with an unliberated bourgeois bayonet in their ribs. Also in the south there developed, in the early 1990s, an opposition movement known as the Fasci, which was to give its name to a movement of later times. In the north there had been a tradition of mainly middle-class radicalism since the days before unification. Socialism, however, had taken a grip in the Romagna, where Andrea Costa had formed a socialist party in 1881. But it was in Lombardy, and in particular in Milan, that socialism made its greatest advances at this time, fuelled by the growth of an industrial proletariat in the area. The Partito Operaio Italiano (Italian Manual Workers' Party) was formed in 1882, to be followed in 1891 by the first Camera del Lavoro, a workers' organisation founded by Osvaldo Gnocchi-Viani.

The disparate strands of Italian opposition, from bomb throwers to intellectuals, came to be dominated by socialism, and were given a co-ordinated and coherent dimension by organisers such as Antonio Labriola and Filippo Turati, who, at a congress held in Genoa in August 1892, formed the Partito dei Lavoratori Italiani (Italian Workers' Party), which was the precursor of the Partito Socialista Italiano (Italian Socialist Party), founded in 1895 and still in existence today. 1895 also saw the publication of the socialist Programma Minimo, around which the democratic movement rallied. This was a progressive and enlightened, but also to modern eyes largely moderate, programme for change, which included amongst its demands universal suffrage, payment for elected representatives, factory reform, progressive taxation, and old age pensions for all. Socialism brought an organised political dimension to the often violent dissent which had been maturing since the late 1880s, the most visible manifestations of which had been bombings in Florence and Pisa, an insurrection at Pesaro, and an attempt at Naples on the life of King Umberto, who had succeeded to the throne in 1878 on the death of his father. (Incidentally, the Pizza margherita is named after his wife, Queen Margherita.) In the early 1890s a serious rebellion broke out in Sicily, with the Fasci in the front line. Crispi reacted to this in a typically heavy-handed and indeed almost paranoiac fashion, sending large numbers of troops to the island to crush all opposition, and setting up military tribunals which passed inordinately heavy sentences on anybody suspected of complicity. He used similar tactics to deal with a revolt of the marble-workers at Carrara.

This unsubtle approach naturally proved to be counter-productive, since what was being addressed was in fact the symptoms rather than the causes of the malaise. The causes essentially lay in the failure of the Liberal state to capture the imagination of the people and to tackle the real problems which plagued their daily lives. Italians increasingly saw the state for what it was: a collection of often corrupt individuals whose principal concern was to safeguard their own interests and those of a restricted section of the population. The majority of the people were therefore becoming increasingly alienated from the state, which they regarded as largely irrelevant to their aspirations and needs – the system was palpably failing to 'make Italy out of Italians'. Crispi's repression therefore served only to increase support for the socialists. The predictable reaction to the failure of these tactics was to provide more of the same, and in October 1894 Crispi banned the socialist organisations, 271 of them in all. He now retreated more and more into his own bunker, purging electoral registers to fix the outcome of elections, and taking increasing personal charge of the functions of government.

If in domestic affairs Crispi revealed insensitivity and delusions of grandeur, in his foreign policy he additionally showed distinct signs of megalomania and even paranoia. His support for Germany led him to sign a treaty with Bismarck, and to reject a commercial treaty with France to the detriment of the Italian economy. A large-scale outflow of capital ensued, contributing considerably to the country's economic crisis. He followed this with a period of tilting at windmills, convincing himself that the French were about to invade, which they in fact were not, and working himself up into a frenzy about the whole issue. But the aspect of foreign policy which most centrally characterised and conditioned his regime was his vain and disastrous attempts to turn Italy into an imperial power in Africa. Italian interest in the continent in fact predated Crispi's premiership. In 1882 the Italians had captured Assab Bay, on the Red Sea. Three years later, with British encouragement, they had added Massawa to their possessions, only for their colonial ambitions to suffer a serious setback in January 1887 when a company of 500 Italian soldiers was massacred by the Abyssianians under Ras Alula at Dogali. National pride was wounded by this incident, prompting Crispi to respond in typical fashion by aggressively consolidating Italian territory into the new colony of Eritrea, capturing more land in Somalia, and declaring Abyssinia an Italian possession. The new citizens of the empire again proved to be less than accommodating, however, and a major rebellion broke out under the leadership of the supposedly compliant king of Abyssinia, Menelik. General Baratieri was despatched to sort out the insurgents, who unfortunately slaughtered his troops on 1 March 1896 at Adowa. The Italian troops took with them to their desert graves Crispi's political career. This enigmatic character, the risorgimento hero who found it difficult to control his own emotions, and who took ideas of the grandeur of both his country and of himself a little too far, ended his days in anonymity and poverty.

The fall of Crispi did little to stem the spread of the new socialist opposition, which grew in confidence and popularity. Another attempt was made to assassinate the king and there was widespread civil disturbance throughout the country. The disruption reached a climax in 1898, when the country seemed for a time to be on the verge of revolution. A rising in the south was suppressed by General Pelloux, but then spread to the rest of the country, with the result that half of the fifty-nine provinces were placed under martial law. The most serious incidents occurred in Milan, where the military fired on the crowd, killing almost 100 people. For a period Italy was on the verge of military rule, under, amongst others, General Pelloux, who was prime minister from 1898–1900. This outcome was in the end averted by a consensus government under Giuseppe Saracco. The situation in the kingdom calmed down, but not before King Umberto had been assassinated at Monza in July 1900, to be replaced by Vittorio Emanuele III. A new face now appeared on the political scene: Giovanni Giolitti.

The Age of Giolitti 1900–1914

If Depretis and Crispi had been cynical and not a little devious in their manipulation of the parliamentary system, then Giovanni Giolitti (1842–1928) was the original slippery eel, the 'minister of the under-world' as his contemporary, the historian Gaetano Salvemini, referred to him. He kept himself in power by continuing the established practice of trasformismo, and indeed taking it a step further. The main opposition to his Liberal regime came, on the left, from the socialists and, on the right, from the Clerical Party (the precursors of the modern Christian Democrats), which had emerged as an electoral force after Pope Pius X (1903–14) had relaxed the Catholic boycott of the state in November 1904. Giolitti effectively stole the thunder from the Left by adopting many of their social policies, while keeping the Right happy by supporting some of their pet causes and preferred areas, such as the army, and occasionally making direct deals with them, as he did in 1913. In this way he ensured an almost continuous majority for himself in parliament. Another facet of his deviousness was the way he tended adeptly to withdraw from the heights of the political scene just when affairs were about to become difficult, leaving others to take the heat while he himself sat out the crisis at a safe distance. With his carefully constructed and persistent majority, he was really the éminence grise of Italian politics at the start of the twentieth century, in power even when he was out of it, so to speak. He was clearly the dominant figure in the country from 1901 until the outbreak of the Great War. On the domestic front, his periods of office were characterised by important social reforms such as the regulation of child and female labour, improvements in primary education and in life insurance, and, above all, the introduction of universal male suffrage on 25 May 1912.

Nevertheless, Giolitti's not inconsiderable domestic achievements were overshadowed by the cynical detachment which his often corrupt, unprincipled and generally dubious use of patronage and manipulation of parliament engendered among the mass of the Italian people. He was, to an extent, only following and perfecting the tradition which had been established by his predecessors in the Liberal state ever since unification, but the outcome was a fundamental detachment between the parliamentary state and the people which it purported to represent. This phenomenon was to prove of great significance for the country for, when the state came under threat from the Fascists in the 1920s, many Italians were to ask what the system had to do with them, if it worked in their best interests and whether they should support it. The answers were inevitably negative: the people therefore did not defend the state and it collapsed. Giolitti was not the root cause of this fatal malaise but he contributed to it, and certainly did little to stem it. The seeds of the decline of the Liberal state and of the rise of Fascism had been sown.

The irony of this situation was that conditions in Italy were in fact improving. The first years of the twentieth century are sometimes referred to as the country's 'belle époque'. Economic prosperity had increased considerably, and this was the case not only for the entrepreneurial class who were spearheading the Italian industrial revolution, now in full swing fuelled by cheap hydroelectric power, but also for skilled workers, civil servants, and many agricultural workers, who had experienced improvements in their working conditions and increases in their pay. The arts were again flourishing. Verdi's operas continued to be popular, reaching a peak with his collaborations with the librettist Arrigo Boito in *Otello* (1887) and *Falstaff* (1893), but those of Giacomo Puccini (1858–1924) were also enjoying their heyday (*La Bohème* had appeared in 1896, *Tosca* in 1900 and *Madama Butterfly* in 1904) under the baton of Arturo Toscanini (1867–1957) and sung by such as Enrico Caruso (1873–1921) – the precursors of a long line of distinguished stars that includes Victor de Sabata, Tullio Serafin, Carlo Maria Giulini, Amelita Galli-Curci, Beniamino Gigli, Tito Gobbi, Renata Tebaldi and Luciano Pavarotti, to name but a few. Two other ever-popular operas of the period were *Cavalleria Rusticana* by Pietro Mascagni (1863–1945) and *I Pagliacci* by Ruggiero Leoncavallo (1858–1919). Poetry too was again enjoying widespread popularity, with the 'Crepuscolare' (twilight) school (Corazzini, Gozzano) dolefully reflecting the ennui of middle-class life. The poetic alternative was provided by the zany futurists (such as Marinetti), but the most influential poet of the period was undoubtedly the artistically gifted, colourful, even sensual, but also in many ways distasteful Gabriele D'Annunzio (1863–1938).

Mass culture and entertainment were for the first time developing in Italy. The film studios of Rome, Turin and Milan were beginning to churn out their products, and film stars such as Lidia Borelli were emerging. Sport was extremely popular with the mass of the people, as of course it still is today: football, cycling and motor-racing were the major areas of interest, the last establishing manufacturers such as Fiat, Maserati and Alfa Romeo as household names. This 'Italietta', as it was known, existed in a context of financial rectitude on the part of the state – a situation rarely paralleled in Italian history. But crucially, real life in this mini golden age was divorced from the political and parliamentary scene in the country. In any case it was not to last.

An unfortunate, but perhaps inevitable, feature of this 'belle époque' was the growth of an aggressive brand of Italian nationalism. This was the era of Bismarck's 'blood and iron', and of the cult of force, with super people living in a super state, and the spin-off reached Italy. Here the movement was fuelled by the writings and life style of D'Annunzio, and by an emerging right-wing press epitomised by publications such as *Il Tricolore*, *Grande Italia* and Corradini's *L'Idea Nazionale*. These preached ideas about the greatness and superiority of the Italian race, and advocated state control (ironically, since the Italians had always hated it), militarism (of which the Italians, Piedmont excepted, had little experience or tradition), and colonialism (which would provide a solution for the problem of mass emigration). The earliest and easiest outlet for this nationalism was predictably to be found in colonialism, and in September 1911 Italy duly embarked on an imperialist war against Turkey, to capture Libya. The war was generally popular, and there were all the familiar gung-ho scenes as the troops departed. The only dissent came from isolated voices such as the historian Gaetano Salvemini, who described Libya as a huge 'sand-pit' which was certainly not worth shedding blood for, and from the socialists, including a youthful Benito Mussolini. The war spun on for longer than expected, was extremely costly, and brought little real reward as people began to realise the possibility that Libya might indeed be a big 'sand-pit'. In addition, it did not end with the official conquest and ceasefire (which was sealed with the Treaty of Ouchy in 1912), for nationalist guerrilla activity meant that a sizeable and costly military presence had to be maintained in the north African desert.

The Libyan war threw Italy's finances into serious deficit, helping to undermine Giolitti's political position. The 1913 election, the first under the new universal male suffrage, was in many ways a masterpiece of Giolittian manoeuvring, returning a majority which included the widest range of opinion. But this time Giolitti's coalition proved to be too heterogeneous to provide the required stability. When, in 1914, the country was again hit by a series of strikes, compounded by civil disturbance in Ancona and the Romagna, he took refuge in his usual fashion: he resigned, leaving others to deal with the deficit, the disturbances, and the agitation of the socialists whose newspaper, *Avanti*, was now edited by Mussolini. This was to all intents and purposes Giolitti's final throw. He was out of high office for seven years, during which Italy was to involve itself in the Great War, although typically the old fox still retained the overall support of the majority of parliamentary deputies throughout the period.

Italy in the Great War

When the western world was plunged into total war, following the murder of Archduke Ferdinand of Austria in Serbia on 28 June 1914, Italy at first adopted a stance of neutrality. The Triple Alliance with Austria and Germany had crumbled into insignificance over the years, the Germanic countries increasingly mistrusting Italy's overtures to France, not to mention its ambitions over Trieste. The Austrians, for their part, had maltreated Italians living in Trieste, and Italy had not even been consulted over the decision to declare war. Therefore the neutralist tendencies in the country, which consisted mainly of the Catholic Party, the big industrialists and Giolitti himself, had little difficulty in initially winning the day. In any case, the country was totally unprepared, militarily, financially, and in terms of morale, for a major war.

However, a substantial portion of the country's opinion-makers were all for intervention, and their pressure and influence gradually forced Italy to become involved. The nationalists, the freemasons and some socialists, led by the increasingly influential figure of Mussolini, all, for their own different reasons, wanted war. But war against whom? To many of the nationalists it did not really seem to matter, as long as war there was. The natural side for Italy would have been the Austro-German one, but as we have seen the Triple Alliance had all but disintegrated. Austria continued to rebuff Italy's claims to Trieste, there was growing pro-French sentiment in the country, and the best bet for satisfying Italy's lingering colonial ambitions seemed to lie in support for France and Britain. So the new premier, Antonio Salandra, chose to ally

Italy to the eventual winning side. Through his foreign minister, Sidney Sonnino, he concluded the secret Treaty of London in April 1915, pitching Italy into the allied camp in return for the promise of substantial territorial gain on the victorious cessation of hostilities. Italy was to receive the Trentino, including the Brenner Pass, Trieste, and land and islands along the Dalmatian coast, as well as colonial possessions in Africa and Asia Minor. The generally apathetic Italian public were roused to a fever pitch of nationalist fervour by the media and by the rousing speeches of D'Annunzio, and on 23 May 1915 Italy declared war on Austria.

The country was as ever totally unprepared for this massive venture. The army was nowhere near being on the appropriate footing, and money for armaments was scarce. Nevertheless, the Italian armies marched into Austrian territory in the north-east, with some success against armed forces who had their hands full elsewhere. The poorly-armed and badly-led peasant conscripts fought bravely on the Isonzo, in the Adige valley, and around Asiago, with the same fatalistic resignation to which they had become accustomed in the fields. However, a prolonged stalemate quickly developed which was not broken until the end of 1917. Then the Austrians and Germans, freed from the burden of the Russian front, attacked, inflicting a humiliating defeat on the Italians at the Battle of Caporetto. The Germanic armies moved south to threaten the peninsula, as their predecessors had done on several other occasions over the centuries; Italy seemed to be in grave peril, and British and French troops were despatched to the rescue. The Italians, however, responded to the challenge with great fortitude and spirit. Before the arrival of the Allied forces, the greatly outnumbered Italian army halted the Austro-German advance on the River Piave – a military feat which has gone down in nationalist folklore, and which was celebrated in the patriotic song 'Il Piave mormorò ... non passa lo straniero' (The Piave whispered ... the foreigner shall not pass). By the autumn of 1918 the Italian and Allied forces were driving the Austrians back towards the north. A notable victory was achieved at the Battle of Vittorio Veneto, and on 4 November an armistice was concluded with Austria, and the war was over. Italy was on the winning side, but victory had been costly: the effort of mobilising more than five million men over

3½ years had involved great personal and financial sacrifice. There had been nearly 700,000 casualties; the longer-term cost for democracy in Italy was to be even greater.

In the end, the gains from the war certainly did not justify the enormous cost, since the Paris peace conference proved to be a massive comedown for the Italians. They had been foolish to place too much trust in a secret treaty drawn up in the middle of a war, for the US president, Woodrow Wilson, refused to recognise its validity, and the other Allies failed to support the demands of the indecisive and diplomatically naïve Italian representatives, Vittorio Orlando and Sonnino. In the Treaty of Versailles of January 1920 Italy emerged with the promised important gains in the north-east of the country up to the Brenner pass, and with some fairly useless territory in north Africa, but with none of the other territory promised in London. Nationalist opinion in the country was infuriated by the settlement: Italy had won the war, but had lost the peace. It was another nail in the coffin of the Liberal state.

Fascism

Within a few years the Liberal state had been swept away by Mussolini's Fascists, and the country had been plunged into a disastrous period of ultra-right-wing rule. What caused this dramatic volte-face?

COLLAPSE OF THE LIBERAL STATE

As we have seen, the state had long since lost touch with the people. The roots of the malaise can be traced back to the chicanery of the likes of Depretis, Crispi and Giolitti; it was thus fundamentally weak. What finally precipitated its collapse was a mixture of unfavourable historical circumstances, mismanagement, political ineptitude and sheer chance. An important immediate cause was the deep disappointment which followed the humiliating and public rebuff which the government had received in the post-war settlement. This clearly undermined its credibility and popularity, but it also gave carte-blanche for right-wing extremists to inflict further humiliation. A particular source of rancour was the failure to obtain Fiume (Rijeka, in what is now Yugoslavia). In September 1919, when it became clear that it was not to be Italian,

Gabriele D'Annunzio led a collection of nationalist fanatics to occupy the city, and set up a comic parody of a regime there. D'Annunzio held firm for an extended period, until Fiume was declared independent by the Treaty of Rapallo in November 1920 (it was annexed by Italy in 1924), hordes of extremists of every variety flocking to hear his demagogic oratory, in which he spat venom at the timidity of the government under Francesco Nitti (whom he referred to as 'cagoia', or filthy coward) and Giolitti, who were both powerless to control him. It is tempting from a distance to regard D'Annunzio's quasi-fascist regime as a surreal aberration, but it in fact left a deep impression on the Italians, and provided a model for the real thing later on. The 'leader' personally made decisions 'on the hoof', and he adopted several dictatorial trappings such as the Roman salute, the castor-oil treatment for dissenters, and the ridiculous war cry 'Eia eia alalà'. The bands of desperadoes who flocked to D'Annunzio's side spent their time in Fiume in constant festivity and ceremony, partying and strutting around in cloaks and daggers, to the chagrin of the bemused local population. It has been called a kind of right-wing May 1968, but it was also a huge slap in the face for the state, and a public demonstration of its impotence.

The final straw for the moribund Liberal state was its failure to manage adequately the economic transition which the country had to make from war to peace. Matters were not helped by the actions of big industrialists such as the Perrone brothers, the owners of the Ansaldo company, who, fearing that their own position would be undermined by disarmament, sabotaged the state by financing right-wing agitation of all kinds.

The government's policy, if we are generous enough to assume that it actually had a policy in these chaotic times, consisted of entrusting the solution of the problems of post-war restructuring to a semi-market economic regime, leaving the various industries to cope unprotected with international competition. This was a challenge for which much of Italian industry was clearly unprepared. Accustomed as they were to secure government arms contracts, many industrialists did not respond as they might have done, but rather just gave up. The result was a host of bankruptcies, including that of Ansaldo in 1921. The government was blamed, as it was for the mass unemployment which followed from demobilisation, for the galloping inflation of the immediate post-war period, and for the declining wages and living standards of those who were fortunate enough to be in work. The desperate economic situation resulted in widespread strikes and rioting, as the trade unions and the socialists stepped up their involvement and organisation, aware of recent events in Russia and of the possibility of precipitating revolution in Italy as well. But the revolution, when it came, was not to be of the Left. The government responded to the crisis with the time-honoured tactic of trying to buy off trouble by compromise and absorption. This only succeeded in buying time, and in the process the middle classes were alienated as they were forced to look on in dismay at the strikes, and at actions such as the halving of food prices by the Camere del Lavoro. A section of the middle class began to look to strike-breakers and right-wing extremists as the best, and possibly only, way to safeguard their interests in the midst of this chaos.

RISE OF THE FASCISTS

Thus the Right began to gain the support of influential sections of the population. In any case its power and organisation had been growing rapidly. In March 1919 Benito Mussolini, now running his own paper, *Popolo d'Italia*, in Milan, formed the first Fascio di Combattenti (Band of Fighters) of 150 men, many of them veterans of the Fiume escapade and anxious to stamp out the 'red menace'. At the same time the nationalists and 'patriots', including D'Annunzio and his 'Arditi', formed similar groups, and soon numerous Fasci were springing up throughout the country, terrorising all who dared to disagree, with their batons and their doses of castor oil. The government, by now more divided and removed from reality than ever, did absolutely nothing. If anything, Giolitti tolerated the Fascists as a way of defeating the perceived 'red menace' of the socialists. The carabinieri and the army thus stood by while the Fascist 'blackshirts' burned down the offices of the socialists, violently hijacked the peasant and industrial unions, and ejected the socialists by force from their municipal strongholds in major cities such as Bologna and Milan. Here the leaders of the 'squadristi', the 'Ras' as they called themselves, such as the villainous Roberto Farinacci in Cremona, Balbo in Ferrara and Arpinati in Bologna, set themselves up

Benito Mussolini

as the new local bosses. In May 1921 Giolitti called new elections, hoping as usual to absorb Mussolini and his mob of Fascists into his multicoloured coalition. This time he failed.

The election was inconclusive and Giolitti once again resigned. His successors, Ivanoe Bonomi and Luigi Facta, carried on, constructing a series of unstable and short-lived coalitions while public order fell to pieces – fiddling while Rome burned. Late in 1821 Mussolini, who had just been elected to parliament with thirty-four other Fascist deputies, formed the Partito Nazionale Fascista (National Fascist Party), with a complete programme of government based on the principles of sound finance, an authoritative (and authoritarian) state, social reform, a high foreign policy profile, strike-breaking, and rigid control of the economy within a strict capitalist framework. By the end of 1921 the PNF had over 200,000 members, by May 1922 over 300,000. Mussolini was thus assured a political base for Fascism, which now additionally began to take on its crucial personal dimension, as a personality cult grew around the myth of 'Il Duce' as a 'strong man'.

Who exactly were these original Fascists? Mussolini himself (1883–1945) came from a working-class background near Forlì. His father was a blacksmith with strong socialist views which his son inherited. He became a party activist, and after terms of imprisonment for revolutionary activity, in 1912 he became editor of the national socialist paper *Avanti*. He split with the socialists over their neutral stance in the war and moved to the right. There is disagreement about the precise identity of his supporters, but the evidence suggests they were predominantly from the middle classes: landowners, white-collar workers, shopkeepers, and a large number of students. Tacit support also came from key officers of the state, such as judges, the military and the police. The whole can be regarded as a new bourgeois movement to fill the void left by the disintegrating Liberal state. Middle-class the Fascists might have been, but they also relied heavily on militant trade unionists, as well as peasants and the mob to act as their enforcers. By June 1922 the Fascist National Confederation of Syndical Corporations had amassed 500,000 members.

THE MARCH ON ROME

Terrorism had given Mussolini power on the ground in the country. Soon his opportunism, aided and abetted by the amazing confusion and divisions in the ranks of the Liberals and the socialist opposition, was to allow him to seize power in parliament as well. The government was in a state of collapse, which was compounded by the withdrawal of Vatican support for the Popular Party by the new pope Pius XI, when in August 1922 the trade unions which still retained their independence called a general strike. This was just the sort of situation which the Fascist squadristi relished, and they proceeded to smash the strike and assume control of essential services. By October they controlled all the key points of communication between Rome and the north. At this point they decided to exert real pressure on the state: a quadrumvirate of leading Fascists – Bianchi, Balbo, De Vecchi and De Bono – set out, with Mussolini's personal approval, to march on Rome with their squadristi to seize power. Mussolini himself conveniently remained in Milan so that he would be in a position to flee to Switzerland in case something went wrong. On 28 October the prime minister, Facta, urged the king to declare martial law. The king agreed, but then mysteriously changed his mind, perhaps fearing that the army would mutiny. Mussolini boarded a sleeping-car in Milan and travelled to Rome to accept the king's invitation to form a government on 29 October 1922.

The new government was given a vote of confidence by parliament by 306 votes to 116. Those who voted against included the men of the past, Giolitti, Orlando and Salandra, as well as some men of the future, notably Alcide de Gasperi. Mussolini had trodden the path from membership of the socialist party to the opposite end of the political spectrum. He had seized power and brought a Fascist state to Italy. His former colleagues would be made to pay dearly for their mistakes. It is important to note at this point that the rise of the Duce had been accomplished with the support, active or tacit, of the Italian establishment; it could not have happened had it not been for the attitude of big business, the judges, the army, the police, the bureaucrats, and the Church. The role of the king was also crucial: had he not changed his mind on the morning of 28 October, it is possible that there might never have been a Fascist regime.

FASCISM IN ITALY

At first few people thought that Mussolini would last very long: he would sooner or later either disappear from the scene or be absorbed into the system like everybody else before him. There was a distinct air of complacency surrounding what was happening to the country; some observers, in fact, including the lifelong socialists Gaetano Salvemini and Anna Kuliscioff, welcomed Mussolini as a moderating influence on the squadristi. As things turned out, he did moderate the excesses of the extreme Fascists like Farinacci, but he also managed to consolidate his own position and to remain at the helm of the right-wing state for over twenty years. That he succeeded in consolidating his position to the point that the Fascists held a total monopoly over Italian politics and society was in no small measure due to the good fortune which he enjoyed on the economic front. The last rights of the Liberal regime had been administered against a backcloth of economic crisis, but from 1922 until about 1929 the United States and European economies rallied and, in an increasingly interdependent world, Italy's economy was dragged up in the slipstream. As a result, the economic policy of the early fascist era, based on privatisation, deregulation, wage cuts and tax cuts, allied to external tariff protection and currency stabilisation, met with some success. By the end of the decade, industrial production in Italy had increased by 50%, with chemicals (mainly the Montecatini company), synthetic fibres (Snia Viscosa), and automobiles (Fiat) doing particularly well. Unemployment fell as industry expanded, and there was also significant recovery in agriculture. The more favourable economic situation made it easier for the Fascists to liquidate opposition and establish a right-wing authoritarian state. So too did the support of the middle and upper classes, who had benefited most from the economic recovery.

The process of turning Fascism into a regime began in 1923, when a parallel army, the Fascist Militia, was recruited, mainly from ex-squadristi, many of whom were becoming restless at what they perceived as a sell-out of the revolution by their leader. The Grand Council of Fascism was then turned into an organ of state, and in July a new electoral law ensured a parliamentary majority for the Duce and his followers. The election which followed in April 1924 returned the Fascist 'listone' (approved list of candidates) with a large majority, but in its aftermath came the first crisis – Mussolini's Watergate, as it has been called. On 30 May Giacomo Matteotti, the new leader of the socialists, condemned the elections as a farce. On 10 June Matteotti disappeared, his body eventually being discovered in August in a ditch near Rome; he had been murdered by the Fascists, and the so-called 'Matteotti affair' had begun. Mussolini was accused of personal involvement in the crime by the press, in particular by Amendola's *Il Mondo* and Albertini's *Corriere della Sera*. He became increasingly isolated, and during the autumn he appeared to be in real political danger. Unlike Nixon, he rode out the crisis, and retorted in startling fashion, delivering a brazen speech to parliament on 3 January 1925 which effectively restored the confidence of the establishment in his regime. From now on the die was cast.

Between January 1925 and the beginning of 1929, the Italian state was transformed into an authoritarian regime, with the slogan 'Everything within the state. Nothing outside the state. Nothing against the state.' The freedom of the press was curbed, partly by censorship and partly by compliant proprietors sacking uncooperative editors. Local government was subjected to increasing control, with appointed *podestà* replacing the elected mayors. The opposition parties, who in any case had been largely supine in front of the Duce, were banned in 1926, and leading dissenters were exiled either abroad (the 'fuorusciti') or to remote parts of the south. Here many intellectuals discovered the existence of the 'southern problem'. One of them, Carlo Levi, subsequently wrote *Cristo si è fermato ad Eboli* (Christ Stopped at Eboli), based on his experiences in the south during the Fascist years. The police and the secret police (the OVRA) naturally persecuted all and sundry who were suspected of having the temerity to disagree with Mussolini, in a typical week carrying out some 20,000 'knocks on the door in the dead of night' and similar operations. 'Secret associations', including the freemasons, were banned; the bureaucracy was purged of suspect elements; and even the Mafia in the south was attacked by the Duce, who, incidentally, is the only person who had come anywhere near to breaking their stranglehold over the Mezzogiorno. Membership of the 'Party', the PNF, became an essential prerequisite for getting on, to the extent that it was sarcastically said that the initials stood for 'Per Necessità Famigliari' (For Family Reasons). Yet even the PNF itself was not immune, with several large-scale expulsions being carried out. The workers were kept happy by sport, 'ideologically sound' popular music, and by the *dopolavoro* (working men's clubs), while the last free trade union was dissolved in the name of the state's sham corporatism. At the apex of the Fascist pyramid was the Duce himself, who 'was always right', and harangued the population in his radio transmissions, his speeches from the balcony overlooking Piazza Venezia, and through his slogans, such a 'Work nobilitates' and 'Better one year as a lion than one hundred years as a lamb'. In 1929 the Church ended its isolation when, in the Lateran Agreements, Pope Pius XI and Mussolini agreed to the creation of the Vatican State and papal recognition of the kingdom of Italy. The only opposition came from underground sources, in fact four attempts were made on Mussolini's life during 1926.

Although by the end of the 1920s Mussolini's state was of course right-wing and authoritarian, it was in many ways not really a 'fascist state' as such. Although crucial traditional freedoms and rights had been abolished, most of the old institutions of the Liberal period had survived. Since power was almost completely concentrated in the person of the Duce himself, it kept alive in the dwindling ranks of the opposition the lingering hope that Fascism might collapse if Mussolini were to disappear from the scene. He did not, and Fascism persisted for long enough to plunge Italy into the devastation of the Second World War. (One should note in passing that events in Italy were actually warmly welcomed in some circles abroad. In Britain, Winston Churchill stated that he would probably have been a fascist if he had been Italian, while prime minister Baldwin was quick to defend Churchill's statement.)

In contrast to the 1920s, the 1930s were a period of general economic recession, epitomised by the Wall Street crash in the USA. The Italian economy suffered accordingly, and the Fascists responded with an important about turn in policy. In addition to continuing protectionism, they decided to restrain private expenditure and expand public spending, thus effectively establishing a siege economy with a large state sector. This period, in which it is sometimes claimed that the true Fascist revolution took place, thus saw the demolition and rebuilding of large parts of Rome, in the typically ugly monumental Fascist style, as well as a mass of other public works and road-building. It also saw the rescue by the state of several ailing private firms by means of the Istituto per la Ricostruzione Industriale (IRI), which still exists today as an important state holding company. The political repercussions of this change in policy, particularly between 1936–8, were distinctly to increase the authoritarian and totalitarian nature of the regime.

FASCIST WAR, RESISTANCE AND THE FALL OF MUSSOLINI

Fascism might have 'made the trains run on time' (sometimes), but it also turned Italy into a vulgar, corrupt, cynical and conformist society, in which fear and intellectual poverty predominated. Worse was to come, for Fascism also led Italy into war. In a sense this was a purely logical development, for Fascism was above all a militaristic philosophy, if one can grace it as a philosophy. 'War alone', said Il Duce in 1932, '. . . places the seal of nobility on those peoples who have the courage to meet it.'

Mussolini himself took charge of foreign policy. In the 1920s he concluded a number of commercial treaties with European countries, including the Soviet Union in 1924, in between organising the bombardment and occupation of Corfu. In the 1930s Italy played the role of a major actor on the European diplomatic scene, albeit occasionally an overambitious one, until Mussolini's instinct for expansionism got the better of him in 1935 and he invaded Abyssinia. This action was condemned by the international community, which applied sanctions, but the largely useless (for the Italians) territory of Abyssinia was captured in May 1936, when the Duce declared from his balcony overlooking Piazza Venezia that the Italian Empire had been founded. By now a kindred spirit, Adolf Hitler, was well established in Germany, and the famous 'Axis' between the two powers was sealed in the same year, after both Germany and Italy had intervened in the Spanish Civil War in favour of the future dictator Francisco Franco.

The axis, despite Mussolini's rhetoric, was not a partnership of equals. Il Duce very much played second fiddle to the Führer, towards whom it seems he developed a distinct inferiority complex. Thus Italian Fascism, as the junior partner in the alliance, proceeded to absorb many aspects of Nazi doctrine and policy, to its cost and that of the country. Italy was increasingly drawn into the Nazi camp and away from its First World War allies. In 1937 the Anti-Comintern pact was concluded between Italy, Germany and Japan, and in the following year Italy adopted the Nazi policy of persecuting Jews. The latter development was perhaps the most tragic and inexplicable of the regime's acts: despicable, unpopular, counter-productive, and an insult to the openness of the Italian character. But by now there was no turning back. The Duce had decided that the future glory of the Italian people lay in war side by side with Germany, even though he himself was aware that the Italian army was not ready for a protracted struggle, and that his militaristic regime had therefore failed in one of its primary objectives, to turn Italy into a military machine. He tried to buy time, but in the end was swept forward inexorably by events, caught in a trap of his own making, a victim of his own delusions. Like a lemming he jumped over the cliff into the Second World War, dragging the unfortunate country behind him.

In April 1939 Mussolini occupied Albania, and then signed the 'pact of steel', committing Italy to war in support of Germany. When hostilities broke out in September he bided his time, finally entering the war on 10 June 1940, after the easy German victories in France, and with an opportunism which was as blatant as it was distasteful. 'Do you want war! ... ?' boomed the Duce from his balcony. 'Yes,' screamed the chorus of sycophants from down below.

The course of the Second World War is well known. Suffice it to say that the badly prepared troops, despite some individual acts of bravery, did not distinguish themselves on various fronts in Africa and Greece. Most of the soldiers adopted a defeatist posture from the start, regarding the hostilities as a Fascist war rather than a genuine national struggle. A particularly serious blow was the bloody defeat suffered by the army of 110,000 which had been sent to the Russian front in 1942. By the beginning of 1943 half of these wretched souls had been massacred by the Russians or by the cold. At home war exposed the corruptness and bankruptcy of the regime, and it was profoundly unpopular, ultimately facilitating the emergence of an anti-Fascist movement. It was against the basic instincts of most Italians to sacrifice for a pointless cause, particularly when the sons of the Fascist hierarchy were seen to be usually avoiding the draft.

In the initial stages the voice of the opposition had been scattered and modest in size, consisting mainly of the underground activities of the Communist Party, which had been founded in 1921 by a schism from the socialists, and which was the sole group to have developed at this stage a coherent analysis of the situation in the country. The principal theoreticians of the party were the future leader Palmiro Togliatti, and Antonio Gramsci, whose programme was adopted by the party congress held at Lyons in 1926, and who in the same year was incarcerated by the Fascists. From his gaol, where he remained until his death in 1937, Gramsci wrote his influential *Letters from Prison*. Opposition also came from a group of *fuorusciti*, who organised against Mussolini, mainly from France; the best known of these were Benedetto Croce, Gaetano Salvemini and Carlo Rosselli, who founded the group 'Giustizia e Libertà' (Justice and Liberty).

By 1943 the situation at home had become really grim. Food was

Antonio Gramsci

extremely short, and Mussolini was displaying distinct signs of personal degeneration. Matters were brought to a head by the Allied landings in Sicily, and on 25 July 1943 Mussolini was forced to give up his dictatorial powers by the Fascist Grand Council. The compliant king now pathetically turned to Marshal Pietro Badoglio to form a new government; it dithered, but eventually concluded an armistice with the Allies on 8 September. The next day the Allies landed at Salerno. The Germans poured troops into Italy and occupied Rome, kidnapping Mussolini on 11 September and setting him up at the head of the puppet Salò Republic ('Italian Social Republic') in the north. Badoglio moved his capital to Brindisi and on 13 October declared war on Germany. Italy was again the battleground for foreign armies.

From the Italian point of view, this part of the war is memorable for the emergence of the resistance, which fought a brave and often costly underground war on the side of the Allies and against what were now the Nazi invaders. These partisans spearheaded what took on the dimensions of a genuine national movement, an outlet for the frustrations of twenty years, which salvaged some pride and dignity for Italy from the war and rendered the post-war settlement much less unfavourable than it might otherwise have been. Unlike that of France and Yugoslavia, which relied heavily on the charisma of inividuals like De Gaulle and Tito, the Italian resistance was held together by political parties. At its height it numbered 200,000 people, and it spanned the full spectrum of political opinion, from communists, through socialists, to Christian Democrats and the intellectuals of the Action Party. It contained many sincere and brave anti-Fascists, as well as the predictable opportunists who were turning with the tide – a well-known contemporary joke refers to how all Italians at the time were in the resistance, including the pope! In May 1944 the Allies took Monte Cassino after a bitter struggle and advanced on Rome, which was liberated in June. The final offensive came in the spring of 1945, during which the partisans occupied and liberated Milan, Turin and Genoa. The guerrillas of the resistance took heavy losses in the face of Nazi resistance and indiscriminate reprisals, but they persevered, to salvage many of the northern cities from the sabotage of the retreating Germans. Towards the end Mussolini's Social Republic became more despicable than ever, with Farinacci instituting the persecution of Italian Jews. Finally the Duce was captured by partisans at Lake Como as he was trying to flee to Switzerland dressed in a German uniform. On 28 April, on the orders of the Committee of National Liberation, he was shot, along with Farinacci and other Fascist leaders. He was strung up upside down in Piazzale Loreto, the scene of Nazi atrocities in Milan, together with his mistress, Clara Petacci – a gruesome symbol to end an unfortunate episode of Italian history.

CHAPTER EIGHT

Post-War and Contemporary Italy

The aftermath of war was difficult, but not as difficult as it might have been. The 1947 settlement deprived Italy of her possessions in Africa and the Dodecanese islands, and of Fiume and Istria. However, Italy kept Trieste, the South Tyrol and, despite De Gaulle's ambitions, the Val d'Aosta. In addition, Britain and the USA forwent their reparations, and indeed the Americans supplied generous amounts of aid to help Italy over its immediate plight. And plight it was, for the war had predictably left the peninsula physically devastated, and its economy torn by inflation and mass unemployment. Nevertheless, the partisan action had at least saved key structures in the north from the sabotage of the retreating Nazis, so there was something to build on. All in all, Italy emerged more favourably from the defeat of the Second World War than it had from the victory of the First.

THE ITALIAN REPUBLIC

The most pressing question, certainly from the political viewpoint, was the exact form which the new state would take. In many ways Italy in 1945 was at a political crossroads. Would the Italians emerge from the war with a new radical democratic state in place of the old Liberal regime, under the auspices of the Left, the communists, the socialists and the Action Party for whom the resistance had been a great success, and with policies to match? Or would they place their faith in conservatism, reverting to a modified version of the structures and policies of the ancien régime? There was a strong regional dimension to the choice. The resistance had been an almost exclusively northern phenomenon; most partisans were on the Left; therefore it was from the north of the country that the new radical energy was coming. The south, on the other hand, was a bastion of conservatism, in which the old order remained largely intact and in which the power of the Church was strongest.

At first it seemed that the Left might have a fighting chance of success. Their organisation was strong and they were also widely popular following the ad hoc victories of the local Committees for National Liberation (CNLs). The five-month government of Ferruccio Parri, himself the leader of the Action Party, included many of the resistance leaders and was arguably the most radical in Italian history. But it achieved very little in concrete terms, and its purges against former collaborators quickly lost it the support of the establishment – there were relatively few Italians who did not have some skeleton or other in their cupboard from the Fascist period. Parri was forced to resign in November 1945, to be succeeded by Alcide De Gasperi, the leader of the Christian Democrats, the first Catholic prime minister of Italy since unification.

The future political direction of Italy was to a large extent decided on 2 June 1946, when the election took place for the constitutent assembly which would draw up the new constitution. Women, incidentally, had the right to vote for the first time. The Christian Democrats (DC) gained 31% of the vote, and won a substantial majority over the Socialists (20%) and the Communists (PCI, 19%); the Action Party was virtually wiped out. The Partito dell'Uomo Qualunque (The Qualunquisti, or Party of the Ordinary Man), the representatives of the right-wing white-collar workers in the centre–south who were worried by the anti-Fascist purges (and the precursor of the neo-Fascist Italian Social Movement (MSI)), significantly obtained 30 seats out of 556. The government of the CNLs was over, and an enduring electoral pattern had been established, with three major parties dominating a variety of smaller ones. On the same day Italians voted in a referendum on the 'Institutional Question', that is whether the country was to remain a monarchy or become a republic. The vote was in favour of the republic by 12.7 million to 10.7 million, and Umberto II, who only one month earlier had acceded to the throne on the abdication of his father Vittorio Emanuele III, packed his bags to go into disgruntled exile. Mazzini had finally been vindicated.

The constitution was debated over nearly two years. On paper the Left could have dominated the Assembly, but in practice they were far too deeply divided to have any chance of forming a compact parliamentary unit. There were fundamental ideological differences between Togliatti's PCI and the Socialists, and in any case the latter were in the process of splitting in two over whether to support Moscow or Washington in the deepening East–West conflict. In January 1947 the pro-American Giuseppe Saragat left to form what was to become the Italian Social Democratic Party (PSDI), while the remaining, more left-wing socialists formed the Italian Socialist Party (PSI) under Pietro Nenni. As a consequence the DC called the tune, at the head of a colition of the three main parties plus the Republicans (PRI), until May 1947 when, under pressure from the USA and the Vatican, De Gasperi expelled the PCI.

The final outcome was a constitution which looked remarkably like that of the old Liberal state, minus the king. The nominal head of state was to be the President of the Republic, elected by parliament for a period of seven years, but the real power lay with the Council of Ministers and the legislature, which consisted of a Chamber of Deputies and the Senate, both now elected by proportional representation. The judges were to be independent, controlled by a Supreme Council of the Judiciary. There was to be a Constitutional Court, and citizens would have the right to challenge laws by means of popular referenda. Regional governments were to be set up, and the bureaucracy was to be decentralised. The DC in effect won a major victory by incorporating into the constitution the 1929 Lateran Agreements with the Vatican, granting the clergy special privileges and outlawing divorce. In the end the Assembly approved the constitution by a massive majority of 453 votes to 62. The question which must be asked is why the PCI voted in favour of a constitution which included such an illiberal concordat? The answer lies partly in Togliatti's propensity for compromise, and partly in the fundamental rights which were now enshrined in the constitution. This contains the statement that 'sovereignty belongs to the people', and it establishes the right of citizens to a whole variety of goodies: employment, free education, a living wage, free health care, and profit-sharing; it also abolished the latifondi. For the most part, these were empty generalisations, which the DC traded in exchange for real concessions to the new clerical conservative establishment.

Consolidation, 1948–1960

The constitution came into effect on 1 January 1948. The first President of the new Italian Republic was Luigi Einaudi, an economist and former governor of the Bank of Italy, and not a member of the DC. The first parliamentary elections were held on 18 April and the DC were returned with a clear majority, polling over 48% by pushing the 'red scare' tactic for all it was worth in the aftermath of the Soviet seizure of Czechoslavakia. The 'Popular Democratic Front' of the PCI and Nenni's PSI polled 31%.

DE GASPERI

Alcide De Gasperi held power without interruption between 1948 and 1953. His governments, based on a number of coalitions, laid the essential foundations of post-war Italy. Apart from being a statesman, he was himself an agile and resourceful politician in the tradition of many of his predecessors – the length of his period in office, almost without parallel in post-war Italy, testifies to that. He maintained himself and the different strands of the DC in power in the time-honoured fashion of compromise, negotiation and patronage. One could almost think of it as a watered-down variety of trasformismo, adapted to the twentieth century.

In espousing this 'politics of accommodation', De Gasperi set an example to his successors in the DC, who were to have more and more need of political agility in the years to come as the DC vote declined from its 1948 high. He was a devout Catholic, but wise and far-sighted enough not to pander totally to the wishes of the Church. Thus in his eight cabinets he included non-Catholics as well as Liberals, Republicans and Social Democrats, often to the chagrin of extreme elements in the Vatican. By means of his personality and his influence, De Gasperi not only succeeded in holding together the sometimes incongruous factions of the DC, but he also provided Italy with the political stability which was necessary for reconstruction. Compromise usually has a cost,

Alcide De Gasperi

however, and during the De Gasperi period stability was paid for by the impossibility of any radical change. The state could not even begin to think about tackling the vested interests and privileges of key sections of society, and in particular the Church and the civil service, the latter being totally inadequate to cope with the exigencies of a modern society.

The most pressing challenge for the new republic and its clerical government was of course economic reconstruction. The country had been devastated by Fascism and war. It was still predominantly agricultural (44% of the active population worked on the land in 1947), particularly in the south, and many Italians lived lives of poverty in depressing conditions: overcrowded and very basic rural houses which were often shared with the animals, and foul slums in and around the big cities; a considerable number of people were even forced for a period to make their homes in caves. The industry that survived the war was antiquated and after years of fascist militarism and protectionism, it faced all the serious problems involved in adapting to peacetime production in an increasingly interdependent world. Most of industry was in fact miniscule in size, 90% of firms employing five people or less. Unemployment and underemployment were also rife, with the official number of jobless – almost certainly a gross underestimate – amounting to two million. In addition there was the glaring problem of the north–south divide, now posing an immense social and political as well as economic problem.

In the event, reconstruction was considerably facilitated by a number of favourable factors. In the first place, Italy received large amounts of Marshall and other aid from the USA, which helped to support the Lira, to develop efficient steel and cement industries, and to mitigate the worst of the post-war social and economic deprivation. Currency stability gave Italians the confidence to save, which in turn permitted the investment necessary for development to be financed. Secondly, natural gas was discovered in the Po valley. The discovery was largely due to the single-minded and unconventional efforts of Enrico Mattei, one of the most intriguing characters of post-war Italy. Given the brief of dissolving Mussolini's Oil Exploration Agency, Mattei in fact continued drilling on his own initiative and against the wishes of his superiors. This idiosyncratic behaviour paid handsome dividends as large amounts of methane came on stream in the late 1940s. Such an important discovery was in itself of great importance to a country with few natural resources. However, Mattei used the finds as a springboard for greater things. Resisting political pressure from the USA, he secured an Italian monopoly of exploitation over the most promising areas and built up an enormous public-sector empire, the Ente Nazionale Idrocarburi (ENI), which he ran in a typically individualistic and autocratic fashion, almost above parliamentary control, before his death in a mysterious air crash in 1962.

A further factor which helped Italy's economic recovery was a natural resource which had always existed in large quantities: its vast reserves of labour, mainly in the south, which could be used to fuel the country's industrial growth without fears of wage inflation. In addition, many of these workers had a long tradition of craftsmanship, which made it easier for them to adapt to changing industrial techniques. These resources, therefore, allied to some unpopularly tight, but in the long run necessary, macroeconomic control by Einaudi and his successors at the Bank of Italy, permitted the Italian economy to move positively and strongly into the post-war era, and economic resurgence proved to be more rapid and painless than anyone had dared hope. The Italian growth rate of around 6%, albeit from a low base, was one of the highest in the world, and in the context of relative price stability to boot. Freed from the burden of the huge military expenditure and restrictions of the Fascist era, the economic system was beginning to deliver the goods.

And what an eclectic economic system it was! The market and economic liberalism were mixed with large doses of state involvement and intervention. Apart from the Mattei empire, there was also the huge state holding company, Instituto per la Ricostruzione Industriale (IRI), which was retained from Fascist times and gave the state control over a large portion of the economy. This included airlines (Alitalia), cars (Alfa Romeo), ships, motorway construction, machine tools and, crucially, the banks and credit institutions which provided industry with cheap loans in the middle of a general credit squeeze. Politically, this large state sector was very useful to the DC as a means of patronage – the state corporations provided convenient jobs in which to place the faithful. Economic policy was equally pragmatic. Einaudi & co. believed in free trade, but they were quite prepared in 1950 to impose a tariff with an average incidence of around 24% to protect Italy's infant industries. This was not totally removed until the creation of the European Economic Community in 1957, and it effectively protected the domestic market and allowed the country's nascent industries to develop relatively untroubled by foreign competition. Protectionism is usually counter-productive since it is met by retaliation; in this context, however, it worked, for 1950–1 saw the Korean War boom, which permitted increased sales abroad and thus established Italian goods in foreign markets. In addition, the tourist industry was expanding, with north Europeans flocking to soak up the sun in resorts such as Rimini, Iesolo, Capri and Viareggio, and to visit Italy's immense historical and artistic heritage. The result was that the country found itself in a position to import the technology which was required for growth, without running into balance of payments problems.

The regional problem of the Mezzogiorno, however, remained, and was arguably exacerbated by the widespread emigration which took place towards northern Europe and the factories of Turin and Milan. Migration might have fuelled growth and kept labour costs down in the north, but it also involved great personal and social costs, and there is little evidence to suggest that it did very much to promote growth in the source areas of the south, despite the remittances of migrants which undoubtedly contributed to the relief of poverty. At least, however, some attempts were beginning to be made to deal with the issue. In 1950 the Cassa per il Mezzogiorno was set up to direct infrastructural investment to the south. The 1954 Vanoni plan, although it was never presented to parliament, established the objective of creating a rate of growth in the south which was double what it was in the north. Additionally, the Ministry of State Participations (nationalised industries) was set up in 1956, with a brief to locate 60% of all new state investments in the south. All in all, huge amounts of money were poured into the south. Important strides forward were undoubtedly made in key areas, but much of the money, perhaps as much as a third, was directed into unco-ordinated and inappropriate channels. Expenditure was often corruptly allocated, or distributed according to political imperatives, with the result that it would be wasted on pointless projects such as building villages in which nobody ever lived, roads to nowhere, and dams with no purpose. The state corporations frequently built 'cathedrals in the desert', capital-intensive and high social-cost projects which employed few people, bought their components in from the north, and sold their products in other markets. The southern landscape was thus filled with eyesores in return for little real local benefits.

Apart from overseeing the beginning of the reconstruction of the economy, De Gasperi was responsible for steering Italy into the position it currently holds within the international community – a firm member of the western alliance and a staunch supporter of the process of European integration. In this he was aided by his internationalist foreign minister Carlo Sforza, who had been in the Action Party before joining the minority Republican Party. Between them, De Gasperi and Sforza took Italy into NATO in 1949, and laid the foundations for the country to become a founder member of the European Coal and Steel Community in 1952 and the EEC in 1957. Indeed, the treaty which established the Community in that year was actually signed in the Italian capital. The price for stability of the De Gasperi period may have been the avoidance of any radical change, but he did not altogether ignore social issues. Perhaps his most daring measure was an attempt at agrarian reform in the 1950s, in the course of which nearly two million acres of uncultivated land were purchased by the state and redistributed to smallholders.

The 1953 elections saw a serious drop in the DC vote to around 40%, which ended De Gasperi's political career. He died the following year and his departure from the scene left a void in Italian politics which remained substantially unfilled. There was no one who could carry out the necessary political balancing act with quite the same skill. The same could be said about Luigi Einaudi, whose presidency ended in 1955, and who arguably was not adequately replaced until the election of Sandro Pertini in 1978. A whole array of governments and prime ministers came and went between 1953 and 1960: Pella, Fanfani (three times), Scelba, Segni (twice), Zoli and Tambroni, all contributing to the DC's retention of power with their political acrobatics. Meanwhile the DC were building up a massive web of patronage in the country, filling the bureaucracy and the major institutions with their own supporters, as well as liberally bestowing 'pensions' in order to consolidate their hold over the real functioning of the country, and thus make any true change difficult to achieve, no matter what might happen in parliament in the years to come.

It is tempting to assume that with all this governmental and prime ministerial musical chairs, Italy was a politically unstable country. Not so. The actors might change, but the script remained essentially the same. In any case the actors did not really change very much: the basic personnel of successive governments remained remarkably similar. Continuity and stability was achieved, Italian style. This phenomenon persists to the present day, as does a deceptive continuity in macroeconomic policy-making, with the Bank of Italy faithfully steadying the ship. Continuity or not, the political system failed to capture the imagination of the public or to impinge on their day-to-day reality, and it was very much based on apathy. Italians cared little about formal or 'high' politics at this stage: one opinion survey of the period found that 40% of adults did not even know the name of the prime minister, while one journalist estimated that only some 1500 people in the whole country read the political pages of the newspapers.

THE PARTIES OF OPPOSITION

What of the Left? The PCI under Togliatti remained by far the most important of the Left groups, despite the ideological anguishes which it suffered over its relations with the USSR (especially after the invasion of Hungary), and over how to handle the growing success of Italian capitalism. They had been excluded from government at an early stage by De Gasperi, but they maintained a large membership and a formidable organisation on the ground. They failed to provide a genuine alternative government, or even an effective parliamentary opposition, even though together with the revolutionary socialists they controlled one-third of the seats in the Chamber of Deputies. But then that was not their prime objective. They in fact picked up a good deal of support from ideologically uncommitted people from every class, who saw them as an outlet for their increasing alienation and dislike of clericalism. They also enjoyed the support of many of the artists and intellectuals of this period: Pasolini, Visconti, De Sica, Moravia, Quasimodo, Levi and Guttoso were fellow-travellers, to name but a few. Perhaps the PCI's greatest successes were in local government, where they came to be regarded as the party of good and incorruptible rule: Bologna, Florence, Milan, Turin and Genoa all came under their control. A big disadvantage for the PCI was the fragmentation of the Italian trade union movement, which in 1949 split into three groups along party lines, thus depriving the PCI of the opportunity to control a strong and united movement. The PCI remained in control of the CGIL, while the DC now controlled the CISL, and the PCI the UIL.

The Socialists fared worse than the Communists. The breakaway of the Social Democrats of course weakened the PSI as an electoral force. They managed to maintain their share of the vote at around 12–14% throughout the 1950s, but it is clear that in their ideological identity crisis they had ceded the leadership of the anti-DC movement to the PCI. On the extreme right, the standard-bearers of neo-fascism, the MSI, polled around 5–6% of the vote. A slight cause for concern perhaps, but not a really significant proportion on a national scale.

The 'Economic Miracle': Italy in the 1960s

The economic recovery of the late 1940s and 1950s had been impressive and relatively painless, but it was nothing compared to what came next. For in the years 1959–62 the economy really took off, and the basis was laid for Italy to occupy its current position amongst the élite of the industrialised world. This period is often referred to as the Italian 'economic miracle', although rapid expansion continued, albeit in fits and starts, throughout the decade. The take-off had been brewing throughout the post-war period, and was precipitated by the factors we have already discussed: American aid, appropriate macroeconomic policies and direct state involvement, cheap and compliant labour (there were no strikes at FIAT between 1954–62), cheap steel and energy, entrepreneurial panache, and a good slice of luck. In any event, the country's Gross Domestic Product more than doubled and industrial production more than trebled between 1951–63. It was an export-led boom, spearheaded by the 'flagships' of Italian industry: FIAT, Montecatini-Edison, Olivetti. But it was also about the Italian spirit of improvisation and enterprise coming to the fore: new firms mushroomed and whole industries, such as motor-scooters, washing machines and refrigerators, emerged seemingly from nowhere to dominate world markets. One could almost think of it as 'l'arte dell'arrangiarsi' (the art of getting by) channelled into the formal economic system. The flight from the countryside to the cities accelerated, with less than 20% of the working population left on the land by the end of the 1960s, by which time the north at least had become a modern and wealthy industrial environment.

The political background to this economic renaissance was more DC control, but with a slightly different emphasis. The response of the DC to the conditions of the 1950s had been to create a series of centre–right governments. This approach was brought abruptly to an end in July 1960, when the Tambroni government which was supported by the neo-fascists, was brought down by an outbreak of riots and popular discontent. From this point the DC, pragmatic as ever, turned its sights towards the Left. Pope John XXIII had removed the prohibition against political dealings with Marxists, and the 1962 Fanfani administration tried to woo the Socialists. Pietro Nenni finally led his PSI troops into coalition with the DC in late 1963, himself becoming deputy prime minister in the new Moro administration. Centre–left government, or more cynically the DC using left-of-centre parties to keep itself in power and the PCI out of it, has continued with one or two interruptions up to the present day.

ALDO MORO

The dominant political figure of the 1960s, and the linchpin of the DC's opening to the Left, was Aldo Moro, who was prime minister from December 1963 to June 1968. The major issues which he and his administrations had to deal with were the slowdown of the economic miracle and the fundamental social changes which were affecting Italy, and for that matter the rest of the West, in the 1960s. The economy went into recession after 1962. To an extent this downturn constituted a natural phase of the trade cycle after the remarkable expansion of the previous years. However, many of the favourable circumstances which had permitted the economic miracle to take place had also disappeared. The 'reserve army' of labour had become smaller, with official unemployment down to half a million by 1963, and the workers and their trade unions were growing in confidence. The price of labour therefore increased, rendering Italian goods less competitive on world markets and bringing the export-led boom to an abrupt end. The state sector led the way in wage inflation, and there was little way in which the DC government could control their activities. The public corporations were protected from the discipline of the market, and at the same time their activities were virtually unconditionally underwritten by the DC, which had used them as a source of both patronage and income, and which could not now allow any of them to go bankrupt. At the same time, large sections of the Italian bourgeoisie became alarmed at the prospect of the Left being allowed into government, with the wealth taxes and increased controls which might result. There was consequently a massive 'flight of capital' from Italy to places such as Switzerland, as rich Italians in true patriotic fashion fell over themselves to stash their wealth somewhere that they considered safe. Share prices halved between 1961 and 1972, and the balance of payments went into serious deficit. Nevertheless, the recession must be seen in perspective: despite the difficulties, income and the standard of living of the population continued to improve.

The social changes of the 1960s influenced Italy in a particularly deep way. The traditional rural Catholic society was gradually shaken apart by the effects of growing industrialisation and prosperity, by increased exposure to other cultures and ideas as a result of travel and migration, and by the mass communications revolution. Most Italians were better off and could afford to own TV sets; for those who could not there was always a set available at the local bar. The country shrank in size and, arguably for the first time, 'Italy was made'. With these changes came increased awareness, increased confidence, and greater aspirations among workers and, particularly, the young. A subservient and modest life in a society controlled by the clergy and by often cynical and corrupt politicians was no longer enough. People demanded a better standard of living, and in increasing numbers began to reject the status quo and the establishment, including the government, the DC, the Church, the traditional parties of the Left, and even their own trade unions. The weak government of compromise responded to the changes which were occurring with its habitual 'immobilismo'. It was clearly in no position to tackle the fundamental issues, and the ruling DC were losing what public confidence they still commanded as scandal after scandal undermined their credibility. The result was that by the late 1960s key functions in the cities, such as housing, schools, universities, transport, welfare and medical services, had virtually broken down and the country was in turmoil. Italy was about to enter a period of extreme turbulence.

Italy in the 1970s: Hot Autumn, Cultural Revolution and Terrorism

The outbreak of the 'turbulence' can be traced back to November 1967, when shipyard workers went on strike in Genoa and Trieste. This paved the way for a massive outbreak of unofficial strikes, protests and occupations, as the anger of the workers spilled over in a way which the official unions could not handle. The 'tiger' of grass-roots activism was out of the cage, and the bureaucrats in the CGIL, CISL and UIL were in no position to ride it.

At the same time the students were in ferment. The university system had practically ceased to function. The number of students increased by over 50% in the three years following 1968, from 416,000 to 631,000. The quantity and quality of provision at best remained unchanged, however, and in most places deteriorated substantially. In addition, employers were becoming increasingly suspicious of the quality of the degrees which were being awarded – for example, the militants at Milan Polytechnic forced the authorities to introduce 'collective assessment' at one stage; they therefore began to employ fewer graduates. By the mid-1970s industry was employing half the number of graduates it had done in 1969, and only 2% of the total graduate output. Thus a large pool of disaffected and relatively well-educated young people was created; their anger and their frustrations found expression through the active and radical 'movimento studentesco', which brought the universities to a virtual standstill, with colourful but often violent demonstrations and occupations.

The autumn of 1969 was the 'hot autumn' for Italy, as the country lived through an enormous wave of strikes, occupations and demonstrations, particularly in the north. Similar developments were of course occurring throughout the rest of Europe, and in particular in France. What was different in Italy was that the agitation, tension and change did not die down in the early 1970s, but rather continued for most of the decade, spreading even to schools. The troubles brought unity to the trade union movement, as its baffled leaders struggled to keep up with the demands of their membership, and victories which were really significant, on the surface at least, were won by the protestors. Wages increased rapidly. In 1972 the bulk of the workforce became entitled to 150 annual hours of paid education. The right not to be dismissed on economic grounds was established by the extension of the 'Cassa Integrazione Guadagni' in 1975, to guarantee at least 80% of full pay to laid-off workers. Now those who were made redundant would turn up to the workplace, play cards all day, and go home with a virtually full wage packet. Italy became the 'Pompeiian economy', its workers frozen in place like the statues in the famous Roman city. Perhaps most important of all, in 1975 the 'scala mobile' was set up, automatically index-linking the pay of most employees.

Nor were the changes limited to the labour market. In the social sphere, divorce became legal in 1970, and was confirmed as such in a fiercely fought referendum in 1974, much to the chagrin of the Vatican. The traditional Catholic nuclear family was further challenged by a rapid growth in the number of civil marriages, and, worse still, by the increasing number of couples who were not bothering to get married at all. Controlled abortion was introduced in 1978 in response to the demands of the growing women's movement, and was again confirmed by referendum in 1981.

Another bastion of Italian society to suffer serious setbacks in this period was the Church. Its restrictive teachings and norms became increasingly irrelevant to many people in an age of growing awareness and personal freedom. The Vatican was rebuffed over the issues of divorce and abortion. Regular attendance at Sunday mass continued to decline, and the general influence of the clergy over people's lives substantially diminished, particularly in the cities of the centre–north.

A real cultural revolution had occurred, driven from below, and Utopia had arrived. Needless to say, it did not last. The large pay increases of the 'autunno caldo' increased production costs and priced many Italian goods out of the market. Profits slumped, bankruptcies increased, investment plummeted. Inflation was over 20%, and was frozen into the system by indexation. The state corporations made huge losses, IRI alone losing 500 billion lire in 1975, and a staggering 2200 billion Lire, equivalent to 6% of national income, in 1980. At one stage, it was estimated, each Alfasud car which was sold was subsidised by the state to the tune of over £1000. Unemployment was high, and was exacerbated by the reluctance of firms to hire people whom they could not lay off. Naturally the young were worst hit, and there was no social security safety net to fall back on, so there were yet more protests and crime increased. In short, the economy and the basic fabric of society were in tatters. Yet in the midst of all this chaos, and despite a fall of 3.7% in 1975 (the first actual fall since the war), national income remarkably still managed to increase by an average of about 3% pa during the 1970s, much more slowly than in the 1960s but quite fast compared to some other European countries. Furthermore, the 'informal' economy grew to take some of the pressure from the situation.

The already precarious position of the state was made critical by perhaps the most salient feature of the decade: terrorism. Italian terrorism began on the extreme right. The events of the 'autunno caldo' frightened and angered many middle-class people, who looked to the fascists for protection, just as they had done in 1920. The MSI vote increased to over 8% in 1972 and right-wing terrorist squads such as 'Ordine Nuovo' and 'Rosa dei Venti' appeared on the scene – all well financed and with the covert support of influential people within the state. They pursued a 'strategy of tension' – the destabilisation of the state through violence and chaos. Thus they are thought to have planted the bomb at Piazza Fontana in Milan in 1969 which killed sixteen people (the anarchist Pietro Valpreda was arrested for this and spent several years languishing in gaol before being released, prompting Dario Fo's play *The Accidental Death of an Anarchist*). Neo-fascist terrorists also derailed the Rome–Munich express in 1974, killing twelve, and worst of all, they placed a bomb in Bologna railway station in 1980 which killed eighty-four innocent bystanders. There were rumours of a planned coup, but the strategy eventually failed and ultra-right terrorism gradually died away.

Extreme left-wing terrorism grew from the disaffected students and intellectuals in the universities, and from the angry workers in northern factories such as Magneti Marelli and Alfa Romeo in Varese. The number of armed left-wing factions mushroomed, until it was almost possible to permute any three words from workers', red, power, people's, revolutionary, squads, struggle, proletarian, nucleii, fighting, communist and brigades, and have a good chance of coming up with the name of a terrorist group. They either financed themselves through kidnappings and bank robberies, or else received money from rich sympathisers such as Giangiacomo Feltrinelli, who blew himself up trying to cut off Milan's electricity supply by placing a bomb under a pylon at Sagrate. Later they may have received help from abroad. They also enjoyed the tacit support of many on the 'unarmed' left, who often referred to them somewhat sympathetically as 'compagni che sbagliano' (comrades who err). At its height, red terrorism claimed forty victims in a year, in about 2000 incidents. Anyone in authority was fair game, although policemen, managers and DC politicians were the favourite prey. The most famous group were the Red Brigades, founded by Renato Curcio in Milan in 1970; their best-known 'action' was the kidnap and murder of Aldo Moro in 1978, although there were many others, including a daring commando-style raid on DC headquarters in Rome. Perhaps the most colourful, if that is the right word, group were the 'Metropolitan Indians', who grew out of the 'autonomia', or non-aligned radical extra-parliamentary groups, and who were fond of dressing up as North American Indians to shoot their unfortunate victims in the knee-caps. Eventually the Red Brigades and the other groups were broken in the early 1980s by the Carabinieri under General della Chiesa, with the help of confessions and collaboration from 'I Pentiti' (repentant terrorists). The turning-point was the freeing of the American General Dozier from the clutches of his Red Brigades kidnappers in 1981. The state had survived.

What were the government and the political parties doing amid all this chaos? Much as they had always done is the brief answer. The DC vote remained steady at around 38% throughout the 1970s, while the PCI vote increased gradually, reaching a peak of 34.4% in 1976. To maintain power, and keep the Communists out of office, the DC were forced during the early part of the decade to enter into a variety of centre–left coalitions with the smaller parties. There were several prime ministers, the most notable of whom was probably Giulio Andreotti. The DC's task was made easier by the decision of the PCI to enter into the 'historic compromise' in 1976, by which they agreed to maintain a government of national unity, under the DC and with themselves excluded, by abstaining in parliament. This arrangement persisted until 1979, when the PCI changed tack and withdrew their tacit support. It might not have achieved the objectives which Enrico Berlinguer, the PCI's respected leader, had hoped for, but it served to steady the boat during the height of the Red Brigades' challenge to the state. As for the other parties, the vote of the PSI remained unchanged at around 9%, while the MSI vote fell to roughly 5% by the end of the decade. A small, but significant, development here is the emergence of the Radical Party under Marco Pannella, which won eighteen seats in 1979, and exuberantly bartered their votes in parliament in return for the progress of their radical social agenda. They also organised referenda on several radical issues, and perhaps their most far-reaching 'victory' was the ending of the state broadcasting monopoly, previously held by the RAI, in 1976. Henceforth the airwaves of Italy would be filled by a plethora of deregulated private broadcasters, peddling everything from soap powder to hard porn.

Not all cultural developments have been so vulgar, however, for the arts have continued to flourish in post-war Italy. Writers such as Alberto Moravia and Umberto Eco have a genuine international standing. Milan is a major artistic centre. Opera is produced to the highest standards in La Scala and elsewhere. Dario Fo and France Rame have become major and highly inventive 'alternative' playwrights. Above all, perhaps, there is Italian cinema which, apart from spaghetti westerns, has given us major directors such as de Sica, Visconti, Rossellini, Antonioni, Fellini, Pasolini, Rosi, Zeffirelli and Bertolucci, and stars like Anna Magnani, Sophia Loren and Marcello Mastroianni.

Contemporary Italy

Most Italians were probably pleased to see the back of the 1970s. They had been in many ways exciting and heady years, but they had also been troubled and lawless times, in which the economic miracle had ground virtually to a halt, the fabric of society had been shaken apart, and the very existence of the state had been placed in serious doubt.

By contrast the early and mid-1980s were somewhat quiet, a period of retrenchment and regrouping after the storm that had gone before. The decline in the popularity and influence of the Catholic Church was to an extent arrested by Pope John Paul II who, while preaching a conservative dogma, also enthusiastically embraced the possibilities offered by the communications revolution to become a high-profile world figure with his well-publicised journies to the faithful all over the planet. However, the early years of the decade saw continued economic difficulties, with inflation in Italy higher than in most other major countries. The *scala mobile* was still in operation, protecting the living standards of those in work in the 'official' economy, but the whole of the West was in the throes of the monetarist experiment and in recession.

After 1983, with the advent of the Craxi government, the economy picked up, however, and many sectors began to perform remarkably well, giving rise to talk of a second economic miracle. The rate of growth accelerated, inflation slowed down, and the public corporations reduced their deficits. A feature of the economy was the growing importance of the 'underground' or 'informal' economy, which has been estimated to account for between 20 per cent and 30 per cent of national income – perhaps a case of the flair and improvisation of the Italian people refusing to lie down, or else a manifestation of the age-old reluctance of many Italians to be bound by officialdom. Another was the emergence on the scene of big-time entrepreneurs to rival the Agnelli family at FIAT, for example the media giant Belusconi (who, like many of his ilk, has become a household name by buying and financing a football team, in his case A C Milan), Carlo de Benedetti of Olivetti and Raul Gardini (*il contadino* – the peasant) of Ferruzzi-Montedison. In any event, in 1987 the Italians proudly boasted of '*Il Sorpasso*', when the country's national income per head officially overtook Britain's. Italy had finally graduated to the position of a major economic power with a place on the G7 group of countries which try to oversee economic affairs in the Western world. No longer was it 'the most developed of the less developed countries', as Ezio Tarantelli, the economist later murdered by the Red Brigades, was fond of putting it in the late 1970s.

But holding on to the fruits of the mid-eighties' economic advance has, perhaps predictably, proved difficult. In the late 1980s and early 1990s the world economy went into recession, in the wake of events such as the collapse of Communism in East/Central Europe and Russia, the subsequent end of the Cold War, German unification, the US budget deficit, and the collapse of monetarist economics. Italy suffered particularly badly because of the inadequacy and fundamental corruption of its political and bureaucratic system. Furthermore, the Andreotti and Amato governments were forced to take draconian measures on tax, public expenditure and privatisation in an attempt to cut the huge public sector deficit and thus qualify for EC monetary union planned for the turn of the millenium under the Maastricht Treaty, and thus a continuing place in Europe's economic first division. The latter is central to Italian plans for the twenty-first century. Italy is the most fervent supporter of European integration, seeing it as a means not only of consolidating the country's economic achievements and its democracy, but also as the only means of modernising its archaic bureaucracy and system of *clientilismo*. In any event, unemployment increased and living standards fell during this period, and the Lira was forced out of the Exchange Rate Mechanism of the European Monetary System (along with Britain) in September 1992.

Hand in hand with the economic crisis came a political crisis which was to lead to a form of 'velvet revolution' Italian style. It was common knowledge for some time that corruption of various types was endemic in Italian society. There is of course the mafia, but in addition bribes and illicit payments had been used by political parties, and in particular the DC Democrats and the PSI, as a means of both financing their own activities and ensuring the loyalty of their supporters (not to mention lining the pockets of the party hierarchies) – it is no coincidence that Italy, and in particular the Mezzogiorno, has the highest proportion of invalidity pensioners in the world. Blind men who work as chauffeurs and cripples who labour on building sites have long been the subject of resigned and ironic conversation among Italians. From time to time the more glaring cases of corruption would come to the surface, opening up yet more cans of worms of political involvement with organised crime: for example the amusing 'golden sheets' scandal which broke in 1986, and involved inflated contracts placed by the state railway corporation (FS). Italians, it seemed, had learned to live with this state of affairs, as well as with the country's notorious organised crime, with political intrigue typified by the discredited secret services' involvement in the Moro, GLADIO and other affairs, and with a bureaucracy which seems to exist more for the sake of the people who run it than to help the population. The country had after all fared very well despite these aberrations.

At the beginning of the 1990s, however, something changed to end this resigned acceptance of the status quo. The change was precipitated by a determined campaign on the part of the independent judiciary to expose municipal corruption in Milan. This led to large numbers of PSI officials in the city being arrested on corruption charges, and Milan becoming referred to, with typical irreverence, as *tangentopoli* (bribesville). The ramifications of this reached as far as Bettino Craxi, destroying his political career and forcing his resignation in 1993. Buoyed by this success, the judiciary set about exposing corruption of other types and in other places: a host of DC, PSI and other politicians, including many 'untouchable' high profile figures, were systematically exposed and put on trial for dishonesty of seemingly every conceivable type. Even Andreotti, the doyen of the DC and many times prime minister, has been charged with actually being a member of the mafia. The faith of the Italian people in its political leaders, not exactly strong in the first place, collapsed completely.

The general feeling of shock, resentment and loss of confidence in the state was exacerbated by an intensification in the activity of organised crime, with almost daily vendetta killings by its various manifestations: the Sicilian Mafia, the Neopolitan Camorra and the Calabrian 'Ndragh-etta. These organisations are estimated to have been responsible for almost half of Italy's 1,697 murders in 1992. The murder of state officials who dared to challenge organised crime in the South demonstrated gruesomely the inability of the state to overcome this challenge to its authority. General della Chiesa, who was sent to be the Prefect of Palermo as a reward for his efforts in smashing the Red Brigades, had been killed in 1983. But in 1992 the stakes were well and truly raised, and there was a veritable spate of murders of state officials, beginning with the MEP Salvo Lima, Andreotti's right hand man in Sicily, and ending with the outrageous assassination of judges Falcone and Borsellino.

There was now a real attempt by the Amato government to crack down on corruption, particularly at the municipal level, and to challenge the mafia. The attack on organised crime in the South was probably the most concerted one since the days of Mussolini. For example, in November 1992 241 Sicilian gang members were arrested with the help of *pentiti* (informers), and the courts seized mafia assets worth 2000 billion Lire ($1.2 billion) in the course of this year. Several senior bosses, including Salvatore Riina, were arrested, and the interior ministry suspended several municipal councils on the grounds that they were infiltrated by the mafia. It was, however, too late. The anti-corruption judges of 'operation clean hands' continued to expose dirty dealing in all walks of Italian life, from industry to sport, making their leaders such as Antonio DiPietro highly popular national figures in the process. The Amato government collapsed in 1993, and was replaced in 1993 by a 'government of technocrats' headed by Carlo Azeglio Ciampi, formerly of the Bank of Italy. The traditional political parties then suffered catastrophic losses in the 1993 municipal elections, and it became clear that the days of the 'first republic' were strictly numbered.

The 1993 débâcle was the culmination of a period of crisis and decline on the part of most of the traditional main actors in Italy's party system. Racked by continuing scandals (for example P2 and Lockheed), the DC's vote had fallen sharply in 1983 and, despite a marginal recovery in 1987, had fallen to an historical low of 29.7 per cent by 1992. The party was finding the process of maintaining power by alliances that excluded the Communists more and more difficult to manage, so much so that it was forced to concede the premiership to politicians of other parties for much of the previous decade. The first beneficiary was Giovanni Spadolini of the Republican Party. Then, most importantly, came the Socialist Bettino Craxi, who tenaciously held on to the position between 1983–87, and who managed to provide relatively stable government and to oversee economic recovery. There followed a trio of DC Prime Ministers: the youthful Giovanni Goria, Ciriaco de Mita, and the old hand Andreotti yet again, but the latter was succeeded by Giuliano Amato, a Socialist. In a vain attempt to halt the spiral of decline, the party in 1993 attempted the age-old marketing trick of changing its name, in this case to the Partito Popolare (PP).

The principal party of opposition has still to experience government, having been principally concerned with reinventing itself after the collapse of Communism in East/Central Europe and the former USSR. After a protracted period of uncertainty (during which the Party was known as *La Cosa* – the 'thing'), the bulk of the PCI renamed itself the Partito Democratico di Sinistra (PDS, Democratic Party of the Left) and embraced Social Democracy, while a minority of die-hard fundamental marxists broke away and called themselves Rifondazione Comunista (RC). The PDS remains strong in local government, which is particularly significant in Italy, exercising important powers and dispensing around 20 per cent of the national budget. Nationally, however, their share of the vote has been in long term decline since the death of their popular leader Berlinguer. In 1992 they polled only 16.1 per cent, while RC's share of the vote was a mere 5.6 per cent. Under their recent leaders, Alessandro Natta, Achille Occetto, and now D'Alema, the former PCI has still to resolve the question of its attitude to power. It is, however, the only one of the old Italian parties to have retained a reputation for honesty and good government, a fact which should stand it in good stead in the future.

On the left of politics the PCI/PDS had faced stiff opposition from the PSI, who had fared well in the 1980s under Bettino Craxi and the flamboyant disco dancing foreign minister Gianni de Michelis. The 1992 elections could have been their big opportunity to make significant advances on the 14.3 per cent they polled in 1987, but the exposure of their involvement in corruption precluded this and they have now declined to virtual insignificance. The Green Party which, along with similar parties in the rest of Europe, had emerged strongly in the late 1980s, seems to have settled into a role on the fringe of mainstream power politics.

The fascists of the MSI were another group who changed their name in 1993 to Alleanza Nazionale (AN), and under their new leader they continued to command significant support, especially in the South. Support for them has been fuelled by the fears that have resulted over the immigration which Italy has experienced over the last few years. Italy has traditionally been a labour exporting country, of course. But now there are an estimated two million, largely illegal, black migrants in the country, subsisting in the informal economy. These are the *vu cumpra* (*vuoi comprare*, do you want to buy) who trail for miles across beaches under the beating sun attempting to persuade tourists to buy anything from rugs to beads, the hapless young men who wash windscreens at traffic lights, the labourers who work for a pittance at harvest time in the countryside. With immigration has come racism, as well as some violence and thuggery. The state at first reacted in a liberal fashion, granting citizenship to something like one million illegal immigrants, but it has become increasingly restrictive and protectionist under pressure from the Italian electorate and from other EU governments anxious about the influx of outsiders into the new frontier-free Europe. Thus illegal immigrants tend now to be harassed and expelled, and we witness scenes such as the enforced and summary repatriation of boat people from Albania.

The vacuum created by the demise of the now renamed and sometimes revamped traditional parties has been filled by the emergence of new forces. The first on the scene were the Northern Leagues, notably the Lombard League led by the irascible Umberto Bossi. These are right-wing, anti-mafia, anti-Rome, anti-immigrant, anti-tax, separatist parties who gained over 20 per cent of the vote in Lombardy in the 1992 elections. They too have benefited from the new racism that has emerged as a result of immigration. We have also witnessed the creation of the anti-mafia *La Rete* (the Network). Most significant, however, has been the emergence of the *Forza Italia* (Come on, Italy) party led by Silvio Berlusconi. This 'Italian Rupert Murdoch' is a media magnate who, largely through his Finninvest holding company, owns three national television channels, as well as a host of other enterprises, and a plethora of luxury accoutrements such as villas in Sardinia, not to mention the all-conquering AC Milan football club. Forza Italia is basically a right-wing, economically liberal technocratic party, whose rise to prominence has been facilitated by the propaganda skills of its leader and his Finninvest aides. Its popular appeal is based on Berlusconi's promise of change and modernisation, and to the leader's reputation for managerial acumen, the hope that what he did for Finninvest he might be able to do for the country. Cynics claim he entered politics to rescue his financially precarious business interests and to avoid personally the clutches of operation clean hands.

Be that as it may, Forza Italia, in a 'Freedom Alliance' with the Northern League and the neo-fascist AN decisively won the 1994 general election (the coalition polled 42.9 per cent of the vote for the Chamber of Deputies). The centre-left Progressive Alliance of the PDS, RC and La Rete gained only 34.5 per cent, while the PP's Pact for Italy was reduced to a mere 15.7 per cent. The 1994 general election was the first to be contested under a new electoral arrangement, which 82.7 per cent of Italians had supported in a referendum (one of several held on a variety of issues over the last few years) promoted by Mario Segni in 1993. This is a mixture of the British 'first past the post' system and the previous system of proportional representation. It was intended to provide more stable government by ensuring working majorities for the victors. Berlusconi thus became the first Prime Minister of what is sometimes referred to as the 'Second Republic'. In the event, *sua emittenza* (his eminence, the broadcaster) as he has come to be known in Italy, himself came under investigation by the Milan corruption judges, and was forced to resign in late 1994 after being abandoned by his coalition partners from the Northern League.

Berlusconi had offended progressive opinion inside and outside of Italy by allowing the fascists into power. In addition, his regime prompted severe doubts about the real nature of the new order. There was a major row over the conflict of interests between Berlusconi's FINNINVEST holdings (and in particular his media interests) and his state office. Italy also had to endure attacks by his fascist partners on organs of state such as the Bank of Italy, interference in the running of the RAI state media channels, delays in tackling the huge state deficit, anger from the trade unions when attempts were then made to cut pensions, attempts by the Interior Minister Biondi to discredit 'operation clean hands', constant government attacks on the press, and then the arrest of Berlusconi's brother Paolo by the judges of 'clean hands'. Scepticism over Berlusconi's fitness to govern was widespread, typified by a front cover of the high circulation weekly *L'Espresso*, which proclaimed 'An atrocious doubt has arisen: does this man know what he is doing, or is he just a donkey?'

His successor, the former Treasury minister Lamberto Dini, was forced to tread rather more warily. He introduced an economic austerity programme in order to attempt to qualify for the European Monetary Union which is planned around the millennium. He too, however, failed to command a parliamentary majority for very long, and his fall precipitated a general election in April 1996, following the failure on the part of Antonio Maccanico, President Scalfaro's first choice as Dini's successor, to construct a viable parliamentary coalition.

The result was a convincing victory for the centre-left 'ulivo' (olive-tree) grouping which emerged with a clear majority in the Senate, and as the dominant grouping in the Chamber of Deputies. The right of centre Freedom Alliance, dominated by what is left of Silvio Berlusconi's Forza Italia and by Gianfranco Fini's Alleanza Nazionale (formerly the neo-fascist MSI) suffered a convincing defeat, while the separatist Northern League is out of power but retains considerable support in its heartlands. The result is of deep historical significance, since it is the first time that the left of centre parties have held direct power.

L'ulivo is a broad coalition, led by Romano Prodi, the new Prime Minister. He is an economics professor at Bologna University, a member of the small Popular Party, a former head of the IRI State holding company, and he has a sound financial reputation, as well as a track record as a promoter of privatisation. The grouping also includes other paragons of financial rectitude, notably the former Prime Ministers and central bankers Lamberto Dini and Carlo Azeglio Ciampi. In numerical terms it is dominated by the PDS (Partito Democratico di Sinistra, the social democratic majority from the old PCI Communist Party which is led by Massimo D'Alema), and it also includes members of minority groupings, including some left of centre former Christian Democrats. The new government will on the surface have to rely on the support of Rifondazione Communista (the Marxist rump of the old PCI) for a majority in the Chamber of Deputies, although leading members of the coalition (such as Walter Veltroni, Italy's 'baby Blair'), have expressed a willingness to take an eclectic stance to power, forming alliances with LN and even members of the defeated Freedom Alliance on specific issues.

The hope is that the ulivo will provide relatively enlightened and stable government for an extended period of time, whilst at the same time implementing the economic, financial and structural policies and reforms that are required to modernise the Italian state and qualify Italy for EMU. The initial portents were good, and the new government was welcomed by financial markets and by the world media, one suspects both for its own virtues and out of a sense of relief at the defeat of a politician under investigation for corruption and of maverick groups such as AN and LN. The initial euphoria has since been somewhat moderated in light of uncertainties about the stability of the coalition with RC precipitation a crisis over planned welfare cuts. The new government has faced pressure for constitutional change (increased federalism or even the break up of the unitary state) from Umberto Bossi's LN party who refer to Northern Italy as the state of Padania. It has also faced widespread opposition to its plan for further austerity intended to prepare Italy for EMU, which has now become a central economic and political objective of virtually every party and interest group in the country (apart from RC). Most Italians dread the prospect of the humiliation of 'not qualifying for Europe'. The portents here are good, the likelihood being that Italy will in fact succeed in qualifying for the EMU that is planned for the millennium. If it does, this will represent a major collective success, and perhaps a turning point for the country, with significant reform being imposed from without.

What of the future? The emergence of the ulivo provides grounds for some optimism, but there remain fundamental uncertainties surrounding the 'Second Republic'. The old system, for all its failings, oversaw the rapid social and economic development of the country. It also made 'Italy out of Italians', to the extent that this is possible for a people that are so fundamentally irreverent, independent, and attached to their families and their localities. What the new status quo eventually delivers remains to be seen. One of the dangers is that the new order will divide the country. Elections since 1994 have to an extent segmented Italy into three parts: the North (Padania) which is largely controlled by the Northern League (which of course is hostile to the South and the money the state spends on it), the Centre which is dominated by the PDS and the other parties of the Left, and the South, in which the fascists and the PP are particularly strong.

Nevertheless, it is also true that Italy has become the prosperous, thoroughly modern, open and European society that it now is largely in spite of happenings in the political sphere. Italians are deeply interested in politics, but at the end of the day they tend to shrug their shoulders and get on with their activities and the serious business of enjoying life. This seems destined to continue. An interesting development on the social sphere has been the collapse of the birth rate. The average Italian female now produces just 1.2 children – the lowest in the world. This has certainly increased the prosperity of the current generation, but may well produce problems in the future.

This, then, is the Italy of today. We have seen how the Italian people have come to be what they are and where they are at present. Of course there are many problems, old and new. But then, there always have been. In the long run, however, things continue to get better, and overall the Italians are entitled to regard the future with a certain amount of enthusiasm and optimism. There is a big place for their drive, their energy, their flair, their humour and their basic humanity in the context of an ever more integrated Europe, and indeed world. Above all, Italy remains what it has never ceased to be: a good place to live and to visit.

Notes

Notes

Roman Emperors of the Great Period, 27 BC-AD 337

Augustus *27 BC–AD 14*
Tiberius *14–37*
Caligula *37–41*
Claudius *41–54*
Nero *54–68*
Galba *68–69*
Otho *69*
Vitellius *69*
Vespasian *69–79*
Titus *79–81*
Domitian *81–96*
Nerva *96–98*
Trajan *98–117*
Hadrian *117–138*
Antonius Pius *138–161*
Marcus Aurelius *161–180*
Lucius Verus *161–169*
Commodus *180–192*
Pertinax *193*
Didius Julianus *193*
Septimius Severus *193–211*
Caracalla *211–217*
Geta *211–212*
Macrinus *217–218*
Elagabalus *218–222*
Severus Alexander *222–235*
Maximinus *235–238*
Gordian I *238*
Gordian II *238*
Balbinus *238*
Pupienus *238*
Gordian III *238–244*
Philip *244–249*
Decius *249–251*
Trebonianus *251–253*
Aemilianus *253*
Valerianus *253–260*
Gallienus *253–268*
Claudius Gothicus *268–270*
Aurelian *270–275*
Tacitus *275–276*
Florianus *276*
Probus *276–282*
Carus *282 –283*
Carinus *283–285*
Numerianus *283–284*
Diocletian *284–305*
Maximian *286–305*
Constantius *292–306*
Galerius *293–311*
Licinius *311–323*
Constantine *306–337*

Popes of the Renaissance

Avignon

John XXII *1316–1334*
Benedict XII *1334–1342*
Clement VI *1342–1352*
Innocent VI *1352–1362*
Urban V *1362–1370*
Gregory XI *1370–1378*

The Great Schism

Urban VI *1378–1389*
Clement VII *1378–1384* (Avignon)
Boniface IX *1389–1404*
Benedict XIII *1394–1423* (Avignon)
Innocent VII *1404–1406*
Gregory XII *1406–1415*
Alexander V *1409–1410* (Pisa)
John XII *1410–1415* (Pisa)

Rome

Martin V *1417–1431*
Clement VIII *1423–1429* (Anti-Pope)
Eugenius IV *1431–1447*
Felix V *1439–1449* (Anti-Pope)
Nicholas V *1447–1455*
Calixtus III *1455–1458* [Borgia]
Pius II *1458–1464* [Piccolomini]
Paul II *1464–1471*
Sixtus IV *1471–1484* [Della Rovere]
Innocent VIII *1484–1492* [Cibò]
Alexander VI *1492–1503* [Borgia]
Pius III *1503* [Piccolomini]
Julius II *1503–1513* [Della Rovere]
Leo X *1513–1521* [Medici]
Adrian VI *1522–1523*
Clement VII *1523–1534* [Medici]
Paul III *1534–1549* [Farnese]

Emperors of the Renaissance

Henry VII of Luxemburg *1308–1314*
Louis IV of Bavaria *1314–1347*
Charles IV of Luxemburg *1347–1378*
Wenceslas of Luxemburg *1378–1400*
Rupert of the Palatinate *1400–1410*
Sigismund of Luxemburg *1410–1437*
Albert II of Habsburg *1437–1439*
Frederick III of Habsburg *1440–1493*
Maximilian I of Habsburg *1493–1519*
Charles V of Habsburg *1519–1556*

Venetian Doges of the Renaissance

Giorgio ('Zorzi') Marino *1311–1312*
Giovanni Soranza *1312–1328*
Francesco Dandolo *1328–1339*
Bartolomeo Gradenigo *1339–1342*
Andrea Dandolo *1343–1354*
Marino Faliero *1354–1355*
Giovanni Gradenigo *1355–1356*
Giovanni Dolfino *1356–1361*
Lorenzo Celsi *1361–1365*
Marco Cornaro *1365–1368*
Andrea Contarini *1368–1382*
Michele Morosini *1382*
Antonio Venier *1382–1400*
Michele Steno *1400–1413*
Tommaso Mocenigo *1414–1423*
Francesco Foscarini *1423–1457*
Pasquale Malipiero *1457–1462*
Cristoforo Moro *1462–1471*
Niccolo Tron *1471–1473*
Niccolo Marcello *1473–1474*
Pietro Mocenigo *1474–1476*
Andrea Vendramin *1476–1478*
Giovanni Mocenigo *1478–1485*
Marco Barbarigo *1485–1486*
Agostino Barbarigo *1486–1501*
Leonardo Loredano *1501–1521*
Antonio Grimani *1521–1523*
Andrea Gritti *1523–1539*

Kings of Naples of the Renaissance

Robert of Anjou *1309–1343*
Giovanna I of Anjou *1343–1381*
Charles III of Durazzo *1381–1386*
Louis II of Anjou *1386–1400*
Ladislas of Durazzo *1400–1414*
Giovanna II of Anjou-Durazzo *1414–1435*
(Louis II of Anjou *1424–1434*)
Rene of Anjou *1435–1442*
Alfonso I of Aragon *1442–1458*
Ferdinand I (Ferrante) of Aragon *1458–1494*
Alfonso II of Aragon *1494–1495*
Ferdinand II *1495–1496*
(Charles VIII of France *1495*)
Federico of Aragon *1496–1501*
Louis XII of France *1501–1503*

Followed by Spanish governors

Italian Artists, 1200–1600

(In order of birth)

Nicola Pisano *c.1200–c.1284*
Giovanni Cimabue *1240–1302*
Giovanni Pisano *1245/50–after 1314*
Duccio *1255/60–1315/18*
Giotto *1266/7–1337*
Pietro Cavallini *fl.1273–1308*
Pietro Lorenzetti *1280–1348*
Simone Martini *1284–1344*
Tino da Camaino *c.1285–1337*
Andrea Pisano *c.1290–1348*
Pietro Lorenzetti *fl.1306–1345*
Andrea Orcagna *c.1308–1368*
Ambrogio Lorenzetti *fl.1319–1347*
Gentile da Fabriano *1340–1427*
Jacopo della Quercia *1374–1438*
Filippo Brunelleschi *1377–1446*
Lorenzo Ghiberti *1378–1455*
Donatello *1386–1466*
Fra Angelico *1387–1455*
Antonio Pisanello *c.1395–1455/6*
Michelozzo Michelozzi *1396–1472*
Paolo Uccello *1396/7–1475*
Luca della Robbia *1400–1482*
Jacopo Bellini *c.1400–1470*
Domenico Veneziano *d.1461*
Masaccio *1401–1428*
Giovanni di Paolo *1403–1482*
Leon Battista Alberti *1404–1472*
Filippo Lippi *1406–1469*
Piero della Francesca *1410/20–1492*
Andrea del Castagno *1419/21–1457*
Benozzo Gozzoli *1420–1497*
Gentile Belli *1429–1507*
Giovanni Bellini *1430–1516*
Antonello da Messina *c.1430–1479*
Carlo Crivelli *1430/35–1494/1500*
Andrea Mantegna *1431–1506*
Antonio del Pollaiuolo *1432–1498*
Andrea del Verrocchio *1435–1488*
Piero Pollaiuolo *1443–1496*
Sandro Botticelli *1444–1510*
Donato Bramante *1444–1514*
Luca Signorelli *1445/50–1523*
Perugino (Pietro Vanucci) *1446–1523*
Melozzo da Forli *1448–1494*
Domenico Ghirlandaio *1449–1495*
Leonardo da Vinci *1452–1519*
Pinturicchio (Bernardino di Betto) *1454–1513*
Antonio da Sangallo *1455–1534*
Filippino Lippi *1457–1504*
Vittore Carpaccio *1460–1526*
Andrea Sansovino *1467/71–1529*
Fra Bartolommeo *1474–1517*
Michelangelo Buonarroti *1475–1564*
Giorgione *1476/8–1510*
Lorenzo Lotto *1480–1555/6*
Bernardini Luini *1481/2–1532*
Raphael (Raffaello Sanzio) *1483–1520*

Andrea del Sarto *1486–1530*
Titian (Tiziano Vecelli) *1487/90–1576*
Antonio Correggio *1489–1534*
Giulio Romano *1492–1546*
Benvenuto Cellini *1500–1571*
Agnolo Bronzino *1502–1572*
Francesco Parmigianino *1504–1540*
Andrea Palladio *1508–1580*
Giorgio Vasari *1511–1574*
Bartolommeo Ammanati *1511–1592*
Jacopo Tintoretto *1518–1594*
Paolo Veronese (Caliari) 1528–1588
Giambologna (Giovanni da Bologna) *1529–1608*
Ludovico Carracci *1555–1619*
Carlo Maderno *1556–1629*
Agostino Carracci *1557–1602*
Annibale Carracci *1560–1609*
Orazio Gentileschi *1563–1639*
Michelangelo Caravaggio *1573–1610*
Guido Reni *1575–1642*
Francesco Albani *1578–1660*
Bernardo Strozzi *1581–1644*
Guercino (Francesco Barbieri) *1591–1666*
Pietro da Cortona *1596–1669*
Gianlorenzo Bernini *1598–1680*
Francesco Borromini *1599–1667*

Selected Major Artists since 1600

Andrea Pozzo *1642–1709*
Vittore Ghislandi *1655–1743*
Alessandro Magnasco *1677–1749*
Giambattista Tiepolo *1696–1770*
Antonio Canaletto *1697–1768*
Luigi Vanvitelli *1700–1773*
Pietro Longhi *1702–1785*
Francesco Guardi *1712–1793*
Giovanni Battista Piranesi *1720–1778*
Andrea Appiani *1754–1817*
Antonio Canova *1757–1822*
Carlo Carva *1881–1966*
Umberto Boccioni *1882–1916*
Amedeo Modigliani 1884–1920
Giorgio de' Chirico *1888–1978*
Giorgio Morandi *1890–1964*
Marico Marini *1901–1980*
Giacomo Manzù 1908–

Heads of State, Popes and Prime Ministers of United Italy

Heads of State

VITTORIO EMANUELE II, 1861–1878 UMBERTO I, 1878–1900 VITTORIO EMANUELE III, 1900–1946 UMBERTO II, 1946	Kings of Italy
ENRICO DE NICOLA, 1946–1948	Provisional Head of State
LUIGI EINAUDI, 1948–1955 GIOVANNI GRONCHI, 1955–1962 ANTONIO SEGNI, 1962–1964 GIUSEPPE SARAGAT, 1964–1971 GIOVANNI LEONE, 1971–1978 SANDRO PERTINI, 1978–1985 FRANCESCO COSSIGA, 1985–1992 OSCAR LUIGI SCALFARO, 1992–	Presidents of the Italian Republic

Popes

PIUS IX (MASTAI-FERRETTI), 1846–1878
LEO XIII (PECCI), 1878–1903
SAINT PIUS X (SARTO), 1903–1914
BENEDICT XV (DELLA CHIESA), 1914–1922
PIUS XI (RATTI), 1922–1939
PIUS XII (PACELLI), 1939–1958
JOHN XXIII (RONCALLI), 1958–1963
PAUL VI (MONTINI), 1963–1978
JOHN PAUL I (LUCIANI), 1978
JOHN PAUL II (WOJTYA), 1978–

Prime Ministers

CAMILLO DI CAVOUR, 1860–1861
BETTINO RICASOLI, 1861–1862
URBANO RATTAZZI, 1862
LUIGI FARINI, 1862–1863
MARCO MINGHETTI, 1863–1864
ALFONSO LAMARMORA, 1864–1866
BETTINO RICASOLI, 1866–1867
URBANO RATTAZZI, 1867
LUIGI MENABREA, 1867–1869
GIOVANNI LANZA, 1869–1873
MARCO MINGHETTI, 1873–1876
AGOSTINO DEPRETIS, 1876–1878
BENEDETTO CAIROLI, 1878
AGOSTINO DEPRETIS, 1878–1879
BENEDETTO CAIROLI, 1879–1881
AGOSTINO DEPRETIS, 1881–1887
FRANCESCO CRISPI, 1887–1891
ANTONIO DI RUDINI, 1891–1892
GIOVANNI GIOLITTI, 1892–1893
FRANCESCO CRISPI, 1893–1896
ANTONIO DI RUDINI, 1896–1898
LUIGI PELLOUX, 1898–1900
GIUSEPPE SARACCO, 1900–1901
GIUSEPPE ZANARDELLI, 1901–1903
GIOVANNI GIOLITTI, 1903–1905
ALESSANDRO FORTIS, 1905–1906
SIDNEY SONNINO, 1906
GIOVANNI GIOLITTI, 1906–1909
SIDNEY SONNINO, 1909–1910
LUIGI LUZZATTI, 1910–1911
GIOVANNI GIOLITTI, 1911–1914
ANTONIO SALANDRA, 1914–1916
PAOLO BOSELLI, 1916–1917
VITTORIO ORLANDO, 1917–1919
FRANCESCO NITTI, 1919–1920
GIOVANNI GIOLITTI, 1920–1921
IVANOE BONOMI, 1921–1922
LUIGI FACTA, 1922
BENITO MUSSOLINI, 1922–1943
PIETRO BADOGLIO, 1943–1944
IVANOE BONOMI, 1944–1945

FERRUCCIO PARRI, 1945
ALCIDE DE GASPERI, 1945–1953
GUISEPPE PELLA, 1953–1954
AMINTORE FANFANI, 1954
MARIO SCELBA, 1954–1955
ANTONIO SEGNI, 1955–1957
ADONE ZOLI, 1957–1958
AMINTORE FANFANI, 1958–1959
ANTONIO SEGNI, 1959–1960
FERNANDO TAMBRONI, 1960
AMINTORE FANFANI, 1960–1963
GIOVANNI LEONE, 1963
ALDO MORO, 1963–1968
GIOVANNI LEONE, 1968
MARIANO RUMOR, 1968–1970
EMILIO COLOMBO, 1971–1972
GIULIO ANDREOTTI, 1972–1973
MARIANO RUMOR, 1973–1974
ALDO MORO, 1974–1976
GUILIO ANDREOTTI, 1976–1979
FRANCESCO COSSIGA, 1979–1980
ARNALDO FORLANI, 1980–1981
GIOVANNI SPADOLINI, 1981–1982
AMINTORE FANFANI, 1982–1983
BETTINO CRAXI, 1983–1987
GIOVANNI GORIA, 1987–1988
CIRIACO DE MITA, 1988–1989
GIULIO ANDREOTTI, 1989–1992
GIULIANO AMATO, 1992–1993
CARLO AZEGLIO CIAMPI, 1993–1994
SILVIO BERLUSCONI, 1994
LAMBERTO DINI, 1995–1996
ROMANO PRODI, 1996–

Chronology of Major Events

B.C.	
c. 200,000	First traces of human life in the peninsula
c. 60,000	Middle Palaeolithic period; Neanderthal humans
c. 30,000	Upper Palaeolithic period; first humans in Sicily
c. 10,000	Cro-Magnon human life
c. 5000	Mesolithic period
c. 3500–2500	Neolithic period
c. 2000–1800	Copper Age; Palafitte culture
c. 1800–1000	Bronze Age; Terramare and Apennine cultures
c. 1400	Mycenaean traders in Sicily
c. 800	Iron Age; Villanovan cultures; Greek settlement in Sicily and the south
753(trad.)	Foundation of Rome by Romulus
753–617(trad.)	First four Roman monarchs
c. 700	Beginning of Etruscan period
c. 650	Etruscan expansion in the south
616–510	Etruscan rule in Rome
524	Battle of Cumae; Greeks halt Etruscan expansion to the south
509	Beginning of the Roman republic; Roman domination of Latium
501	First Republican dictator in Rome
c. 500	Etruscan expansion in northern Italy
494	First plebeian secession in Rome
471	Tribunes and Plebeian Council officially recognised
451–450	Twelve tables of law published in Rome
433	Temple of Apollo
420	Etruscan cities in south fall to Sabellians
400	Celtic penetration of Etruscan territory in north begins
396	Veii captured by the Romans
390	Gallic sack of Rome

350	Felsina taken by the Romans
334–264	Roman conquest and colonisation of Italy
312	Via Appia and Aqua Appia
308	Tarquinii falls to the Romans
289	Roman mint established
280	Tomb of Scipios
289–275	Roman war with Pyrrhus
265	Volsinii captured by the Romans; end of Etruscan period
264–241	First Punic war
241	Sicily made first Roman province
238	Provinces of Sardinia and Corsica
229–219	Illyrian wars
225	Gallic invasion of Italy; battle of Telamon
221	Circus Flaminius
218–202	Second Punic war
202–191	Conquest of Galia Cisalpina
200–197	Second Macedonian war
197–133	Lusitanian and Celtiberian wars
191–188	Syrian war
184	Cato censor
172–168	Third Macedonian war
149–146	Third Punic war; destruction of Carthage
136–132	First slave war in Sicily
133, 123–122	Gracchi tribunates
121	Province of Galia Narbonensis
120	Temple of Fortuna in Praeneste
118–117	Dalmatian campaigns
112–105	Jugurthine war
107, 104–100, 86	Marius consul
104–102	Second slave war in Sicily
101	Defeat of Germanic invasion
91–89	Social war
87–84	Cinna consul
81–79	Sulla dictator
73–71	Spartacus in revolt
60	First Triumvirate
50	Julius Caesar crosses the Rubicon
49–44	Julius Caesar dictator

A.D.

27 BC–AD 68	Julio–Claudian emperors

42	Annexation of Mauretania
43	Britain occupied
64	Fire of Rome
69–117	Flavio–Trajan emperors
66–73	Jewish revolt
79	Vesuvius erupts; Colosseum completed
86–92	Dacian wars
114	Armenia annexed
117–193	Antonine emperors
122–142	Hadrian's Wall built in Britain
128	Rebuilding of Pantheon completed
134	Hadrian's Villa at Tivoli completed
165	Province of Mesopotamia formed
167	Barbarians invade Dacia
193–235	Severan emperors
219	Caracalla's Baths built
259–273	Rebel Gallic state
271	Aurelius builds walls around Rome
272	Goths take Dacia
287–296	British rebellion
293	Diocletian establishes tetrarchy
303–305	Persecution of Christians
313	Freedom of worship for Christians
315	Constantine's Arch built in Rome
324–337	Constantine sole emperor
376	Goths permitted to settle in empire
395	Final East–West division of empire; Visigoths invade Greece
402	Imperial seat moved to Ravenna
410	Sack of Rome by Alaric
439	Vandals rule Carthage
455	Sack of Rome by Vandals
476	Last western emperor, Romulus Augustulus, deposed; Odoacer becomes king of Italy
490	Theodoric invades Italy
490–552	Ostrogothic kingdom of Italy
526	Death of Theodoric
535–540	Byzantine reconquest
552	Last Ostrogothic kings die
568	Lombard invasion under Alboin
568–774	Lombard kingdom of Italy
590–604	Pope Gregory I
643	Rothari's edict
700–720	Monasteries built at Farfa, San Vincenzo and Montecassino

754	Pepin III invades Italy
773–774	Charlemagne conquers Italy
800	Charlemagne first Holy Roman Emperor
827	Arab invasion of Sicily
839–849	Civil war in Benevento
855–875	Louis II emperor
876	Start of Byzantine reconquest of south
888–905	Civil war against King Berengar
899	First Hungarian invasion
902	Arabs complete capture of Sicily
903	First royal charter of incastellamento
924	Hungarians sack Pavia
962–973	Otto I first German emperor
1012–28	Pope Benedict VIII; height of aristocratic papacy
1024	Sack of royal palace of Pavia; symbolic end of Italian state
1034	Aversa granted to Normans by the duke of Naples
1053	Normans defeat Leo IX at Civitate
1059	Robert Guiscard invested with Apulia, Calabria and Sicily
1061–91	Norman conquest of Sicily
1071	Normans capture Bari; end of Byzantine rule
1072	Normans take Palermo
1073–85	Pope Gregory VII (Hildebrand)
1075	Normans capture Salerno
1077	Henry IV humiliated at Canossa
1081	Henry IV invades Italy
1082	Florence goes to war against Siena
1084	Henry IV crowned emperor by Antipope; Norman sack of Rome
1085	Robert Guiscard dies
1088–99	Pope Urban II
1101	Count Roger I of Sicily dies; Roger II succeeds him
1111	Henry V crowned emperor
1122	Concordat of Worms
1130	Roger II becomes king of Sicily
1130–43	Pope Innocent II
1130–38	Anacletus II Antipope
1135	Amalfi sacked by Pisa
1147–49	Second Crusade
1154–59	Pope Adrian IV (Nicholas Breakspeare)
1154–66	William I king of Sicily
1155	Rome under Interdict; Frederick Barbarossa crowned emperor
1158	Diet of Roncaglia

1162	Milan burned by Barbarossa
1166–89	William II king of Sicily
1176	Barbarossa defeated by Lombard League at Legnano
1183	Treaty of Constance; legal position of Communes established
1189	Tancred succeeds William II in Sicily
1190	Barbarossa dies on Third Crusade
1190–1225	Growth of Popular Communes
1191–96	Henry VI emperor
1194	Henry VI conquers Sicily
1198	Frederick II becomes king of Sicily
1198–1216	Pope Innocent III
1204	Sack of Constantinople on Fourth Crusade
1216	Dominican Order founded
1220	Frederick II crowned emperor
1223	Franciscan Order founded
1226	Death of St Francis of Assisi
1227–41	Pope Gregory IX
1237	Lombard League defeated by Frederick II at Cortenuova
1250	Death of Frederick II
1252	First European gold coins minted in Florence
1260	Battle of Montaperti, Siena defeats Florence; Charles of Anjou invades Italy
1265–1321	Dante Alighieri
1265	Charles of Anjou invested with Naples and Sicily
1266	Charles defeats Manfred at Benevento
1268	Charles defeats Conradin at Tagliacozzo
1271–76	Pope Gregory X
1282	Revolt of Sicilian Vespers
1284	Battle of Meloria, Genoa defeats Pisa
1292–94	Pope Celestine V
1294–1303	Pope Boniface VIII
1295	Matteo Visconti signore of Milan
1296	Building of Florentine Duomo begins
1298	Marco Polo returns to Venice
1301	Palazzo Vecchio in Florence completed
1302	Treaty of Caltabelotta
1303	Boniface VIII seized at Anagni
1304–74	Petrarch
1305–77	Exile of Papacy
1310–40	Construction of Doge's Palace in Venice
1312	Henry VII crowned emperor in Rome; Can Grande della Scala Imperial Vicar of Verona and Vicenza

1313–75	Boccaccio
1314–21	Dante writes *Divina Commedia*
1328	Louis IV crowned emperor in Rome
1337	Death of Giotto
1343	Giovanna I Queen of Naples
1347	Cola di Rienzo tribune in Rome
1348–9	Black Death rages in Italy
1348–53	Boccaccio writes the *Decameron*
1353–57	Cardinal Albornoz restores authority of Pope in central Italy
1354	Cola di Rienzo murdered
1367–70	Temporary return of Urban V to Rome
1375–1406	Colluccio Salutati chancellor of Florence
1377	Brunelleschi born
1377	Gregory VII returns to Rome
1378–1415	The Great Schism
1378	Revolt of the Ciompi in Florence
1380	Venice defeats Genoa at Chioggia
1385	Gian Galeazzo Visconti becomes ruler of Milan
1386	Donatello born
1402	Death of Gian Galeazzo Visconti
1406	Florence annexes Pisa
1409	Council of Pisa
1414–18	Council of Constance ends schism
1420	Pope Martin V returns to Rome
1433–34	Exile of Cosimo de' Medici
1434	Cosimo de' Medici rises to power in Florence
1436	Cupola of Florence Duomo completed
1440	Donation of Constantine proved a forgery
1442	Alfonso of Aragon captures Naples from Angevins
1444	Federigo Montefeltre duke of Urbino
1444	Sandro Botticelli and Donato Bramante born
1450	Francesco Sforza becomes ruler of Milan
1452–1519	Leonardo da Vinci
1454	Treaty of Lodi between Milan and Venice
1455	The Italian League
1458–64	War of succession between Angevins and Aragonese
1465	First Italian press established at Subiaco
1469	Lorenzo de' Medici becomes ruler of Florence; Machiavelli born
1470	Venetian defeat at Negroponte
1474–1533	Ludovico Ariosto
1475–1564	Michelangelo Buonarroti
1478	The Pazzi conspiracy

1478–80	War between Florence, Venice, Milan and the Papacy, Siena, Naples
1480	Lodovico Sforza comes to power in Milan
1483	Sistine Chapel consecrated
1483–1520	Raphael
1486–87	The Barons' war in Naples
1487	Titian born
1494	Charles VIII of France invades Italy; the Medici expelled from Florence
1498	Savonarola burnt as a heretic
1499–1503	Cesare Borgia captures Romagna
1499	Louis XII invades Italy
1500	Lodovico Sforza captured and banished from Milan
1500	Benvenuto Cellini born
1508–09	League of Cambrai
1509	Venetian defeat at Agnadello
1508–12	Michelangelo paints ceiling of the Sistine Chapel
1512	Medici return to Florence; Battles of Ravenna and Novara
1513	Giovanni de' Medici becomes Pope Leo X
1521	Imperial troops drive French from Milan
1525	Battle of Pavia
1527	Sack of Rome by Charles V; symbolic end of Renaissance
1527–30	Florentine Republic
1530	Treaty of Cambrai
1530–37	Alessandro de' Medici rules Florence
1532	Machiavelli's *Il Principe* published
1534–49	Pope Paul III
1535–44	War between Charles V and Francis I
1537–41	Michelangelo paints the Last Judgement
1540	Jesuit Order founded
1542	Roman Inquisition
1544–95	Torquato Tasso
1545	Pier Luigi Farnese made duke of Parma
1545–63	Council of Trent
1548–1600	Giordano Bruno
1555–59	Pope Paul IV
1559	Treaty of Cateau-Cambrésis
1559–80	Emanuele Filiberto becomes duke of Savoy
1564–1642	Galileo Galilei
1567–1643	Claudio Monteverdi
1571	Battle of Lepanto
1595–1631	Federico Borromeo Archbishop of Milan
1597	Clement VIII annexes Ferrara

1598–1680	Gianlorenzo Bernini
1606–7	Interdict on Venice by Paul V
1612–17	Wars of Monferrato and Valtellina
1618–48	Thirty Years War
1627–31	Second war of Monferrato
1630	Sack of Mantova
1631	Urbino annexed by Urban VIII
1633	Galileo condemned in Rome
1641–44	War of Castro
1647–48	Revolts in Naples and Palermo
1659	Peace of the Pyrenees
1674	Revolt in Messina
1676–1741	Antonio Vivaldi
1684	French fleet bomb Genoa
1700–13	Wars of Spanish succession
1706	Battle of Turin
1707–93	Carlo Goldoni
1713	Peace of Utrecht; end of Spanish domination; Italy partitioned
1714–18	Venice at war with Turkey
1720	Peace of Cambrai; Piedmont becomes Piedmont–Sardinia
1732	Don Carlos of Bourbon becomes duke of Parma
1732	Don Carlos crowned Charles II of Naples
1737	End of Medici; Francis of Lorraine ruler of Florence
1748	Peace of Aix-la-Chapelle
1749–1803	Vittorio Alfieri
1755	Genoa sells Corsica to France
1764	Cesare Beccaria publishes *Dei Delitti e delle Pene*
1764–66	Pietro Verri edits *Il Caffè*
1770	Enlightenment reformer Leopold, Grand Duke of Tuscany
1773	Clement XIV dissolves Jesuits
1785–1873	Alessandro Manzoni
1792–1868	Gioachino Rossini
1796–97	Napoleon's first Italian campaign
1797	Treaty of Campo Formio; Venice given to Austria; Cisalpine, Ligurian and Roman republics
1798	French Parthenopean Republic in Naples
1798–1837	Giacomo Leopardi
1799	Austrians and Russians expel French from Italy; persecution of republicans in south
1800–1	Napoleon recaptures Italy
1801	Treaty of Luneville
1801–2	Italian Republic

1805	Kingdom of Italy
1806	Joseph Bonaparte becomes king of Naples
1807–82	Giuseppe Garibaldi
1808	Joachim Murat king of Naples; French capture Rome
1809	Pius VII exiled
1812	Constitution of Cadiz
1813–1901	Giuseppe Verdi
1815	Congress of Vienna; Murat executed
1817	Macerata revolt
1818–19	*Il Conciliatore* published
1820	Revolts at Nola, Avellino and Naples
1821	Revolt in Piedmont; repression follows end of revolts
1831	Mazzini founds Giovine Italia; revolt in Modena and Bologna
1833	Repression of Mazzinians in Piedmont
1843	*Il Primato* published by Vincenzo Gioberti
1844	Expedition of the Fratelli Bandiera
1846–78	Pope Pius IX
1848	Revolts in Sicily and Milan; Republic of Venice declared
1848–49	First War of Independence; Piedmontese defeated by Austrians
1849	Republic of Rome; despotism restored
1849–78	Vittorio Emanuele II
1852	Cavour prime minister of Piedmont
1854	Piedmontese involvement in the Crimean War
1857	Piscacane's expedition
1858–1924	Giacomo Puccini
1858	Plombières meeting between Cavour and Napoleon III
1859	Second War of Independence; Battle of Solferino; Peace of Villafranca
1859–60	Piedmont annexes most of northern Italy; Nice and Savoy ceded to France
1860	Garibaldi and the Thousand capture Sicily and the south
1861	Vittorio Emanuele II king of Italy; first elections and parliament of united Italy
1861–76	Right in parliamentary power
1862	Garibaldi wounded at Asapromonte
1865	Capital moved from Turin to Florence
1866	Venice becomes part of Italian kingdom after Third War of Independence
1866–1852	Benedetto Croce
1867	Garibaldi defeated at Mentana
1867–1936	Luigi Pirandello

1870	Rome captured and becomes capital; unification complete; Law of Guarantees
1876–1915	Radicals dominate the parliamentary scene
1876–1887	Depretis and *trasformismo*
1878–1900	Umberto I
1878–1903	Pope Leo XIII
1882	Triple Alliance
1885	Occupation of Massawa
1887–96	Crispi's premierships
1890	Eritrea colonised
1892	Filippo Turati founds Italian Socialist Party
1893	Civil unrest in Sicily
1895–1937	Antonio Gramsci
1896	Battle of Adowa
1898	Riots in Milan, breakdown of law & order in much of country
1900	Umberto I assassinated; Vittorio Emanuele III king
1901–15	Giolitti's premierships
1902–7	Widespread strikes
1909	Marinetti launches futurism
1911	Electoral reform extends franchise
1911–12	Conquest of Libya
1912	Mussolini becomes editor of *Avanti!*
1915	Italy enters World War I
1917	Defeat of Caporetto
1918	Victories of the Piave and Vittorio Veneto
1919	Italy snubbed at Versailles; D'Annunzio seizes Fiume; proportional representation adopted; Mussolini organises Fascist group
1920	Rapallo conference; squadristi appear
1921	Mussolini forms Fascist Party; PCI formed
1922	March on Rome; Mussolini prime minister
1923	Corfu incident
1924	Murder of Matteotti
1925–27	Fascist state established
1925	Treaty of Locarno
1929	Lateran Agreements
1935–36	Abyssinian war; League of Nations sanctions
1936–39	Intervention in favour of Franco in Spanish Civil War
1936	Axis formed between Italy and Germany
1939	Pact of Steel with Germany; occupation of Albania
1940	Italy enters World War II on German side
1941–43	Italians fight in Yugoslavia, Russia and Africa; defeat in

	Africa; Allies land in Sicily; anti-Fascist action; Badoglio government; Republic of Salò; Badoglio declares war on Germany
1944	Anzio landings; Allies take Rome
1945	Resistance movement; liberation of Florence; German surrender
1946	Abdication of Vittorio Emanuel III; referendum rejects monarchy; Umberto II exiled; Italian Republic set up
1946–	Christian Democrat domination of government
1946–53	De Gasperi premierships
1947	Saragat founds Social Democratic Party, splitting from Nenni's Socialist Party
1948	Attempt to assassinate Togliatti; Einaudi first President of the Republic
1949	Italy becomes a member of NATO
1954	City of Trieste returned to Italy
1955	Vanoni plan; Gronchi elected President
1956	Italy joins European Community
1959–63	The 'economic miracle'
1960	Tambroni government accepts fascist support; riots
1963–68	Centre–left coalition government; Aldo Moro prime minister
1964	Death of Palmiro Togliatti (succeeded by Longo); Saragat elected President
1966	Floods in Venice and Florence
1968	Dario Fo and Franca Rame set up independent theatre company
1968–76	Crisis governments, centrist & centre–left coalitions
1968–69	Student and workers' struggle
1969	Fascist bomb at Piazza Fontana, Milan; anarchist Pietro Valpreda arrested; autunno caldo
1970	Renato Curcio founds Red Brigades in Milan
1972	Enrico Berlinguer becomes leader of the PCI
1974	Referendum approves divorce; collapse of *Sindona* empire
1974–78	PCI leads rise of 'Eurocommunism'
1975–77	Decentralisation through regional laws
1976	PCI gains 34.4% of vote at the general election
1976–79	PCI enters 'historic compromise' with DC; governments of national unity
1977	Height of power of Autonomia, extra-parliamentary youth movement
1978	Kidnap and assassination of Aldo Moro by the Red Brigades; Sandro Pertini elected President; Karol Wojtya elected Pope

	John Paul II
1979	Seveso disaster
1979–	Centre–left governments
1979–81	Carabinieri under General della Chiese break Red Brigades
1980	Earthquake in Campania; fascist bomb at Bologna station
1981	Licio Gelli's P2 Masonic lodge exposed; Calvi arrested; General Dozier kidnapped by Red Brigades and then freed by Carabinieri; referendum sanctions abortion
1982	Italy wins football World Cup (1934, 1938)
1983	Carlo Alberto della Chiesa murdered by the Mafia in Palermo; Toni Negri elected MP for Radical Party
1983–87	Bettino Craxi first Socialist prime minister
1984	Death of Berlinguer; Natta new PCI leader
1985	Francesco Cossiga elected President
1987	Giovanni Goria youngest ever prime minister at the age of 44; 'Il sorpasso', Italian GNP greater than that of the UK; general election, recovery of DC, decline of PCI
1988	Ciriaco De Mita prime minister, forming 47th post-war government; Occhetto new PCI leader; 'Golden sheets' scandal
1989	DeMita resigns as PM, succeeded by Andreotti
1990	PCI renamed PDS (Partito Democratico di Sinistra), Moro letters surface
1991	Albanian boat people repatriated; Italian warplanes participate in Gulf war; Andreotti resigns and then forms new government; GLADIO scandal; Banco Ambrosiano trial
1992	Intensification of mafia activity: MEP Salvo Lima and judges Falcone and Borsellino murdered; Bank of Italy made independent; privatisation plans for IRI; municipal corruption in Milan and other cities revealed – PSI implicated; general election: Giuliano Amato PM, Oscar Luigi Scalfaro new President, austerity programme, fight against mafia and corruption
1993	Arrest of mafia boss Salvadore Riina; Craxi resigns as leader of PSI; 82.7% vote in favour of electoral reform in referendum, operation 'clean hands' intensifies, faith in traditional political parties collapses, Carlo Azeglio Ciampi moves from Bank of Italy to become Prime Minister in 'government of technocrats', traditional Parties suffer heavy losses in municipal elections, Christian Democrats renamed the Partito Popolare, MSI renamed Alleanza Nazionale
1994	Forza Italia founded, right-wing coalition of Forza Italia,

	the Northern Leagues and Alleanza Nazionale (neo fascists) wins general election, Berlusconi new Prime Minister; ruling coalition wins Euro election, attempt to cut public expenditure; Roberto Baggio's goals take Italy to final of World Cup; Italian birth rate lowest in the world. Berlusconi investigated by corruption judges, falls out with Northern League and resigns
1995	Year begins with unresolved political crisis. In January, Lamberto Dini invited to form a new government; austerity programme to meet Maastricht convergence criteria
1996	Dini government falls; Maccanico fails to form government; general election brings left to power for first time in the form of the Ulivo (olive tree) coalition dominated by the PDS; Romano Prodi new Prime Minister; ore austerity measures to qualify for EMU; antics of separatist northern League who rename Northern Italy 'Padania'
1997	Demonstrations against the government's austerity programme, Lira rejoins the ERM; Prodi survives threatened defection of RC from his government; earthquake seriously damages parts of central Italy including Assisi; Versace murdered; Berlusconi charged with corruption; DiPietro comes under investigation by operation clean hands
1998	Progress towards meeting EMU convergence criteria

Election Results to the Chamber of Deputies, 1946–92

Percentages and seats

	1946*	1948	1953	1958	1963	1968	1972	1976	1979	1983	1987	1992
DC	35.18 (207)	48.48 (304)	40.08 (262)	42.35 (273)	38.27 (260)	39.09 (265)	38.74 (266)	38.8 (263)	38.3 (262)	32.9 (225)	34.3 (234)	29.7 (206
PDS & RC (PCI)	18.96 (104)	—	22.64 (143)	22.73 (140)	25.31 (166)	26.96 (177)	27.21 (179)	34.4 (227)	30.4 (201)	29.9 (198)	26.6 (177)	21.7 (142
PSI	20.72 (115)	31.03 (183)	12.73 (75)	14.26 (84)	13.87 (87)	14.51 (91)	9.63 (61)	9.7 (57)	9.8 (62)	11.4 (73)	14.3 (94)	13.6 (92)
PSDI	—	7.09 (33)	4.52 (19)	4.56 (22)	6.11 (33)	—	5.15 (29)	3.4 (15)	3.8 (20)	4.1 (23)	3.0 (17)	2.7 (16)
PRI	4.37 (23)	2.49 (9)	1.62 (5)	1.38 (6)	1.37 (6)	1.97 (9)	2.86 (15)	3.1 (14)	3.0 (16)	5.1 (29)	3.7 (21)	4.4 (27)
PLI	6.79 (41)	3.38 (19)	3.02 (13)	3.55 (17)	6.99 (39)	5.83 (31)	3.89 (20)	1.3 (5)	1.9 (9)	2.9 (16)	2.1 (11)	2.8 (17)
Monarchist	2.7 (16)	2.78 (14)	6.86 (40)	4.87 (25)	1.77 (8)	1.31 (6)	—	—	—	—	—	—
Northern League	—	—	—	—	—	—	—	—	—	—	—	8.7 (55)
MSI	[5.3] (30)	2.01 (6)	5.85 (29)	4.77 (24)	5.11 (27)	4.46 (24)	8.67 (56)	6.1 (35)	5.3 (30)	6.8 (42)	5.9 (35)	5.45 (34
PR	—	—	—	—	—	—	—	1.1 (4)	3.4 (18)	2.2 (11)	2.6 (13)	—
New Left	—	—	—	—	—	—	1.33 (0)	1.5 (6)	2.2 (6)	1.5 (7)	1.7 (8)	—
PSIUP	—	—	—	—	—	4.46 (23)	1.95 (0)	—	—	—	—	—
Greens	—	—	—	—	—	—	—	—	—	—	2.5 (13)	2.8 (16)
LR	—	—	—	—	—	—	—	—	—	—	—	1.9 (12)
Others	5.9	2.74	2.68	1.53	1.2	1.41	0.57	0.6	1.9	3.2	3.3 (7)	6.3 (13)

* 1946 Constituent Assembly; 1948–87 Chamber of Deputies

DC	= Democrazia Cristiana	MSI	= Movimento Sociale Italiano
PCI	= Partito Comunista Italiano	PR	= Partito Radicale
PSI	= Partito Socialista Italiano	PSIUP	= Partito Socialista di Unità Proletaria
PSDI	= Partito Socialista Democratico Italiano	PDS	= Partito Democratico di Sinistra
PRI	= Partito Repubblicano Italiano	RC	= Rifondazione Comunista
PLI	= Partito Liberale Italiano	LR	= La Rete (anti-Mafia)

Election Results to the Chamber of Deputies, 1994–1996

Percentages and seats (total seats: 630)

	1994		1996
Freedom Alliance (Forza Italia, Northern League & AN)	42.9 (366)	Olive Tree (inc PDS, PPI, Dini List, Greens)	40.5% (284)
Progressive Alliance (PDS, RC, & La Rete)	34.5 (213)	Freedom Alliance (Forza Italia & AN)	36.3% (246)
Pact for Italy (Including PP)	15.7 (46)	Northern League	10.1% (59)
Others	6.9 (5)	Refounded Communists	8.6% (35)
		Others	4.5% (6)
		l'Ulivo has 157 seats out of 315 in the Senate	

Selected Reading in English on Italian History

Agnelli, S. *We Always Wore Sailor Suits* (London, 1975)
Albrecht-Carrie, R. *Italy from Napoleon to Mussolini* (New York, 1950)
Allum, P. *Italy –Republic without Government?* (London, 1973)
Battaglia, R. *The Story of the Italian Resistance* (London, 1957)
Beales, D. *The Risorgimento and the Unification of Italy* (London, 1971)
Bosworth, R.J.B. *Italy: The Last of the Great Powers* (Cambridge, 1980)
Bruckner, G.E. *Renaissance Florence* (New York, 1969)
Carocci, G. *Italian Fascism* (Harmondsworth, 1974)
Cary, M. & Scullard, H.H. *A History of Rome* (London, 1979)
Cassells, A. *Fascist Italy* (London, 1969)
Clark, M. *Modern Italy 1871–1982* (London, 1984)
Cogan, N. *A Political History of Post War Italy* (New York, 1981)
Davis, J.A. (ed.) *Gramsci and Italy's Passive Revolution* (London, 1979)
Ginsborg, P. *A History of Contemporary Italy* (Harmondsworth, 1990)
Goldthwaite, R.A. *The Building of Renaissance Florence* (Baltimore, 1980)
Haycraft, J. *Italian Labyrinth* (Harmondsworth, 1987)
Hearder, H. *Cavour* (London, 1972)
Hearder, H. & Waley, D. *A Short History of Italy* (Cambridge, 1963)
Hibberd, C. *Garibaldi and his Enemies* (London, 1965)
James Gregor, A. *Italian Fascism and Developmental Dictatorship* (Princeton, 1979)
Kent, P. *The Pope and the Duce* (London, 1981)
La Palombara, J. *Democracy Italian Style* (London, 1987)
Longworth, P. *The Rise and Fall of Venice* (London, 1974)
Mack Smith, D. *Cavour and Garibaldi* (Cambridge, 1986)
Italy, A Modern History (Ann Arbor, 1969)
Mussolini (London, 1981)
Victor Emanuel, Cavour and the Risorgimento (London, 1971)
Martines, L. *Power and Imagination* (London, 1980)
Pinto, D. (ed.) *Contemporary Italian Sociology* (Cambridge, 1981)
Procacci, G. *History of the Italian People* (London, 1970)
Ridley, J. *Garibaldi* (London, 1974)

SALVEMINI, G. *Mazzini* (London, 1956)
SARTI, R. *The Ax Within* (New York, 1974)
SASSOON, D. *Contemporary Italy* (London, 1986)
STINGER, C.L. *The Renaissance in Rome* (Bloomington, 1985)
VASARI, G. *Lives of the Artists* (Harmondsworth, 1971)
VIOTTI, A. *Garibaldi* (Poole, 1979)
WICKHAM, C. *Early Medieval Italy* (London, 1981)
WISKEMANN, E. *Fascism in Italy: Its Development and Influence* (London, 1970)
WOOLF, S.J. *A History of Italy 1700–1860* (London, 1979)
(ed.) *European Fascism* (London, 1968)
(ed.) *The Rebirth of Italy 1943–50* (London, 1972)

Historical Gazetteer

Numbers in bold refer to the main text

Agrigento Notable for its remarkable Vale of Doric temples from the 5th century BC, probably the best examples outside Greece. Legend has it that the city was founded by Daedalus. Under the Greeks it was called Akragas, and was involved in a series of wars with the Carthaginians between 480–340 BC, capturing Carthage after victory at Himera (480), and being itself destroyed by Hannibal in 406. Captured by the Romans in the third century BC and renamed Agrigentum, it remained in Roman hands until the end of the empire, and was then taken by the Saracens in 827, and then by Count Roger in 1087. Birthplace of the ancient poet and philosopher Empedocles (490–430 BC), and of the modern playwright Luigi Pirandello (1867–1936). **9**

Alba Now a centre of wine production (barbera, dolcetto and barbaresco), this medieval city has a 14th-century Duomo and is the birthplace of the 16th-century painter Macrino.

Alberobello The town of the Trulli, round hut-like houses which are still lived in, and which probably originate from the Saracens or the Mycenaeans.

Alessandria Founded in the 12th century by nobles from Monferrato, who named the town after Pope Alexander III, the bitter enemy of their foe Barbarossa.

Amalfi First city to emerge from the dark ages. The Amalfi Republic was founded in the 6th century; by the 9th century it was a major trading power. Occupied by the Normans, and then sacked by Pisa in the 1130s, the city never really recovered. Devastated by an earthquake and freak storms in 1343, when much of the old city was engulfed by the sea. Of interest is its remarkable Duomo, started in the 9th century, which contains the head of Sant' Andrea, taken in the sack of Constantinople in 1204. **66, 70**

Ancona Founded in the 5th century BC by Greek colonists from Syracuse, and then built up by the Roman emperor Trajan. A leading commune in the 12th century, it fell under Papal rule in 1532. Suffered heavily from bombing during World War II, and then from an earthquake in 1972. Now a busy port and regional capital. Historically significant features include an arch dedicated to Trajan, and the pretty Cathedral of San Ciriaco, built in the 11th century, overlooking the old city on the site of an ancient temple to Venus. Now the home of a large university and of the Museo Nazionale delle Marche. **4, 7, 9, 44, 106–7, 125, 134, 141, 148, 187**

Aosta Founded by the Romans in 23 BC as Augusta Praetoria, as a medieval city it was the seat of the dukes of Aosta, allies of the Savoys. Its strategic position near to the Alpine passes has given considerable historical importance to the city. Contains the excavations of the 6th-century Basilica di San Lorenzo, a Roman bridge, wall and amphitheatre, and a much rebuilt cathedral with 12th-century mosaics. **15**

Aquileia Major Roman city founded in 181 BC. Now just a small settlement, but also the most important archaeological site in the north. Augustus spent considerable time here, but the city declined in importance after being sacked by Attila the Hun in 452 and the Lombards in 568. Contains an impressive 11th-century Basilica, and important Roman and palaeo-Christian excavations.

Arezzo One of the major cities in the Etruscan Dodecapolis, and then the Roman city of Arretium. In the Middle Ages, a free commune and rival of Florence, which captured the city in 1384. Birthplace of Maecenas, a patron of Horace and Virgil, of Guido D'Arezzo, Petrarch, Vasari and Pietro Arretino. Historical features include a Gothic Duomo and the church of San Francesco, which contains some of the best frescoes by Piero della Francesca. **13, 28, 60, 99**

Ascoli Piceno Centre of the ancient civilisation of the Piceni, razed to the ground by the Romans in 89 BC and then rebuilt by them in the form of a rectilinear castrum, the form it in essence retains today. A defensive strongpoint in the Dark Ages, the city established itself as a strong free commune after 1100. Stagnated under Papal rule from the 15th century. Features include several towers and a 13th-century Palazzo del Popolo, as well as the 12th-century Cathedral of Sant' Emidio. **60**

Assisi City of St Francis (1182–1226) and an impressive medieval town built on Mount Subasio. Of historic interest is the Basilica of St Francis, started in 1228, which consists of two superimposed churches. The saint is buried there and it contains some of Giotto's most significant frescoes and a Cimabue Crucifixion. Also of note is the 12th-century Cathedral of San Rufino, in which Emperor Frederick II was christened. **106**

Asti Birthplace of the poet Vittorio Alfieri (1749–1803), and once the rival of Milan. The Duomo is 14th-century Gothic, and there is the 9th-century Crypt of Sant'Anastasio. The city is known for its sparkling wine, and hosts an annual *Palio* which dates back to 1257. **70, 71**

Bari Founded by the Illyrians and then a Greek and Roman city (Barium). Held in turn by the Ostrogoths, the Byzantines, the Saracens and Robert Guiscard's Normans, who took it in 1071. Seat of the Captanate, it later became a major port and sea power, rivalling Venice in the 11th century. Control of the city continued to change regularly: Frederick II, the Angevins, the Sforza all held it before it became part of the kingdom of Naples in 1558.

Devastated by a plague that killed 80% of its inhabitants in 1656–7. Now the second largest city in the south, it is noted for its university and for the Basilica of San Nicola, built by the Normans in 1087 to house the remains of St Nicholas of Myra, the patron saint of Russia, stolen from Asia Minor by sailors from Bari.

Benevento Capital of the ancient Samnites, who called it Maloenton, and then a Roman city called Malventum (ill wind), and then Beneventum (good wind) after the Romans had defeated Pyrrhus of Epirus here in 275 BC. Later a Lombard city and the capital of the duchy of Benevento. Captured by the Normans around 1060, and devastated over the years by earthquakes and World War II. Home of Strega liqueur. Contains a Roman theatre, a fine triumphal arch built in honour of Trajan in 117, and an interesting Samnite museum. **57, 59, 60, 66–7**

Bergamo Birthplace of the painter Lorenzo Lotti, the 15th-century *condottiere* Bartolomeo Colleoni and the composer Donizetti, and the home town of many of Garibaldi's mille. Was under the control of Venice from 1428–1797. Now a charming city whose attractions include the Cappella Colleoni, the Basilica of Santa Maria Maggiore, begun in 1137, and the 12th-century Palazzo della Ragione. **92**

Bologna Founded by the Etruscans as Felsina, near the prehistoric settlement of Marzabotto, and named Bononia by the Gauls. Became a major commune in the 12th century, and part of the Papal States in 1278. Controlled by the Bentivoglio family in the 15th century. Charles V was crowned Emperor here in the Basilica of San Petronio, which overlooks the city. Home of the oldest university in the world, founded in the 11th century, and still a major centre of learning. Birthplace of Guglielmo Marconi (1874–1937), the inventor of the radio. Traditional strongpoint of the Italian Left, the city was forcibly taken over by the Fascists in the early 1920s, and is now the 'model' of Communist local government. Its station was bombed by right-wing terrorists in 1980. A major culinary centre, home of spaghetti alla Bolognese and many other delicacies. Many features of historical interest include 35 km of arcades (*portici*), the earliest of which dates back to the 12th century; two imposing medieval towers near the university (the highest, the Torre degli Asinelli is 97 metres and was built in 1119); various medieval palaces; a 10th-century Duomo di San Pietro; the Basilica of San Petronio; and a fascinating Museo Civico Archeologico. **4–6, 14, 19, 68, 71, 74, 76, 89–90, 101, 106, 119, 139, 142, 191, 211, 217**

Brescia Originally settled by the Gauls, who named it Brixia, and flourished under the rule of Augustus. Capital of a Lombard duchy under Desiderius, then a member of the Lombard League in the 11th century. Under Venetian rule it became a major centre of munitions production. Contains the remains of Roman Brixia and an 11th-century Duomo Vecchio. **3, 59–60, 92, 139**

Capua Founded by the Oscans, this ancient town was once the second city of Italy. An ally of Hannibal in 216 BC, the city was totally destroyed by the

Arabs around 830. Contains the remains of a large Roman amphitheatre. The place where Spartacus began his revolt against Rome. **18**

Carrara Along with nearby Massa, the source of the marble used in many Renaissance and other works of art, including those of Michelangelo. Features a 13th-century Duomo. **182**

Catania Sicily's second city, on the foothills of Etna. Originally a Sickel village, colonised by the Greeks in 729 BC. A rival of Syracuse, it was taken by the Romans in 263 BC and flourished during the reign of Augustus. Suffered from earthquakes in 1169 and 1693, and from a major eruption of Etna in 1669 Birthplace of the composer Vincenzo Bellini (1801–35) and the writer Giovanni Verga (1840–1922). Features include the Duomo of Santa Agata, founded by Count Roger in 1094, and a Roman theatre and amphitheatre. **9**

Cerveteri Ancient Etruscan town of Caere. Contains an important necropolis with the famous 'Tomb of the Capitals' and 'Tomb of Shields and Chairs'.

Chieti Now a provincial capital, this ancient city was founded on the site of a bronze age settlement. Home of the Museo Nazionale Archeologico di Antichità, and of a Roman baths. **1**

Chius Etruscan Camars and Roman Clusium; home town of Lars Porsena. Home of the Museo Nazionale Etrusco. Good examples of Etruscan tombs at nearby Pitigliano, Saturnia and Sorano. **13, 19**

Città d: Castello Ancient town of the Umbrians, now a thriving and attractive town in the Upper Tiber Valley. The medieval centre contains 14th-century palazzi (del Governo & Communale), a Duomo the oldest part of which dates back to the 6th century, and a very good Pinacoteca (art gallery) with Renaissance works by Raphael, Signorelli, Ghiberti and Della Robbia.

Como The birthplace of Pliny the Elder, this ancient city was captured by the Romans from the Gauls in the 2nd century BC. Later a commune, and from 1335 ruled by Milan. Has a magnificent Duomo. **71**

Cortona Ancient Etruscan city perched on a hilltop surrounded by stunning scenery. Now an Umbrian provincial capital with an interesting museum which contains a magnificent Etruscan candelabra. Also a centre for the study of fine art. **13, 15, 99**

Cosenza Capital city of the Bruttians, and where Alaric died in 410, in the Middle Ages the city was ruled by the Arabs, Normans and French. Boasts an interesting Cathedral built in 1222.

Cremona Founded by the Romans in 218 BC. The birthplace of the composer Claudio Monteverdi, in the 16th to 18th centuries the town was famous for its violin-makers, the Amati, Guarneri and Stradivari families, of whom the greatest was Antonio Stradivari (1644–1737). There is an interesting 12th-century cathedral and baptistry, and the bell-tower, the Torrazzo, built in the 13th century, is, at 112 metres, the tallest in Italy. **69, 70, 72, 76, 101, 191**

Crotone Once a major city of Magna Grecia (Croton), and the home of Pythagoras in the 6th century BC. **9, 10**

Cumae First Greek city in Italy,

taken by the Samnites in 421 BC. Traditional home of the Sibylline books and the scene of major naval battles in ancient times. Razed to the ground by Arabs in the 9th century, only ruins now remain. **8, 9, 19**

Cuneo Provincial capital and market town largely rebuilt in the 18th and 19th centuries. Most interesting historical building is the Church of San Francesco, built in 1227.

Ferrara Medieval and Renaissance city, ruled by the Este 1250–1597. A centre of the Renaissance, the city was then under the control of a papal legate. In the 20th century the birthplace of the Metaphysical school of artists, which includes De Chirico and Morandi. Historical features include the Castello Estense, begun in 1385, and various Renaissance palazzi, notably the Palazzo Schifanoia and the Palazzo di Lodovico il Moro. The home of the poets Ariosto and Tasso, patronised by the Este in the 16th century. **72, 89, 92, 95, 100, 105, 108, 119, 130, 139, 144, 191**

Fiesole Perched on a hill overlooking Florence, and now virtually a suburb of the city, Fiesole is of Etruscan origin and became the Roman Faesulum. A stronghold in the Dark Ages, it contains the escavations of a Roman theatre, as well as an 11th-century Duomo. Nearby San Domenico now houses the European University Institute. **60, 72**

Firenze (Florence) One of the most important historical cities in the world. Probably founded by the Etruscans, and razed to the gound by Sulla during the Roman Social Wars. Flourished during the Roman empire and during the time of Charlemagne. Became a commune in 1115, and then a major Republic. By the middle of the 13th century the city was one of the foremost banking and commercial powers in Europe. Characterised by sectarian strife (between Guelphs and Ghibellines, and then between 'blacks' and 'whites'), the city became dotted with towers in medieval times. Its 'golden age' came as the capital of the Italian Renaissance, when it was governed by the Medici, produced a wealth of characters such as Savonarola, and great artists and intellectuals, ranging from Dante and Boccaccio to Botticelli and Leonardo da Vinci. The real history of the city ended with the Renaissance. Thereafter it became a provincial backwater, and was annexed by Piedmont in 1859. Capital of united Italy between 1865–70. Now a wealthy city which lives almost exclusively from tourism. Historical features are to be found everywhere. The best-known are: the Duomo, begun around 1290, and with Brunelleschi's famous Cupola and Giotto's bell-tower; the Baptistry, which dates back to between the 7th–9th centuries; the Palazzo Vecchio, restored by Giorgio Vasari in the mid-16th century; the Bargello, begun around 1250; the Uffizi palace, again the work of Vasari; the Ponte Vecchio, built in 1345 to replace a wooden structure dating from around 970; a whole host of Renaissance churches such as Santa Maria Novella, Santa Croce, San Lorenzo, and Santo Spirito; the Forte Belvedere and Piazzale Michelangelo; and the Palazzo Pitti, built in 1457. And, of course, innumerable museums and art galleries filled

with many of the best-known paintings and sculptures in the world. **11, 16, 68–9, 72, 75–9, 83, 90, 95–100, 112, 119, 121, 125, 129, 211**

Foligno Ancient town, and the Roman Fulginia, was one of the first centres of printing in Italy in the 15th century. Badly damaged in World War II, it still boasts a good Duomo and the old church of Santa Maria Infraportas.

Frascati Originally Tusculum, ruled by the Latins, the Etruscans and then the Romans, and destroyed in 1191. Now a lovely medieval town on the hills above Rome, and a centre of wine and olive production. Features the 17th-century Villa Aldobrandini. **18**

Genova (Genoa) Ancient maritime city and republic. The chief city of the Ligurians, it was trading with the Phoenicians and the Greeks by the 6th century BC; then part of the Roman empire and sacked by Hannibal. Taken by the Lombards in 641, the city rose to prominence in the 12th century by capturing Sardinia and Corsica and helping the Normans take Antioch. Thereafter it became a major trading power, establishing its superiority in the west Mediterranean by defeating Pisa at Meloria in 1284 and then Venice at Curzonali in 1298, and enjoying a golden age at the beginning of the 14th century. Simone Boccanegra, hero of Verdi's opera, came to power in the city in 1339. From the 15th century the city developed into a centre of banking under the leadership of the Bank of Saint George, and for a while was Europe's leading economic power. The leading personality of this period was Andrea Doria (1468–1560), who helped the Spanish Emperor Charles V to defeat Francis I of France and was the leading patron of the Renaissance in the city. Taken by the French in 1668 and the Austrians in 1734, the city became part of Piedmont in 1815 and was thereafter a major centre of the risorgimento. Now a busy metropolis, Italy's largest port and the home of the famous trennette al pesto, the city boasts many buildings of historical interest, notably the 13th-century Church of Sant'Agostino, the palaeo-Christian Santa Maria di Castello, a Palazzo Ducale, the Cathedral of San Lorenzo which was begun in the 12th century, and a whole host of imposing palazzi. **30–1, 66, 69–72, 76, 89, 92, 94, 101, 119**

Gubbio Imposing hill town, a centre for the ancient Umbrians and then a medieval commune. Captured by Duke Montefeltro of Urbino in 1384, and then part of the Papal States. Home of the famous ceramics artist Maestro Giorgio. A wealth of historical features include a 1st-century Roman amphitheatre, a 13th-Century Bargello, the 14th-century Palazzo dei Consoli and Palazzo Pretorio, the 13th-century Duomo, and the Palazzo Ducale built by Luciano Laurana for Federico da Montefeltro. Birthplace of Pope Marcellus II (1555). **7, 8**

Herculaneum (modern Ercolano) Roman town destroyed with Pompeii by the eruption of Vesuvius in 79. Fascinating excavations of the ancient city. **21**

Imperia Formed in 1923 by Mussolini by the fusion of Porto Maurizio and Oneglia. Birthplace of the Genovese admiral Andrea Doria.

Ivrea The headquarters of Olivetti, which was founded in the city in 1908. Contains an 11th-century cathedral and a castello built in 1358.

L'Aquila Hilltop city founded by Frederick II in 1240. Resisted the Aragonese in 1423 and was richly rewarded by Queen Giovanna II, becoming the second city of the kingdom of Naples. Rose against the Spanish in 1529 and was then devastated by an earthquake in 1703. Retains many features of historical interest, including a 99-headed fountain built in 1272 (the number has a special significance for the town), a castello built in 1535, and the Basilica of San Bernardino.

Lecce Beautiful and historically important town, founded by the Messapians and known to the Romans as Lupiae. In the Middle Ages flourished as the centre of the Salento peninsula, and then under the Spanish and the Bourbons, while always maintaining a strong degree of independence as a succession of revolts against oppressors from 1648 to 1848 testifies. Now the city features major examples of Baroque architecture, built mainly in the 16th century by the likes of the Zimbalo brothers. A good example is the Church of Santa Croce, begun in

1549 and completed in 1680. There are also the remains of a large Roman amphitheatre.

Livorno (Leghorn) Founded in 1571 by Cosimo de' Medici as a port to replace Pisa, which he linked with a canal. Became one of Italy's major ports, with strong trading connections with England. Birthplace of the painter and sculptor Modigliani. **99, 125, 129, 134**

Loreto Town dominated by a large sanctuary, begun in 1460 and dedicated to the Virgin Mary, whose house is supposed to have flown there from Nazareth in 1294.

Lucca Beautiful and interesting Tuscan city of Roman origins. A leading commune in the Middle Ages and a rival of Florence, especially under Castruccio Castracani in the 14th century. An independent state after the Treaty of Cateau-Cambrésis. Boasts an impressive set of walls, a pleasant Duomo begun in the 11th century, and a Roman amphitheatre. Now a centre of olive oil production. **65, 68, 70–1, 76, 89, 92**

Mantova (Mantua) Birthplace of the poet Virgil. Rose to fame in the 11th century under Countess Matilda. A city-state ruled by the Gonzaga family from 1328, it patronised artists such as Mantegna and humanist teachers such as Vittorino da Feltre (1379–1446). Sacked by the Habsburgs in 1630 and taken by the Austrians in 1707. Features include the Basilica of Sant'Andrea built by Leon Battista Alberti in 1472, the Rotunda di San Lorenzo built by Countess Matilda in 1082, and the Palazzo Ducale which dates from the late 13th century. **92, 95, 112, 119, 132, 139**

Messina Founded by the Greeks as Zancle on the site of a sickel settlement. A port for the Crusaders, it flourished until losing its privileges after a revolt against the Spanish in 1674. Has suffered greatly from natural catastrophes, culminating with the great earthquake of 1908 which killed 84,000. Contains a Duomo built by Roger II, consecrated in 1197 and restored after the earthquake. The setting of Shakespeare's *Much Ado About Nothing*. **9, 134**

Milano (Milan) Ancient city on old trade routes, called Mediolanum by the Romans. Diocletian's preferred city and the place where Constantine officially accepted Christianity in 313. Home of the 4th-century St Ambrose, to whom the Milanese owe their folk name of Ambrosiani. One of Italy's first communes in the 11th century, the city was sacked by Barbarossa in 1158 and again in 1160, the Milanese getting their revenge by leading the Lombard League to defeat the infamous Redbeard at Legnano in 1176. One of the first communes to fall into the hands of the signori, when the Della Torre took control in 1247. Thereafter the fief of the Visconti family, in particular the famous Gian Galeazzo, and then of the Sforza. It was Ludovico Sforza (1451–1508) who commissioned much of Leonardo da Vinci's work, including the Last Supper. After the Renaissance the city was ruled by a Spanish viceroy until 1712 when it was taken over by the Habsburgs and was the scene of enlightenment reform. Capital of the Napoleonic Cisalpine Republic, and then a centre of the 1848 revolts, Milan was the home of the writer Alessandro Manzoni. After unification, the city became Italy's leading industrial city, a position which it still enjoys today, and a stronghold for the Socialist Party. It is also the city in which Mussolini founded the Fascist Party. Bombed heavily during World War II, it was liberated by the partisans, who displayed Il Duce's body in Piazzale Loreto. Now a leading artistic as well as commercial centre, and one of the leading European cities. Full of buildings of historical interest, but one should not miss the Duomo, founded by Gian Galeazzo Visconti in 1386 and since overhauled several times; La Scala Theatre, completed in 1778; the Brera Gallery; the Castello Sforzesco, rebuilt in 1450; the 15th-century Santa Maria delle Grazie, which houses the Last Supper; the Basilica di Sant'Ambrogio, where the patron saint of the city lies; the Leonardo da Vinci Museum; and the Renaissance gate of Porta Romana. **30, 48, 51, 59, 62, 68–73, 76, 87–9, 94, 100–5, 118–120, 124, 128, 135–6, 138–9, 157, 165, 169, 181, 183, 191, 194, 201, 208, 211, 217, 218**

Modena Now one of the richest cities in Italy, the home of Ferrari and Maserati cars, ceramic tiles, Luciano Pavarotti, and gastronomic delicacies. The Roman city of Mutina, came under the control of Countess Matilda Da Canossa in the 11th/12th centuries, before becoming an independent commune and a Ghibelline stronghold. Taken over by the Este of Ferrara in 1288, in whose control it remained until 1796. Historical features include the famous Duomo di San Geminiano, begun in 1099 and completed in the 13th century, and the Palazzo dei Musei which houses the Biblioteca Estense and the Galleria Estense. **41, 68, 72, 76, 119, 138, 148, 157, 159, 164**

Monreale Home of one of the great churches of the Middle Ages, the Cathedral built by the Norman William II in 1172–76. **80**

Montecassino Famous monastery founded by St Benedict in 529 and destroyed at regular intervals ever since, latterly by the Nazis in 1944.

Napoli (Naples) A Greek colony founded by Cumae in 750 BC, Neapolis was then ruled by the Samnites and the Romans. Captured for the Byzantines by Belisarius in 536, the city then became the capital of an independent duchy in 736. Seized by the Normans in 1139 and then in the hands of the Hohenstaufen, who were in turn displaced by the Angevins in 1266 when Charles of Anjou beheaded Conradin in Piazza del Mercato. Capital of the kingdom of Naples, the city was in Spanish hands from 1435 to 1707, when it passed to Archduke Charles of Austria after the Spanish War of Succession. Thence back to the Bourbons from 1734 until unification. Now the city of the 'scugnizzi' (urchins), beautiful but chaotic, and ruined by uncontrolled speculative building, but still famous for its 'song' and the restaurants along Santa Lucia. Historical features include the Castel Nuovo, built in 1282, and its triumphal arch which dates from 1467; the Certosa di San Martino; the Palazzo Reale, begun in 1600; one of Europe's oldest universtities, founded in 1224 by the Emperor Frederick; a fascinating if ill-maintained Museo Nazionale; the tomb of the poet Virgil; and a series of catacombs from Roman times. **9, 66, 82, 109–11, 118–9, 124, 126, 130–3, 136, 138–9, 140–2, 145–7, 149, 167, 175, 181**

Novara Ancient city with Duomo built in the 19th century by Antonelli on the site of a Romansque church. Inside it are the 12th-century chapel of San Siro and a 5th-century baptistry.

Orvieto The Etruscan city of Volsinii, this hilltop stronghold was taken by the Romans in 280 BC. In the Middle Ages a key city in the Papal States and a haunt of several popes. Contains an impressive Duomo started in 1290, with a superb façade only completed in 1600, and the Museo Civico has several interesting Etruscan exhibits. **13, 14, 18, 20, 28**

Ostia Ancient Rome's port, founded in the 4th century BC, grew into a major city, which then declined into extinction by around 800. Now one of the major archaeological sites from the Roman period, with virtually the full layout of the old city surviving. **44, 66**

Padova (Padua) Birthplace of Livy, the city has one of the oldest and most famous of the European universities, founded in 1222 and boasting illustrious former lecturers such as Galileo, Dante and Petrarch. More recently a centre of student militancy, and the home of the ultra-left intellectual, and alleged terrorist, Toni Negri. Historically important buildings include the Basilica del Santo, begun in 1232, and the Oratorio di San Giorgio, dating to 1377. The Cappella degli Scrovegni is decorated with 38 frescoes by Giotto. **72, 89, 92**

Paestum Founded originally in the 6th century BC as the city of Poseidonia by the Sybarites, and then taken by the Romans in 273 BC, Paestum flourished in Roman times, only to be devastated by the Saracens and completely abandoned in the 9th century. It was submerged by forest until discovered by chance by road-builders in the 18th century. It is chiefly notable for a series of imposing temples, the only Greek ones on the Italian mainland. The Temple of Neptune, which dates from the 5th century BC, is one of the best preserved in Europe. **9**

Palermo Ancient Panoramus, a Phoenician colony from around the 8th century BC, then a Carthaginian stronghold, taken by the Romans in 254 BC. Reconquered by the Byzantines in 535, and then taken by the Saracens in 831, becoming a splendid city under their rule. Captured by the Normans under Tancred de Hauteville in 1072, it became a trading centre, and then an intellectual centre under the Hohenstaufen Frederick II. Scene of the outbreak of the rebellion of the Sicilian Vespers against Charles of Anjou in 1282, it passed to the Spanish, then to Vittorio Amadeo of Savoy after the Treaty of Utrecht in 1713, and then to the Bourbons in 1718. A centre of rebellion in 1820 and 1848, it was 'liberated' by Garibaldi in 1860. Now the capital of Sicily. Badly damaged in air raids in 1943. Birthplace of the composer Alessandro Scarlatti (1660–1725). Features a cathedral founded in 1185 by the English archbishop Walter of the Mill, several fine churches (notably the Norman San Giovanni degli Eremiti) and Palazzi, and an interesting Museo Archeologico Nazionale. The Palatine Chapel in the Palazzo dei Normanni, built between 1130–1140, is a wonderful example of Arab-Norman decoration. **80, 83, 126, 156–7, 167, 220**

Parma Now a major gastronomic centre, the home of Parmesan cheese and Parma ham. A small Roman outpost, it developed into a medieval city which was at various times ruled by the major families of the time: the Visconti, Sforza, Este and Della Scala. Incorporated into the Papal States in 1521, and then made into a duchy by Pope Paul III for the benefit of his son Pier Luigi Farnese. It was ruled by the family until 1815, when Napoleon's widow Maria Louisa took over. Contains a 13th-century Duomo and Baptistry, as well as four famous castles nearby. Birthplace of the conductor Arturo Toscanini (1867–1957), and the city in which the violinist Niccolò Paganini (1782–1840) is buried. **59, 121, 144, 148, 157, 159, 164**

Pavia Originally the Roman city of Ticinum, this is a place of major historical importance. Capital of the Gothic Kingdom of Italy, the city in which Odoacer was crowned. In the 6th century captured by the Lombards, who made it their capital city. Charlemagne, Berengar and Frederick Barbarosa were all crowned here. Birthplace, in 1005, of Lanfranc, the first Norman Archbishop of Canterbury. Later a Ghibelline commune, taken by Milan in 1359. Major historical buildings include the magnificent Certosa, founded by Gian Galeazzo Visconti in 1396, the Castello Visconteo built in 1360, several medieval towers, and the Basilica di San Michele, which dates from 661 and was rebuilt in the 12th century. The university was founded in 1361. **54–6, 59, 62–3, 70–2, 75, 101, 137**

Perugia Ancient Umbrian town, taken by the Etruscans around 500 BC and with the name of Peiresa becoming one of the cities in the Etruscan League. Assimilated by the Romans in 310 BC, it was burned down and rebuilt by Augustus, who renamed it Augustia Perusia. A major commune in the Middle Ages, when control of the city was contested by the Baglioni and Oddi families. Taken by the mercenary Braccio Fortebraccio in 1414, it was eventually incorporated into the Papal States. Features of historical interest include the 13th-century Palazzo dei Priori, the 15th-century Cathedral of San Lorenzo, Museo Archeologico Nazionale dell'Umbria, and the 13th-century Torre degli Scirri. The university was founded in 1307. **13, 76, 89, 102, 106**

Piazza Armerina Central Sicilian city with some interesting Baroque monuments, but chiefly known for its truly splendid Roman Villa Imperiale, which may have belonged to the Emperor Maximinianus, and which is comparable to Hadrian's villa at Tivoli. Contains wonderful mosaics. **21**

Pisa Now famous for its 12th-century leaning tower, the city was founded by the Romans around 100 BC. By the 11th century it had developed into a major trading power, with possessions which included Corsica and Sardinia. Conqueror of Amalfi in 1135, the city was itself defeated by Genoa at Meloria in 1284. Captured by the Visconti in 1396, it was seized by the

The birthplace of Federico Fellini, it features the Tempio Malatesta, converted from a 13th-century church by Leon Battista Alberti. **5, 105, 208**

Roma (Rome) The 'eternal city' and one of the world's most important historical centres. Founded, legend has it, by Romulus; ruled by three Etruscan kings; the home of the Roman republic; the city responsible for the first unification of Italy; the centre of the Roman empire; the home of Catholicism, the Papacy and the Vatican; the capital city of united Italy since 1870. Now, as ever, a colourful, cosmopolitan and very alive city, and a political, gastronomic and cultural centre. Brimming with features of historical interest, including the Roman Forum; the Colisseum; the Pantheon; the catacombs; Bernini's Piazza Navona; Piazza di Spagna; Palazzo Farnese; Villa and Galleria Borghese; the church of San Giovanni in Laterano; the Basilica of Santa Maria Maggiore; the Aventine hill; Castel Sant'Angelo; the Vatican – Piazza and Basilica di San Pietro, the Sistine Chapel and the Vatican museums. A 'must' for all who are interested in history, a major feature of this great city is the range of architectural styles which can be found here. **5–6, 8, 11, 18–19, 21–52, 55, 58–61, 67, 81–2, 102, 117–9, 122–4, 130, 140, 157, 159, 165, 167–9, 176, 194, 197, 200–1, 218**

San Gimignano The 'city of the towers', medieval ones, which dominate the town and can be seen for miles around. There were something like 76 of these in the 13th century. This medieval town was a former free commune and then an outpost of Florence and the haunt of the likes of Dante, Savonarola and Machiavelli. Apart from the towers, historically important features include a Palazzo del Popolo, built probably by Arnolfo di Cambio around 1300, and the Collegiata, a church built in 1470. **75**

San Marino Now a tourist trap, this hilltop town was founded by Christians fleeing Diocletian's perse-

cutions in the 4th century. Became an independent state in 1243 and has retained its anomalous position as a separate republic ever since. **5**

Sanremo Capital of the Italian riviera and watering-hole for many among the rich and famous, including exiled monarchs such as Empress Maria of Russia. Here Tchaikovsky wrote his 4th Symphony, and Alfred Nobel died.

Savona Provincial capital and busy port, this is the family seat of the Della Rovere family which produced two popes: Sixtus IV (who built the Sistine Chapel) and Julius II (who commissioned Michelangelo to decorate it). Features a 13th-century tower at the harbour, the Torre di Leon Pancaldo, named after a companion of Magellan who came from Savona, and a 16th-century duomo.

Selinunte Selinus was colonised in 651 BC by the Greeks and was destroyed by Carthage in 409 BC. The excavations of the site were begun by the Englishmen Harris and Angell in 1822–3. Now the remains of the city can be seen, together with a magnificent series of temples. **9**

Siena Beautiful and fascinating city, a mini-Florence with considerably less tourists. Became an independent commune in 1125 and grew wealthy on cloth and banking. Became a Ghibelline city, and was almost constantly at odds, and at war, with Florence, achieving a notable military success over its arch-rival at Montaperti in 1260. Decimated by the Black Death in 1348. The city was torn apart by factionalism, but enjoyed stable rule under the Petrucci family from 1487–1524; captured by an alliance of the Florentines and the Spanish in the mid-16th century, it declined thereafter. Enjoyed its 'golden age' around the 13th and 14th centuries, when it produced great artists and architects such as Duccio di Buoninsegna, Simone Martini, and Pietro and Ambrogio Lorenzetti. Now noted for its colourful *Palio*, an annual horse race around the Piazza del Campo contested vehemently by the various *contrade*, or areas of the city. A multitude of historically significant features can be found here, including the 14th-century Palazzo Pubblico; the Mangia tower; the cathedral, begun in 1065 with its magnificent floor, and its Piccolomini library and chapel built by the Sienese family which produced Popes Pius II and Pius III. **60, 71–2, 75–6, 78, 89–90, 92, 101, 121**

Siracusa (Syracuse) Founded by the Corinthians in 734 BC on the site of a sickel settlement. A major city in classical Greek and Roman times, later destroyed by the Saracens in 878, and taken in turn by the Byzantines and the Spanish. The birthplace of Archimedes (287–212 BC) and the writer Elio Vittorini (1908–66). Of historical note are the 5th-century BC Greek Theatre, Paradise Quarry, and the catacombs of San Giovanni. **9, 30**

Sovana Ancient Etruscan city, now chiefly of interest for the well-preserved and sometimes imposing Etruscan tombs which can be found just outside the town. **14**

Spoleto Now the setting for an annual major international festival of culture, this pretty town was a centre for the ancient Umbrian civilisation.

Spoletium was taken by the Romans in 242 BC, and soon after resisted Hannibal on his way towards Rome after his victory at Lake Trasimeno. Destroyed by the Goth Totila, and then rebuilt by the Lombards who made it the capital of the duchy of Spoleto. Became part of the Papal States in the 14th century. A wealth of historically significant features include a 1st-century Roman theatre, the Arch of Drusus, built in 23, Gattapone's Ponte delle Torri, and an attractive Duomo, built in 1198 by Innocent III and then rebuilt by Federico Barbarossa. **57, 59–60, 106**

Sulmona Ancient capital of the Paeligni tribe, and the birthplace of Ovid (43 BC - AD 17). Features a Gothic aqueduct, and the church of Santa Maria Annunziata, begun in 1320.

Susa This old town between Turin and the French border was known to the Romans as Segusio. The Gaul Cottius settled here and became a Roman prefect. Features include an Arch dedicated to Augustus, and the 11th-century castle of Countess Adelaide and Cathedral of San Giusto.

Taormina Tauromenium was founded in 403 BC by Dionysius of Syracuse, near the site of ancient Naxos. Landing Place of Timoleon in 334 and of Pyrrhus in 278 BC. Sacked by the Arabs in 902 and captured by Count Roger in 1078. Now an up-market resort, featuring a well-preserved Greek theatre, a 13th-century Duomo, and several good churches. **9**

Taranto Founded by a colony of Spartans in 708 BC as Taras, it was a major city in Magna Grecia, defeated by the Romans around 270 BC. A major port again by the time of the Crusades, it is now known for its frenzied dance, the tarantella, and for its mussels, which have in recent years been rendered inedible by pollution. Contains a good Museo Nazionale with items from Magna Grecia. **4, 9, 29**

Tarquinia Ancient Etruscan town, chiefly noted for the painted tombs in its famous necropolis. Also contains a 12th-century church and a rebuilt Roman aqueduct. **10, 13, 130**

Teramo Originally a Roman city, then Angevin in the 14th century. Features the ruins of a Roman theatre and the Church of Santa Maria Aprutiensis, started in the 6th century.

Tivoli In ancient times the city of Tibur, it has traditionally been the resort of the Roman ruling class. Now chiefly noted for the magnificent villa which the emperor Hadrian built there in the 2nd century, and for the Renaissance Villa d'Este, built for Cardinal Ippolito d'Este and renowned for its fountains. **45, 67**

Todi Hilltop town, originally the ancient Umbrian town of Tuter, then captured by the Etruscans. Flourished in the Middle Ages, and is now a craft and gastronomic centre, featuring the Tempio della Consolazione, the 13th-14th-century Palazzi (dei Priori, del Capitano, del Popolo), the 14th-century Rocca, and the duomo. **7, 78, 106**

Torino (Turin) Originally a fortified Roman outpost (Augusta Taurinorum), this elegant and symmetrical Baroque city on the River Po became the seat of the Savoy dynasty when Emanuele Filiberto moved his capital here from Chambéry in 1574. Capital of Piedmont and the first capital of the united kingdom of Italy. Host of many migrant workers from the south. Gramsci was active in the city, which was also the birthplace of the Red Brigades. A major industrial centre, the headquarters of Fiat, the home of Juventus FC and of the noted Egyptian Museum which was founded in 1628 by Carlo Emanuele I. The Cathedral of San Giovanni was built in the 15th century by Tuscan architects and contains the famous Turin shroud. The Palazzo Reale was the city residence of the nobles of Savoy from 1646 to 1865. **68, 169, 176, 201, 208, 211**

Trento Venue of the Council of Trent, the major event of the counter-reformation. Now characterised by its 18th-century Fountain of Neptune, and the 13th/16th-century Castello del Buon Consiglio.

Trieste Founded by the Celts as Tergeste, then a Roman city. Independent from the 9th century, it was Venice's main rival in the Adriatic during the 14th and 15th centuries. Protected by the Austrians, it was made a free port in 1719 by Charles V. The largest port in the Adriatic, a fiercely contested city in both World Wars, it has been home to the likes of James Joyce (1905–14) and Sir Richard Burton (1870–90). Features a 15th-century Castello and the 11th/14th-century Cathedral of San Giusto. **92, 134, 188, 202, 215**

Urbino Magnificent hilltop city, birthplace of Raphael and the fief of the House of Montefeltro, a series of *condottieri* turned dukes. The most famous is Federico, who ruled between 1444–82. Subsequently controlled by the Della Rovere family, and then part of the Papal States from 1626. Nearly blown up with all its treasures by the Nazis in 1944. The best-known of its buildings is the Palazzo Ducale, built by Federico Montefeltro, with its famous art treasures. Also of note are the Fortezza Albornoz, the house of Raphael, and the Cathedral, built in the 1790s. Its university is one of the oldest and most respected in Italy. **111, 130**

Venezia (Venice) Another of the great European historical cities, and a major tourist centre with its canals, its great works of art, its cultural richness and its magnificent churches. Probably founded by groups of people seeking refuge from the Barbarians after the fall of the Roman empire, by 697 it had elected its first Doge. Its citizens bravely resisted the Frankish king Pepin, and then built Venice into the most powerful seafaring, trading and imperial power of its time, fighting a succession of wars against Dalmatian pirates, its former Byzantine allies, and its arch-rival Genoa. The commune of Venice always managed to maintain a vestige of democracy, never succumbing to the signori. Reached the height of its fame and power in the late 15th century; thereafter decline set in, but it was a splendid decadence which the Venetians experienced. It was also slow, the city still managing to win notable victories over the League of Cambrai, and over the Turks at the famous Battle of Lepanto in 1571. Throughout, the Venetians retained their spirit of independence and freedom, for example resisting the counter-reformation like no other Italian city. Became part of the united kingdom of Italy in the mid-1860s.

Now a real open-air museum with such well-known features as the Grand Canal and its palaces; the Ponte dei Sospiri; the Rialto; the Piazza and Cathedral of San Marco; the Doges' Palace; and many more great churches, including Santa Maria della Salute and San Giorgio Maggiore. And, of course, the galleries, with works of the great Venetian painters such as Giorgione, Paolo Veronese and Canaletto. **54, 66, 68–70, 74, 76, 89, 92–5, 108, 115, 123–6, 128, 134–5, 138, 157, 168–9**

Ventimiglia Scene of prehistoric civilisation, fascinating remains of which can be found in the Balzi Rossi caves and in the Museo Preistorico at the entrance to them. Later an important Ligurian capital known to the Romans as Album Intimilium, the ruins of which can still be seen just outside the city. In particular, there is a 2nd-century theatre which is quite well preserved. The city also contains a 12th-century Duomo and Baptistry, and the Romanesque church of San Michele from the same period. **68**

Vercelli Situated in the rice-producing area between Turin and Milan. Flourished in the Renaissance. Contains the Basilica di Sant 'Andrea, begun in 1219 and one of the first Italian churches to be influenced by Gothic style, and a 16th-century Duomo. **35, 70**

Verona Colonised by the Romans in 89 BC, it was the birthplace of the poet Catullus and the architect Vitruvius. A leading city under the Goths and the Franks, it became a free commune in 1107. Ruled by the Della Scala family from 1259 until 1387, when it was captured by Gian Galeazzo Visconti. Then came into the Venetian sphere of influence. A very beautiful city, which inspired the story of Romeo and Juliet (her tomb is in the cloisters next to the church in which they were married), it features a 1st-century Roman Arena in which high-quality opera is regularly performed; several medieval towers and palaces; the 12th-century Romanesque church of San Zeno Maggiore; the Church of Sant'Anastasia (1290); and the Duomo (1187). **1, 54, 59, 68, 74, 76, 87–90, 92, 139**

Vicenza Of Roman origin, Vicenza is now a high Renaissance city – 'Venice on land', as it has been called – largely the masterpiece of the Paduan architect Andrea Palladio (1508–80), who is responsible for many of the impressive buildings, including the Basilica and Loggia del Capitano in the Piazza dei Signori, several of the palaces, the Villa Rotonda, and the Teatro Olimpico. **74, 76, 92**

Volterra Tuscan hilltop town, founded by the Etruscans as Valatri, and then controlled by the Romans. Later under the control of Florence. Now a centre of alabaster production, it has a 15th-century Fortezza Medicea and Duomo, a Roman theatre and baths, and a Palazzo dei Priori built in 1208. **13, 78, 99**

Index

For major cities see Historical Gazetteer

THE TRAVELLER'S HISTORY SERIES

'Ideal before-you-go reading' *The Daily Telegraph*

'An excellent series of brief histories' *New York Times*

'I want to compliment you . . . on the brilliantly concise contents of your books' *Shirley Conran*

Reviews of Individual Titles

A Traveller's History of France
'Undoubtedly the best way to prepare for a trip to France is to bone up on some history. *The Traveller's History of France* by Robert Cole is concise and gives the essential facts in a very readable form.' *The Independent*

A Traveller's History of China
'The author manages to get 2 million years into 300 pages. An excellent addition to a series which is already invaluable, whether you are travelling or not' *The Guardian*

A Traveller's History of India
'For anyone . . . planning a trip to India, the latest in the excellent Traveller's History series . . . provides a useful grounding for those whose curiosity exceeds the time available for research' *The London Evening Standard*

A Traveller's History of Japan
'It succeeds admirably in its goal of making the present country comprehensible through a narrative of its past, with asides on everything from bonsai to *zazen*, in a brisk, highly readable style . . . you could easily read it on the flight over, if you skip the movie' *The Washington Post*

A Traveller's History of Ireland
'For independent, inquisitive travellers traversing the green roads of Ireland, there is no better guide than *A Traveller's History of Ireland*.' *Small Press*

A TRAVELLER'S HISTORY OF FRANCE

FOURTH EDITION

Robert Cole

"Undoubtedly the best way to prepare for a trip to France is to bone up on some history. The Traveller's History of France *by Robert Cole is concise and gives the essential facts in a very readable form"* **The Independent on Sunday**

"Hundreds of thousands of travellers, visit France each year. The glories of the French countryside, the essential harmony of much of French architecture, the wealth of historical remains and associations, the enormous variety of experience that France offers, act as a perennial and irresistible attraction. For these visitors this lively and useful guide provides the essential clues to an understanding of France's past, and present, in entertaining and sometimes surprising detail"
From the Preface by the Series Editor, Denis Judd.

In *A Traveller's History of France*, the reader is provided with a comprehensive and yet very enjoyable, general history of France, from earliest times to the present day.

An extensive Gazetteer which is cross-referenced with the main text pinpoints the historical importance of sites and towns. Illustrated with maps and line drawings *A Traveller's History of France* will add to the enjoyment of every holidaymaker who likes to do more than lie on a beach.

A TRAVELLER'S HISTORY OF PARIS

SECOND EDITION

Robert Cole

Paris, in many people's thoughts, is the epitome of the perfect city – beautiful, romantic and imbued with vitality and culture. It is a wonderful place to visit and to live. A 'pride of place' mentality has characterised Parisians for centuries: 'To be in Paris, is to be' enthused an anonymous correspondent as early as 1323.

Packed with fact, anecdote and insight; *A Traveller's History of Paris* offers a complete history of Paris and the people who have shaped its destiny, from its earliest settlement as the Roman village of *Lutetia Parisiorum* with a few hundred inhabitants, to 20 centuries later when Paris is a city of well over 2 million, at the centre of a conurbation that exceeds 12 million – nearly one-fifth of the population of France.

This handy paperback is fully indexed and there is a Chronology of Major Events, a section on Notre-Dame and historic churches, Modernism, Paris parks, bridges, cemeteries, museums and galleries, the Metro and The Environs. Illustrated with line drawings and historical maps

A TRAVELLER'S HISTORY OF RUSSIA and the USSR

Peter Neville

A Traveller's History of Russia gives a comprehensive survey of that country's past from the earliest times to the era of perestroika and glasnost. The reader first learns about prehistoric Russia and its nomadic invaders, then the story of the city state of Kiev is traced up to the crucial year of 1237 when the Mongol invasion took place. The rise of Muscovy with its colourful panoply of rulers from Ivan Moneybags to Ivan the Terrible, the despotism of the Romanovs and the Russian Revolution are dealt with in depth. The book concludes with an account of the rise of the Soviet state, its world role and current metamorphosis.

There is an A–Z Gazetteer for the visitor which is cross-referenced to the main text and highlights sites, towns and places of historical importance.

Illustrated throughout with maps and line drawings. *A Traveller's History of Russia and the USSR* encapsulates the nation's past and present and is a unique cultural and historical guidebook to that intriguing land.

A TRAVELLER'S HISTORY OF GREECE

Timothy Boatswain and Colin Nicolson

The many facets of Greece are presented in this unique book.

In *A Traveller's History of Greece*, the reader is provided with an authoritative general history of Greece from its earlier beginnings down to the present day. It covers in a clear and comprehensive manner the classical past, the conflict with Persia, the conquest by the Romans, the Byzantine era and the occupation by the Turks; the struggle for Independence and the turbulence of recent years, right up to current events.

This history will help the visitor make sense of modern Greece against the background of its diverse heritage. A Gazetteer, cross-referenced with the main text highlights the importance of sites, towns and ancient battlefields. A Chronology details the significant dates and a brief survey of the artistic styles of each period is given. Illustrated with maps and line drawings *A Traveller's History of Greece* is an invaluable companion for your holiday.

A TRAVELLER'S HISTORY OF ENGLAND

FOURTH EDITION

Christopher Daniell

"This compact volume delivers a solid, comprehensive and entertaining overview of England's history . . . a delightful source." **Library Journal**

Illustrated throughout with maps and line drawings, *A Traveller's History of England* offers an insight into the country's past and present and is an invaluable companion for all those who want to know more about a nation whose impact upon the rest of the world has been profound.

All the major periods of English history are dealt with, including the Roman occupation, and the invasions of the Anglo-Saxons, Vikings and Normans, and the power struggles of the medieval kings. The Reformation, the Renaissance and the Civil War are discussed, as well as the consequences of the Industrial Revolution and urbanism, and the establishment of an Empire which encompassed a quarter of the human race. In this century the Empire has been transformed into the Commonwealth, two victorious, but costly, World Wars have been fought, the Welfare State was established, and membership of the European Economic Community was finally achieved.

A TRAVELLER'S HISTORY OF LONDON

SECOND EDITION

Richard Tames

A full and comprehensive historical background to the capital's past which covers the period from London's first beginnings, right up to the present day – from *Londinium* and *Lundenwic* to Docklands' development. London has always been an international city and visitors from all over the world have recorded their impressions and these views have been drawn on extensively throughout this book.

At different points in London's 2000-year history, it has been praised for its elegance and civility and damned for its riots, rudeness, fogs and squalor. Visitors and London's own residents will enjoy discovering more about the city from this fascinating book.

There are special sections on the Cathedrals, Royal Palaces, Parks and Gardens, Railway Termini, The Underground, Bridges, Cemeteries, Museums and Galleries, The London Year as well as a full Chronology of Major Events, Maps and Index.

A TRAVELLER'S HISTORY OF SCOTLAND

SECOND EDITION

Andrew Fisher

A Traveller's History of Scotland begins with Scotland's first people and their culture, which remained uncrushed by the Roman invasions. Before the Vikings in 900 it was a land of romantic kingdoms and saints, gradually overtaken by more pragmatic struggles for power between the great families of Bruce, Balliol and Stewart. Centuries of strife led up to the turbulent years of Mary Queen of Scots, the Calvinistic legacy of Knox, and the bitterness of final defeat.

The dreams of the Jacobites are contrasted with the cruel reality of the end of the Stuarts and the Act of Union with England. Scotland now saw an age of building, industry and despoliation of their land. The result was much emigration and an obsession fostered by Walter Scott and Burns with the nation's past which glorified the legends of the Highlander and the Clans. In this century, a loss of identity and a drift to the south has been followed by a new surge of national pride with higher aspirations for the future.

A Traveller's History of Scotland explains the roots of Scottish history and is an excellent handbook for visitors.

A TRAVELLER'S HISTORY OF IRELAND

Peter Neville

The many thousands of visitors to Ireland are drawn by the landscape, the people and the underlying atmosphere created by its rich heritage.

The story of *A Traveller's History of Ireland* opens with mysterious early Celtic Ireland, where no Roman stood, through St Patrick's mission and the legendary High King Brian Boru. The Normans came in the twelfth century and this period also marks the beginnings of the difficult and tragic Anglo–Irish relationship. Reading the book helps one understand the complexities of the current political situation.

Its appendices include an A–Z Gazetteer, a Chronology of Major Events, an list of Kings and Queens, Prime Ministers and Presidents, Famous Battles, a full Bibliography and Index. There are Historical Maps and line drawings to accompany the text.

A TRAVELLER'S HISTORY OF SPAIN

THIRD EDITION

Juan Lalaguna

"General yet detailed . . . giving an insight into historical background. Very readable . . . many people would profit from putting contemporary Europe into context in this way and A-Level students will find these excellent for background study" **Books in Schools**

Spain's vibrant and colourful past is as exciting to discover as is taking a fresh look at the tumultuous upheavals of the twentieth century. *A Traveller's History of Spain* will unlock the secrets of the country, its people and culture for the interested traveller.

Juan Lalaguna takes you on a journey from the earliest settlements on the Iberian peninsula, through the influences of the Romans, the Goths and the Muslims, the traumas of expansion and the end of Empire, the surge for national identity – right up to the current dilemmas that face post-Franco Spain.

A Traveller's History of Spain is an essential companion for your trip to Spain.

A TRAVELLER'S HISTORY OF TURKEY

Richard Stoneman

A Traveller's History of Turkey offers a full and accurate portrait of the region from Prehistory right up to the present day. Particular emphasis is given to those aspects of history which have left their mark in the sites and monuments that are still visible today.

Modern Turkey is the creation of the present century, but at least seven ancient civilisations had their homes in the region. Turkey also formed a significant part of several empires – those of Persia, Rome and Byzantium, before becoming the centre of the opulent Ottoman Empire. All of these great cultures have left their marks on the landscape, architecture and art of Turkey – a place of bewildering facets where East meets West with a flourish.

Richard Stoneman's concise and readable account covers everything including the legendary Flood of Noah, the early civilisation of Çatal Hüyük seven thousand years before Christ, the treasures of Troy, Alexander the Great, the Romans, Selcuks, Byzantines and the Golden Age of the Sultans to the twentieth century's great changes wrought by Kemal Atatürk and the strong position Turkey now holds in the world community.

A TRAVELLER'S HISTORY OF JAPAN

Richard Tames

Whether you are going to Japan on business, to study, to teach or simply on holiday, you know that you are going to a country which really does merit the title 'unique'. A century ago the first modern guidebook to Japan warned the visitor that 'he ... who should essay to travel without having learnt a word concerning Japan's past, would still run the risk of forming opinions ludicrously erroneous.' This is still sound advice.

A Traveller's History of Japan not only offers the reader a chronological outline of the nation's development but also provides an invaluable introduction to its language, literature and arts, from *kabuki to karaoke*. Political, social and industrial history and economics are also well covered; this clearly written history explains how a country embedded in the traditions of Shinto, Shoguns and Samurai has achieved stupendous economic growth and dominance in the twentieth century.

There is a Historical Gazetteer, cross-referenced to the main text and particular attention is paid to the classic historical sites which feature on any visitor's itinerary. Special emphasis is given to the writings and reactions of travellers through the centuries. Extra information on Buddhism, National Holidays and Festivals and Food and Drink.

A TRAVELLER'S HISTORY OF INDIA

SECOND EDITION

SinhaRajah Tammita-Delgoda

The Traveller's Histories series' aim is to give a concise but authoritative history of a country from the earliest times right up to the present day. They are excellent for tourists, business travellers and students and are carefully designed for quick reference with the text separated under clear headings plus excellent fact sections at the back of the book.

India, named after the river Indus, is heir to one of the world's oldest and richest civilizations and the origin of many of the ideas, philosophies and movements which have shaped the destiny of humankind.

For the traveller, India is both an inspiration and a challenge. The sheer wealth of Indian culture has fascinated generations of visitors. We see the sweeping panorama of Indian history, from the ancient origins of Hinduism, Jainism, Buddhism, and the other great religions, through the tumultuous political history of India's epic struggle against colonialism, to the ravages of Partition, Non-Alignment, and finally the emergence of India as a powerful modern state still grounded in the literature and culture of an ancient land. *A Traveller's History of India* covers the whole scope of India's past and present history and allows the reader to make sense of what they see in a way that no other guide book can.

A TRAVELLER'S HISTORY OF CHINA

SECOND EDITION

Stephen G. Haw

A Traveller's History of China gives a full and accurate account of this extremely important East Asian country from the earliest times right up to the present day.

China has maintained a distinct civilization and culture through a multitude of upheavals for more than four thousand years. Though often regarded as isolated at the furthest eastern end of the Eurasian land mass, it had at least indirect contact with regions to the west from very early times. Two thousand years ago, Chinese silk was regularly traded right across Eurasia to Rome. Some of the most significant inventions and discoveries of the pre-modern world, including paper, gunpowder and the magnetic compass, originated in China and were transmitted to the West. During the Tang and Song dynasties, the great Chinese cities were the finest and most populous in the world. The rapid development of Europe after the Industrial Revolution coincided with a period of decline in China. During the nineteenth century military defeats by European powers humiliated the last dynasty and the Chinese people. The overthrow of the last Emperor in 1911 ushered in a long period of turmoil. Dramatic changes in political policies since the late 1970s have now made it one of the world's fastest-developing countries, well on its way to superpower status. Its economy is likely to become the largest in the world within the next few years. This book gives insights into how all this has happened and helps to make sense of China as it is today.

For visitors to China, an A–Z Gazetteer gives information about places of historical and cultural significance. Illustrations, maps and reference sections all help to make this great and complex country more readily comprehensible.